Puerto Rico:
The Search for
a National Policy

Also of Interest

†*Politics and Public Policy in Latin America,* Steven W. Hughes and Kenneth J. Mijeski

†*The Dynamics of Latin American Foreign Policies: Challenges for the 1980s,* edited by Jennie K. Lincoln and Elizabeth G. Ferris

†*Latin American Nations in World Politics,* edited by Heraldo Muñoz and Joseph S. Tulchin

Politics and Economics of External Debt Crisis: The Latin American Experience, edited by Miguel S. Wionczek

Mexico's Dilemma: The Political Origins of Economic Crisis, Roberto Newell G. and Luis Rubio F.

†*Cuba: Dilemmas of a Revolution,* Juan M. del Aguila

The Cuban Revolution: 25 years Later, Hugh S. Thomas, Georges A. Fauriol, and Juan Carlos Weiss

Jamaica and the Sugar Worker Cooperatives: The Politics of Reform, Carl Henry Feuer

The Caribbean Basin to the Year 2000—Demographic, Economic, and Resource Use Trends in Seventeen Countries: A Compendium of Statistics and Projections, Norman A. Graham and Keith L. Edwards

†*Revolution and Counterrevolution in Central America and the Caribbean,* edited by Donald E. Schulz and Douglas H. Graham

†*Latin America and the U.S. National Interest: A Basis for U.S. Foreign Policy,* Margaret Daly Hayes

†*Latin America, Its Problems and Its Promise: A Multidisciplinary Introduction,* edited by Jan Knippers Black

†Available in hardcover and paperback.

Westview Special Studies on Latin America and the Caribbean

Puerto Rico: The Search for a National Policy
edited by Richard J. Bloomfield

The issue of Puerto Rico's political status and the need for action on the island's severe economic problems have become urgent. Although any solution for the Puerto Rican situation will have to be based on the principle of self-determination, a decision to change the island's status can only be made by the federal government, in particular by the U.S. Congress. Without voting representation either in the Congress or in the presidential elections, Puerto Rico has been severely handicapped in making its case in the national political arena.

This book explores the main issues surrounding Puerto Rico's political status and economic development from the point of view of the federal government's responsibility. The contributors trace the history of the U.S.–Puerto Rican relationship and analyze why the economic policy tools that made Operation Bootstrap of the 1940s and 1950s a success no longer work. They also discuss the social costs of Puerto Rico's dependent development pattern, suggest why the federal government has traditionally mishandled the Puerto Rico question, propose ways in which the federal and Puerto Rican governments could implement policy tools to improve the island's economic performance, and address the controversial status issue as an international problem for the United States. In the final section of the book, leaders of the four major Puerto Rican political parties outline the concessions they believe the federal government would need to make in order to facilitate a transition to their preferred status for the island.

Richard J. Bloomfield is director of the World Peace Foundation and was a career foreign service officer with ambassadorships to Portugal and Ecuador.

Published in cooperation with the
World Peace Foundation

Puerto Rico:
The Search for
a National Policy

edited by Richard J. Bloomfield

Westview Press / Boulder and London

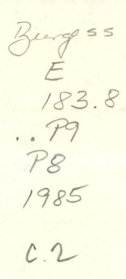
Westview Special Studies on Latin America and the Caribbean

Copyright © 1985 by Westview Press, Inc.

Published in 1985 in the United States of America by Westview Press, Inc., 5500 Central Avenue, Boulder, Colorado 80301; Frederick A. Praeger, Publisher

Library of Congress Cataloging in Publication Data
Main entry under title:
Puerto Rico, the search for a national policy.
  (Westview special studies on Latin America and the Caribbean)
  Includes index.
  1. United States—Relations—Puerto Rico—Addresses,
essays, lectures. 2. Puerto Rico—Relations—United
States—Addresses, essays, lectures. 3. Puerto Rico—
Politics and government—1952–   —Addresses, essays,
lectures. 4. Puerto Rico—Economic conditions—1952–
—Addresses, essays, lectures. I. Bloomfield, Richard J.
II. Series.
E183.8.P9P8 1985   972.95′053   84-23756
ISBN 0-8133-0027-4

Printed and bound in the United States of America

10   9   8   7   6   5   4   3   2   1

Contents

vii

Preface

Puerto Rico: The Search for a National Policy stems from a conference sponsored by the World Peace Foundation of Boston, with the cooperation of Meridian House International of Washington, D.C. The chapters in this book are based on papers presented at the conference, which was held at Meridian House in September 1983.

The conference grew out of a conviction held by several of the participants that the perennial debate about Puerto Rico's "status" (that is, about the island's juridical relationship to the United States and its consequent future political system) had reached a dead end and that a fresh approach was needed. The debate has been going on for decades, in presidentially and congressionally mandated commissions, in academic conferences, and, most intensely, in Puerto Rico's hyperactive political life. In spite of the compact reached between Congress and the people of Puerto Rico in 1952 to provide for local self-government within a "free associated state," the controversy has grown more and more intense in the ensuing thirty years.

That all this thought and discussion has failed to produce any noticeable movement on any of the issues is in itself a clue to what has been wrong with the process of debate. Simply put, the institutions that have the power to do something about Puerto Rico's status have, by and large, not been caught up in the debate. In the final analysis, it is primarily the U.S. Congress that has the power (and the responsibility) to deal with the constitutional, political, and economic issues that make up the status question. The federal executive is also an important actor, as an initiator of legislative proposals and as a manager of federal programs. Both branches of the federal government have shown a consistent reluctance to grapple with the issues of Puerto Rico's future. As a result the recommendations of the various official and private groups charged with advising on the problem have gathered dust.

Sometimes the adage, "don't do something, just stand there," is the best way to deal with a complex, politically controversial problem. In the case of Puerto Rico, however, many now believe, for reasons explained in this book, that the costs of further inaction—in terms of the impact on the moral and physical welfare of the island's inhabitants and on U.S. political values—are too high. All the ingredients for a national political crisis are present in Puerto Rico. That is why the conference at Meridian House focused on the need to find a policy at the national level. Accordingly, the invited participants included members of Congress and their staffs, officials of the executive branch, corporate executives, newspaper columnists, lobbyists—in short, those who make or influence federal policy—as well as Puerto Rican leaders from the island's political and intellectual life.

In keeping with the objective of engaging policymakers in the debate, the conference focused on the federal-commonwealth relationship and, in particular, on the way in which the interaction (or lack thereof) between the two affected the island's political and economic future. A conscious effort was made to avoid repeating the endless debate about the merits of any particular status, whether statehood, commonwealth, or independence.

As a neophyte in Puerto Rican affairs, I had to rely on a great many people for help in organizing this effort. I wish to acknowledge the contribution of three people in particular: Juan Manuel García-Passalacqua, who gave me the benefit of his wise counsel and enormous range of contacts, both in Puerto Rico and on the mainland; Philip von Mehren, who performed the initial chore of cutting and rearranging the original conference papers so that my editorial task was simplified; and Margaret Kourbetis, who, with inexhaustible patience, typed and retyped the manuscript, putting the footnotes in a consistent pattern.

My thanks also to Ambassador John Jova, the president of Meridian House International, for the use of the magnificent facilities of Meridian House in Washington, D.C.; to Nancy Matthews, who coordinated the Washington arrangements; and to Baltasar Corrada, the resident commissioner of Puerto Rico in the House of Representatives, for his general encouragement and for his help in arranging for part of the conference to be held in the Capitol building.

Finally, I extend my gratitude to the trustees of the World Peace Foundation for agreeing to this venture in a new field of study for the foundation. Although a new subject of inquiry for the institution, this project followed in the tradition of the foundation, which for seventy-four years has sought to promote world order by analysis and discussion of critical issues in the international arena.

Richard J. Bloomfield
Boston

1
Introduction

Richard J. Bloomfield

Crises in the U.S. body politic have taken diverse forms, but they have shared one fundamental characteristic. They arise, as Samuel Huntington tells us, when the discrepancy between the behavior of American institutions and the promise of American ideals arouses large numbers of Americans to take direct political action in an effort to overthrow the status quo.[1] To take two examples from our recent history, the challenge to racial discrimination posed by blacks in the early 1960s received broad support among whites because of the wide gap between the American creed's ideal of egalitarianism and the institutionalized practice of racial segregation. Similarly, the storm of protest that erupted against the Vietnam War later in that decade was born in large part in the belief that no matter how worthy the U.S. objective—to counter Communist aggression in Southeast Asia—the means employed had become incompatible with American values.

Puerto Rico also represents a dichotomy between American ideals and institutional reality. Puerto Rico is an anomaly in the U.S. political system. It is not a state of the Union, nor is it a territory whose admission as a state is foreordained. Because it is an "unincorporated territory," Puerto Rico has no independent powers reserved to it by the Constitution, as do the states. Congress can decide which federal statutes will or will not apply there and can even abridge the rights of Puerto Ricans as U.S. citizens. Puerto Ricans are denied the vote in presidential elections.

In spite of the legal and political inequality inherent in these arrangements, Puerto Rico enjoys a degree of self-government not unlike that of a state. Since 1952, Puerto Ricans have had the right to elect a government to manage their internal affairs under a constitution accepted by the U.S. Congress and by the people of Puerto Rico in a referendum. It is also true that federal policies in the two decades after World War II supported a development effort conceived and led by Puerto Ricans that produced a standard of living in Puerto Rico higher than in any country in Latin America.

Yet the powers of local self-government remain, constitutionally at least, contingent upon the discretion of the U.S. Congress, and the economic well-being of Puerto Ricans on the island has in recent years been sustained more by federal transfer payments than by any vitality of the island's economy.

Puerto Ricans from all political factions increasingly attack the current legal status of the island, and many, rightly or wrongly, blame their economic troubles on their political inferiority. The status issue has also become internationalized. Puerto Rico, it is often charged, is a U.S. colony. The United States has denied that this is the case ever since it succeeded in removing the island from the United Nations' list of non-self-governing territories in 1953. Nevertheless, the gap between the ideals of the American Union and the institutional realities of the U.S.-Puerto Rican relationship cannot be defined away. While that gap has continued to be the major political issue in Puerto Rico, the issue has remained latent on the mainland because of a variety of fortuitous circumstances. The questions that should concern us—and that motivated the project of which this book is a part—are how much longer the issue will remain submerged and whether, when it rises to the surface of U.S. political consciousness, its potential destructiveness can be contained.

Destructive elements do exist. Feelings of political inferiority are made sharper and given ideological dimension by Puerto Ricans' strong sense of a distinct cultural identity. To the extent that dissatisfaction among Puerto Ricans regarding their political status reflects anticolonial sentiments, their sense of being a separate and embattled culture can only add to their resentment of the metropolitan power. Similarly, as the relative economic well-being enjoyed by the majority of Puerto Ricans on the island deteriorates and becomes increasingly dependent on federal largesse rather than local enterprise, the status quo loses much of its legitimacy and the paranoid feelings that dependency invariably engenders increase. At some point in this process, the low level of violence practiced for years by small groups of fanatics could become more generalized. One hears with increasing frequency that the American people's immunity from terrorism in their own land will inevitably end. Puerto Rico could be the issue that makes those predictions come true.

As for the mainland, one need only recall the emotions that the debate over the Panama Canal treaties stirred up to realize how negative the response of many Americans would be to attempts by Puerto Rico to gain more equality—whether by becoming a state, an independent republic, or a more autonomous commonwealth—if those attempts were perceived as demands forced on the American people by an "ungrateful"

Puerto Rico. Resentment would be intensified if demands for more autonomy were accompanied by violence.

By all indications, demand for change will become more insistent in the years ahead, and there is the possibility that if that demand is not channeled into a process that offers the hope of political equality and economic progress, the result will be a full-blown crisis. Pointing this out is not taking sides in the three-cornered debate about which status change should be adopted; it is taking a stand for purposeful action to manage the process of change.

But what action and where? A number of the authors in this book point out that a common error running through U.S. policy toward Puerto Rico has been misjudging the locus of responsibility. Washington's defense against charges that Puerto Rico is a U.S. colony has been to pledge to respect Puerto Ricans' wishes as to their status—to promise self-determination, as if that discharged the national government from its responsibility in the matter. On the contrary, these authors argue, since Puerto Rico's dependence on the U.S. government is the central issue, any change in Puerto Rico's political status will require action by Washington. Puerto Rico has a right to help determine its future status, but only the mainland has power to effect the change. Puerto Rican politicians generally understand this difference between rights and power. A number of the Puerto Rican contributors to this book insist that Washington must set forth the conditions it is willing to accept for each status option before Puerto Ricans can make a meaningful choice.

Yet care must be taken that congressional initiative to resolve the status question does not end up as an imposition on the Puerto Rican people. Congress is as capable of acting capriciously or even punitively as it is of acting deliberately or benevolently, as some of the studies in this book demonstrate. Arturo Morales Carrión, in the historical essay that begins this look at the issues, argues forcefully that a compact was forged between Congress and Puerto Rico in 1952 that ended Puerto Rico's position as a possession and created a new legal situation, a status somewhere between colony and independent state. In so doing, he asserts, the U.S. Congress assumed on behalf of the American people a commitment that, although not sanctified by a constitutional amendment, carries much the same political force. Puerto Rico, he says, has shown itself capable of preserving its cultural identity and achieving political autonomy in spite of the overwhelming embrace of the United States. To encourage the federal government to initiate action on the status issue risks upsetting this delicate balance. Instead, he urges mainlanders and islanders to pursue actively a new consensus, similar to that achieved in the 1940s and 1950s.

In the meantime, Puerto Rico's immediate problems will have to be dealt with in the existing constitutional framework. The island's economic situation urgently needs attention. Chapter 3 by Bertram Finn shows that, because of changes in the international economy as well as in Puerto Rico, the old formulas no longer stimulate the island's economy as they once did, and new approaches must be tried.

The Puerto Rican economy is in a parlous state, with chronic unemployment running in the 20 to 30 percent range. As a result, dependency on federal transfer payments has grown rapidly. Yet with no overall economic policy by which the Congress might judge proposed federal legislation and regulations, the island's economy is at the mercy of changes in federal laws that come about for reasons that have little or nothing to do with the needs of Puerto Rico. Two recent examples of this phenomenon—food stamps and corporate tax credits—are examined in this book. Peter Merrill traces the history of the 1982 congressional effort to reduce the tax breaks accorded corporate subsidiaries in Puerto Rico and presents the case for a drastic revision of this type of tax incentive. Nelson Famadas and Miguel Lausell argue the case for preserving the tax credit mechanism. Congressman Thomas Coleman tells why he opposed cashing-out food stamps in Puerto Rico, and Guy Smith describes the impact of the successive reversals in food stamp policy on the island.

Several authors suggest that such twists and turns in federal programs in Puerto Rico are byproducts of a more fundamental lacuna—the absence of a conscious development policy formulated by both the U.S. Congress and the Puerto Rican government. Randolph Mye goes as far as to argue that a federal-commonwealth development effort must precede any resolution of the status question. He proposes giving discretion over the use of federal funds to the island's government and creating a joint presidential-congressional mechanism to achieve better coordination of federal policy toward Puerto Rico.

However, we must question whether more rapid growth of the economy will effectively buy time for resolving the political issue that has agitated the Puerto Rican people throughout this century—their political status vis-à-vis the United States. If one diagnoses the problem as Luis Nieves Falcón does in Chapter 4, the answer is no. He sees the current situation as symptomatic of an acute social disorder brought on by deep feelings of inferiority and helplessness that are in turn a function of extreme dependency.

If the problem is psychological at bottom, a crisis of identity, what can be done? The affirmation of the identity of an entire culture is a political problem, and once again we are brought back to the island's juridical status. Are Puerto Ricans Americans who happen to speak

Spanish? If so, should not Puerto Rico be a state? Or, do the Puerto Rican people make up, at least on the island, a nation and a culture that cannot and should not be assimilated into the American culture and nationality? If that is the case, should not the island be independent? Or, has history, by weaving tight links between island and mainland, foreclosed the choice of independence, making the real alternatives statehood or a more autonomous commonwealth?

This book does not attempt to prolong this debate, in the conviction that all the arguments have been presented over and over again and that the question cannot be resolved in the abstract. Change will come about only when the political institutions of the United States face up to the issues in the normal course of governance. In that spirit, the final section concentrates on what must be done to set in motion a political process that eventually will permit the Puerto Rican people to decide their own status. In one way or another all the authors in this final section recognize that the first problem is to convince the powers-that-be in the congressional and the executive branches of the U.S. government that there is a compelling reason for action. The inertia that has characterized policy on Puerto Rico since the 1950s obeys that immutable law of Washington that only the squeaky wheel gets the grease, and the Puerto Rico issue has not "squeaked enough" to cause high-level concern.

Some expect the requisite noise to come in the future from the international community. After reviewing the history of Puerto Rico as an international issue, Robert Pastor concludes that, although the international costs of maintaining the status quo on Puerto Rico are increasing every year, they still are probably bearable for some time to come. Nevertheless, Pastor makes a case for changing the U.S. position in the United Nations. Pastor argues that there is a different and more compelling reason for changing the U.S. position, namely that the cost to the core values of our political creed is too high. Here Pastor touches directly on Huntington's ideals-versus-institutions gap. He points out that the status of Puerto Rico goes directly against basic U.S. values, such as equality before the law and justice for all. Pastor does not insist, however, that a radical change toward statehood or independence is the only choice. He admits that the majority of Puerto Ricans might quite possibly prefer the current juridical framework. But, he argues, they must be allowed to decide—"the people of Puerto Rico cannot make that decision until the United States agrees to make it with them."

Bringing the national government to that realization is the first hurdle on the path to a solution in Puerto Rico, and a formidable hurdle it is. Juan Manuel García-Passalacqua explains the inertia of the federal government on the status issue in terms of Allison's model of bureaucratic politics as applied to the Puerto Rican case. Such an analysis can be as useful to Puerto Ricans who are trying to penetrate the fog in official Washington as to anyone else, because a frequent assumption on the island is that a monolithic, purposeful actor in Washington is deliberately ignoring Puerto Rico's problems for ulterior motives. Also, clarifying why the federal government behaves as it does may be essential to getting it to act. Besides demystifying the U.S. government's treatment of Puerto Rican issues, García-Passalacqua, like Pastor, proposes a process that involves joint action by Washington and San Juan.

One essential element of a new encounter between mainland and island will have to be a definition of what precisely each status option means in terms sufficiently specific to permit both sides to make rational choices. Legislators and citizens may be in favor of *statehood, independence*, or *commonwealth* in the abstract, but their positions can change when these general concepts are translated into concrete concessions and conditions. What solutions do the proponents of each status propose to such questions as language, taxation, economic assistance, military base rights, and so on? Congressmen, the American people, and Puerto Ricans will have to wrestle with these issues when and if the process of self-determination is worked out.

For that reason, this book ends with a statement from spokesmen for each of the four major Puerto Rican political parties as to what action by the federal government their party believes would be necessary to make possible their preferred status outcome. As might be expected, each party foresees the need for a process of negotiation between Congress and representatives of the Puerto Rican people. The vice president of the Independence party, Fernando Martín, insists that the first step must be a "devolution of sovereignty" to the Puerto Rican people. But the process of recognizing Puerto Rico's independence would be accompanied by a negotiation of "the conditions which shall accompany the devolution of sovereignty as well as the treaties and arrangements that will prevail, at least initially, between the two countries." Héctor Ramos sees the process of statehood following the traditional course, in which Congress makes certain financial concessions to the incoming state. For Puerto Rico, the major concessions would be a twenty-year phase out of the federal income-tax exemption and the assumption by the U.S. government of Puerto Rico's public debt—no small matters for congressional consideration and debate. The Pro-Commonwealth party representative, Miguel Lausell, sees the need for far-reaching concessions of powers to the Puerto Rican government, including the right to enter into international agreements with foreign countries and to impose tariffs and other trade controls. Luis Batista Salas, on behalf of the newly created Puerto Rican Renewal party, would put tackling the economic problem first, but he too urges a process that would engage the federal government in defining acceptable status alternatives.

The process of working out the conditions of a change in status and putting new vitality into the Puerto Rican economy could take years, even decades. It is urgent that we begin now. The United States does not have a good record of anticipating crises and taking action to head them off. In the case of Puerto Rico there is still time, but not much.

Notes

1. Samuel P. Huntington, *American Politics: The Promise of Disharmony* (Cambridge: Harvard University Press, 1981).

2
Puerto Rico and the United States: The Need for a New Encounter

Arturo Morales Carrión

An examination of Puerto Rico's future should begin with a review of the eighty-five-year-old relationship between the United States and Puerto Rico. It is a complex relationship and cannot be understood by looking at only one side of the historical ledger. Mutual assets and liabilities have affected both parties in the relationship. Although the economic dimension of the relationship is fundamental, other factors play a significant role: the strategic importance of Puerto Rico in the Caribbean; the special link between the island and Latin America; and the unique West Indian ethnic, cultural, and social traditions of the Puerto Rican people.

Puerto Rico has the attributes of a cultural nationality: The population shares a common language, a collective memory of past experiences and traditions, and the subjective belief that it belongs to a distinct cultural group. In short, a Puerto Rican ethos exists. Thus, Puerto Rico, as a cultural society, is distinct from the United States. This distinctiveness is particularly characteristic of the Puerto Ricans in Puerto Rico, where they are close to the source of their mores and traditions. After eighty-five years of association, full assimilation into the American cultural matrix has not been achieved in the island. As powerful and pervasive as the American influence has been, Puerto Ricans still adhere to the Spanish language, and their mores and perceptions continue to differ from those of the United States. These facts, stubborn facts, must be considered in any assessment of U.S. policies on Puerto Rico, past, present, or future. The economic web of mutual interest, the strategic imperative, and the presence of a distinct Puerto Rican culture are all historically interrelated. Taken together, these factors create the complexity that characterizes the contemporary situation in Puerto Rico.

The Rise of Colonial Tutelage

The genesis of the present relationship between Puerto Rico and the United States began in 1898. That year Spain ceded Puerto Rico to the United States in the Treaty of Paris, which put an end to the Spanish-American War. The cession of the island was promoted by the jingoists, who argued that the United States had both a right and an obligation to dominate the Caribbean and to penetrate the markets of Asia and Latin America. Jingoism was the ideology of empire building and was fueled by messianic nationalism. The strategic value of Puerto Rico loomed large. Alfred T. Mahan, the prophet of U.S. naval expansionism, put it succinctly: "Puerto Rico, considered militarily, is to Cuba, to the future isthmian Canal, and to our Pacific coast, what Malta is, or may be, to Egypt and the beyond."[1] Thus, the strategic imperative was the main reason for the annexation of Puerto Rico. Furthermore, Mahan's words are still significant: Puerto Rico's strategic influence is still present because of the Marxist takeover in Cuba and the planned withdrawal of U.S. forces from Panama.

Besides the strategic reasons for annexing Puerto Rico, there was also the messianic imperative. President William McKinley saw Puerto Rico and the Philippines as a great trust to which the United States was committed "under the providence of God and in the name of human progress and civilization."[2] Since Puerto Rico was to be permanently attached to the United States, "benevolent assimilation" should follow. Puerto Ricans had to learn the American creed, divest themselves of their past, and in return receive what General Nelson Miles called in a 1898 war proclamation "the blessings of civilization."

There was no room in the spirit of the times for self-determination. In characteristic nineteenth-century fashion, the Treaty of Paris made no allowances for Puerto Rican consent. The political status of the island was to be decided by the U.S. Congress, and no promise was made of eventual U.S. citizenship. Outright annexation was to be followed by outright colonialism. To establish its legal and institutional framework, McKinley in 1899 appointed Elihu Root to be his secretary of war. Root, a conservative corporate lawyer with a sharp mind and consummate legal skills, went to work with General George W. Davis, the last of Puerto Rico's military governors. In his 1899 report, Root framed the theory of colonial tutelage, denying Puerto Rico any legal right but recognizing "a moral right to be treated by the United States in accordance with the principles of justice and freedom which we have declared in our Constitution." Since the people had not been educated in the art of self-government, he thought they had to learn slowly the principles of self-control and respect for constitutional government. He added:

"They would inevitably fail without a course of tuition under a strong and guiding hand. With that tuition for a time their natural capacity will, it is hoped, make them a self-governing people."[3] This doctrine, together with the doctrine of congressional supremacy, as stated in the Treaty of Paris, provided the needed framework for colonial tutelage. Even before Congress acted, the military occupation had centralized administration in the critical areas of education, justice, and security, and had established both the theory and the tone of U.S. colonial rule over the island.

Congress finally decreed civil government in 1900 by approving the Foraker Act. Politically, the act followed strictly from the Root dictum. The omnipotence of Washington prevailed. Both the executive council and the governor were appointed by the president. The Congress added a House of Delegates, elected by the Puerto Rican people. But after much debate in Congress, U.S. citizenship and full incorporation were denied. Puerto Rico was not to be treated like Hawaii or Alaska; nor was it intended to be eventually independent like the Philippines. It was to be a ward of Congress, ruled by presidential appointees as the supreme interpreters of colonial tutelage. According to the Supreme Court in the insular cases, it was to be a nonincorporated territory, belonging to, but not constituting part of, the United States.

The designation of *nonincorporated territory* offered Puerto Rico a flexibility in economic and fiscal relationships that later proved to be advantageous to the island's growth. With its economy in deep disarray and its government facing a fiscal crisis, Puerto Rico was excluded from the federal internal revenue system so that the island could shape its own taxation structure. Furthermore, to allow the government some revenues, customs receipts were diverted into the insular treasury. These unique features, forced by the fiscal crisis, inadvertently became a cornerstone of the relationship between the island and the United States.

With the Puerto Rican government in firm U.S. control, the island was opened to American investment and trade. Because of its 1 million people, Puerto Rico was not an uninhabited land waiting for a tide of enterprising pioneers. It was a new frontier for American investment, particularly in the sugar and tobacco industries. Sugar, above all, looked like a promising crop. The first civil government promptly approved a law chartering foreign corporations, and the first civilian governor, Charles H. Allen, in his annual report insisted that the island's labor surplus would make the returns to capital "exceedingly profitable . . . to the immense and permanent prosperity of the island."[4]

The growth of the Puerto Rican sugar industry was based on free trade as well as protection by U.S. tariff walls. The rapid influx of American corporate capital raised sugar exports from 68,909 tons valued at $4,715,611 in 1901 to 244,257 tons valued at $18,432,466 in 1910. Furthermore, through building roads and railroads and port improvements, much of the needed infrastructure for the sugar industry was provided. Under the Foraker Act, "King Sugar" began his long and profitable reign in Puerto Rico.

The long-term impact of these policies created deep divisions among Puerto Ricans. At the turn of the century, the island was poor and characterized by an agrarian-based economy. Coffee was the major crop, with a profitable market in Europe. Absentee ownership had not yet become prevalent and 93 percent of the island's farms were owner occupied.

The island's liberal elite had gained an autonomous charter from Spain in 1897. Self-government, within a parliamentary system, was just beginning when the war broke out. Even the right to negotiate commercial treaties had been granted by Spain. By 1899, this hard-earned autonomy was dead. The Spanish-American War resulted in the transfer of Puerto Rico from a declining metropole—Spain—to an emerging one—the United States. At first there were great expectations among the political leadership that the island would shortly become a federal state. The Foraker Act, which signaled the end of Puerto Rican autonomy without promising statehood, shook public opinion and led to a polarization of the island's politics. By 1904 support was clearly evident for three political trends: statehood based on cultural assimilation; home rule founded on the recognition of Puerto Rico's unique collective personality; and independence.

While Puerto Rico's coffee economy was being rapidly superseded by King Sugar, with its increasing emphasis on corporate absenteeism, ambivalent feelings developed between tutors and pupils. The new rulers wanted to promote U.S. democracy in the island, yet they were deeply distrustful of the capabilities of the Puerto Rican people. Americanization seemed to be the answer, which meant imposing the English language and casting aside old values and traditions. The army, the schools, and the judicial system were convenient tools for this purpose. Somewhat later, the labor movement, under the powerful influence of the AFL, was also an agent of Americanization, as was the evangelizing fervor of Protestant missionaries.

Yet Americanization forced by colonial rule was bound to be resisted. Although many Puerto Ricans embraced Manifest Destiny and American recolonization, others strongly objected. The quasi omnipotence of the colonial government was resented deeply by the elite. The efforts to implant the English language and the gradual penetration of foreign capital exacerbated tensions on the island. Of course the historical ledger was not one sided: Economic development, the expansion of education, the rise of trade unions, and the birth of a women's movement were bringing Puerto Rico into the twentieth century. Yet tutorial rule, Americanization, and the increasing concentration of wealth were setting the stage for an explosive crisis.

The earliest manifestation of political estrangement occurred in 1909 when the House of Delegates refused to approve the island's budget. President Taft and the U.S. Congress responded by introducing legislation that further limited the political rights of Puerto Ricans. But between 1912 and 1916, sentiment for reform grew in the U.S. Congress. New legislation was introduced that offered Puerto Ricans U.S. citizenship and an elective senate. Action on this legislation was delayed until war became imminent and President Wilson personally intervened. Yet despite this legislation, the substance of colonial tutelage was preserved. Furthermore, when the Jones Act finally passed Congress in 1917 granting U.S. citizenship and an elective senate to Puerto Ricans, Secretary of War Nelson Baker asserted that the bill involved the U.S. moral dominance in the Caribbean. Once again strategic imperatives cast their long shadow over the relationship between Puerto Rico and the United States.

It should be noted that the extension of U.S. citizenship to Puerto Ricans was not a result of the island's cultural absorption by the mainland. Nor was citizenship equated with self-determination. Considerations of the strategic importance of Puerto Rico spurred the redefinition of colonial tutelage. Puerto Rico remained distinct and unassimilated but it was asked to play the role of a Caribbean Malta.

The road to the future nevertheless continued to be rocky and contradictory. U.S. ambivalence toward Puerto Rico was evident in the postwar period. In 1922, in *Balzac* vs. *People of Puerto Rico* (258 U.S. 298), the Supreme Court made clear that citizenship did not convey "an intention to incorporate in this Union these distant ocean communities of a different origin and language from those of our continental people." In the same period, Governor E. Mont Reily, appointed by President Warren S. Harding, was preaching a 100 percent Americanization in Puerto Rico with the supremacy of the English language in the schools and the U.S. political gospel. To accept or not to accept Puerto Rico's cultural reality, that was the question, with American public policy sharply divided on the issue.

In the light of these conflicting trends, no wonder Puerto Rican public opinion became increasingly fragmented. The stirrings for independence began to be solidified with the founding of the Nationalist party and the emergence of a new professional and intellectual elite, deeply critical of the prevailing tutelage. Partisan divisions were accentuated between those who preached statehood and those who saw in the Irish Free State a midway model to promote a permanent association with the

American Union. Efforts to secure an elective governor proved fruitless in the face of presidential indifference and congressional neglect. For both Harding and Coolidge, Puerto Rico was inhabiting the best of all worlds, thanks to American generosity. It was a mark of ingratitude to claim that the island was a "subjected" colony.

But presidential smugness was soon to face an ominous reality. In September 1928, Puerto Rico was hit by San Felipe, a devastating hurricane, and in October 1929, like the rest of the world, it was hit by the Wall Street crash. The period of impressive statistics ended. The ensuing socioeconomic plight of the island would shape all future policy considerations.

Tutelage in Crisis

After 1929, the U.S. government found itself in a quandary concerning Puerto Rico. "Benevolent assimilation" had not worked. In spite of many claims to progress, the economic conditions of the masses were appalling whereas fat profits had been pocketed by the sugar industrialists. To add to the social woes, the population grew from nearly 1 million in 1900 to more than 1,800,000 in 1940. The crisis shattered the rosy dreams of the colonial tutors.

Theodore Roosevelt, Jr. (1929–1931), appointed governor by President Hoover, was the first chief executive to call a spade a spade. He found the rich coastal plain in the hands of the big sugar companies, which had the effect of relegating small and medium-sized farmers to the rugged interior. "Poverty," he claimed in his book, *Colonial Policies of the United States*, "was widespread and hunger, almost to the verge of starvations, common."[5] While praising the progress that had occurred in administration, health, education, and roadbuilding, he criticized official policy in other areas: the refusal of U.S. administrators to speak Spanish; the assumption of American cultural and racial superiority; and the overwhelming dominance of North American capital on the island.

Roosevelt attempted to correct these negative trends by fostering a diversification of agriculture based on aid to small, independent farmers. He also supported the establishment of vocational education and new industries. He saw no reason for continuing "the hopeless drive to remodel Puerto Ricans so that they become similar in language, habits and thoughts to continental Americans." In politics, he favored evolution toward a dominion model. Unfortunately, as the depression hit Puerto Rico with gale force, his far-seeing efforts floundered.

By the time the New Deal arrived under President Franklin D. Roosevelt, the situation was worsening. In a country where 70 percent of the people lived in rural areas, 80 percent were landless. In 1930 the estimated net per capita income in Puerto Rico was $122; the depression lowered it to $85 in 1933. The 1930 level was not reached again until 1940, when defense expenditures improved the island's income.

F.D.R.'s policies were ambivalent. On one hand, thanks to Eleanor Roosevelt's personal interest, an awareness developed concerning the social plight of the island, leading to the extension of relief and rehabilitation measures to Puerto Rico. But Roosevelt made some of the worst political appointments of the tutelage period. Puerto Rican affairs were put under the Interior Department, with Harold Ickes as secretary and Ernest H. Gruening as director of the Division of Territories and Insular Possessions. They were asked to usher in a new period in the island's rehabilitation. But the appointed governors again demonstrated the flaws of colonial tutelage. Robert H. Gore (1933–1934) was a misfit; General Blanton Winship (1934–1939) was an army man with a conservative outlook; Admiral William D. Leahy (1939–1940) was a war appointee. Not until Rexford G. Tugwell (1941–1946) was appointed did the governorship really embrace the New Deal philosophy.

By that time, the critique of tutelage in Puerto Rico had developed strong mass support. Its most strident voice came from the small, tightly knit Nationalist party, led by Pedro Albizu Campos, an uncompromising foe of U.S. rule. Its strongest popular voice came from the liberal groups that sought social and economic reform with political independence. Their eventual leader was Luis Muñoz Marín, a gifted intellectual and writer.

Puerto Rico's legislative assembly during the New Deal period (1932–1940) was dominated by a coalition of statehood-oriented Republicans and Socialists. The Socialist party, with strong ties to the labor movement, was divided and bureaucratized by the end of the 1930s. The strange coalition between labor-oriented Socialists and conservative Republicans, who had been brought together only because of political expediency, made it difficult to implement a rehabilitation program for the island's economy. When the so-called Chardon plan, which called for land reform, agricultural diversification, and industrial development, was finally enacted in 1934, the odds were against its success. The coalition was lukewarm and so was the governor. In fact, the minority Liberal party was the only group that gave unconditional support to the program. As a result, the plan floundered amid squabbles and recriminations between Puerto Ricans and the colonial administration. The assassination of Colonel Francis Riggs by the Nationalists, the Ponce "massacre," in which the insular police killed defenseless Nationalists, and other acts of violence led to a period of reactionary policies under Winship. On the mainland, Senator Millard Tydings of Maryland introduced legislation calling for punitive independence of Puerto Rico.

By 1940, a general crisis in the system of tutelage was clearly evident: The political system was rent by discord; the sugar economy had failed to develop a decent way of life for the workers; health problems were enormous; psychological estrangement between tutors and pupils was deepening. In sum, the historical ledger showed a negative balance.

The Road to Consensus

In the economic and political plight of the 1930s the seeds of a new Puerto Rico were sown. The manner in which the island emerged from that sordid era has had a profound effect on events during the rest of the century. What we call the contemporary crisis cannot be understood without adequate historical insight into the 1940–1960 period, when modern Puerto Rico was built. Extraordinary socioeconomic development took place, together with a profound change in the island's government. To pretend that the political changes from 1950 to 1952 were simply a legitimation of the status quo is to misinterpret historical events. To assert that only now is the process of decolonization under way is to ignore a vibrant period in Puerto Rican history where important achievements took place against great odds, by a mobilization of the people's will. The resolve to change things was a Puerto Rican resolve; it was self-determination in practice before it could be accepted theoretically in the pattern of U.S.–Puerto Rican relations. It was no easy task to wrest powers from a reluctant conservative Congress, jealous of its prerogatives and to create a new framework based on the principles of compact and government by consent of the governed. To hundreds of thousands of Puerto Ricans, these were living principles adopted to guide the course of future relations. They cannot simply be ignored or wiped off the historical record by contemporary analysts.[6]

In 1940, the Popular Democratic party (PPD) led by Muñoz Marín came to power after a narrow victory in the legislature. The party immediately began to implement its program. Land distribution, a minimum wage, and educational reform were among its major objectives. This reformism was supported by Washington. The world was at war and Puerto Rico became one of the keys to Caribbean defense. It was important to surround militarization with good will. Rexford G. Tugwell, a New Dealer, was appointed governor to achieve that objective. He became an ally of populist reform and helped set up a new administrative structure to assure better government.

In 1944, the PPD swept the island's elections and established a democratic hegemony that lasted twenty-five years. The party was the architect of a consensus in both economic and political arenas. Beginning in 1948, a new developmental strategy was pursued—Operation Bootstrap. It created incentives for industrial investment, especially by offering tax exemptions. The domination of the economy by agriculture was permanently broken, and a new middle class was created. Yet many important problems remained—such as unemployment—that fed large-scale emigration. But Puerto Rico was decidedly on the move, as in no other time in its modern history. It was the land of economic planning (*Fomento*) and of great progress in housing, education, and health.

Economic development was buttressed by political evolution: Operation Bootstrap was part of the wider program of defining a new relationship between Puerto Rico and the United States. During the Truman administration rapid progress was achieved in abolishing colonial tutelage. A Puerto Rican was appointed governor in 1946, and in the ensuing years commonwealth status evolved.

The PPD had chosen the middle road in order to both decolonize the political relationship and promote the budding industrialization of Puerto Rico. Operation Commonwealth and Operation Bootstrap were two sides of the same coin.

The idea proposed by the PPD was novel: Congress was to recognize the principle of government by consent. The proposed act (in the language of H.R. 7674) would be "adopted in the nature of a compact so that the people of Puerto Rico may organize a government pursuant to a constitution of their adoption." Puerto Rico was to be self-governing in all internal affairs, doing away with presidential tutelage. It was not to be independent from the Union; Congress still could legislate in federal matters reserved under the law. But internal self-government was to be established. The island, so the Puerto Rican leaders asserted, was to cease being a possession or a territory. They talked about a new dimension of U.S. federalism.[7]

Public Law 600 as finally approved was no mere act of Congress. It needed Puerto Rican approval in a referendum, an obvious sign of the compact concept. Once accepted by the people, a constitutional convention was called, delegates were elected, and the resulting constitution was again submitted for voter approval—373,594 yeas to 82,777 nays. Had Congress made an irrevocable delegation of its powers by entering into the new arrangement? Congressman Meader of Michigan thought so and wanted to amend the Constitution when it came before the House. But his amendment was voted down. Public Law 447, approving the constitution, again reiterated in no uncertain terms that Public Law 600 had been adopted by the Congress "as a compact with the people of Puerto Rico, to become operative upon its approval by the people of Puerto Rico."

There was great Puerto Rican support for the commonwealth, but minority opposition remained in both proindependence and prostatehood groups. To commonwealth supporters the new relations were based on a compact with Congress, as stated in the federal laws and the new island's constitution. To this compact, the majority of the people had consented. To its adversaries, the compact was a hoax, a farce, an impossibility under the U.S. Constitution. Puerto Rico simply remained to them a possession or colony. This issue has been crucial in the status debate. Contemporary anticommonwealth critics either ignore the legislative history of Public Laws 600 and 447 or pretend that the Puerto Rican leaders consented to legislation perpetuating the possession idea.

The new status was tested internationally at the United Nations. In 1953, after long debate Puerto Rico was removed from the list of nonself-governing territories. The United States, with the support of countries like Brazil, Colombia, Ecuador, Peru, and Costa Rica, defended the theory that Puerto Rico had entered into a compact and that, under the new arrangement, the island had achieved not independence but self-government. A message by President Dwight D. Eisenhower made clear that if the insular legislature requested "more complete and even absolute independence" the president would recommend that Congress grant it. Finally, UN Resolution 748 (VIII), sponsored by several Latin American nations, recognized that Puerto Rico had established a mutually agreed association with the United States and had in fact become an autonomous political entity. A significant clause added that due regard would be paid to the will of both the Puerto Rican and American peoples in the event either party might desire any change in the terms of the association. The intent was that the United Nations would still maintain a watch over any future modification of the compact.

So Puerto Rico emerged as a commonwealth or associated free state with international recognition. To those who supported commonwealth, free association was a fact; the relationship was novel. It was thus praised by Chief Justice Earl Warren when he visited Puerto Rico in 1956, and many other prominent U.S. statesmen praised the new relationship and the great socioeconomic strides Puerto Rico had taken.

Presidential supremacy in internal matters had ended. The commonwealth government was run by Puerto Ricans. With the exception of the federal court, the judicial system was also in Puerto Rican hands. Educational policies were determined by insular leadership, not by Washington. Basic economic policies were adopted during the PPD era that responded to Puerto Rico's own criteria. The 1950s were exuberant years. Factories were pouring more than a half million dollars in wages alone into the economy each week. Private investment increased at 36 percent per year from 1950 to 1954 and about 46 percent from 1955 to 1959. Industrial jobs brought unemployment to a record low of 12.4 percent in 1959. A two-way migration movement took place between the United States and Puerto Rico, spurred by cheap transportation and the U.S. economic bonanza. The bulk of the Puerto Rican migrants were unskilled or semiskilled workers, in search of seasonal employment. Governor Muñoz expressed hopes in his State of the Commonwealth message of 1954 that while migration had stabilized population growth, Puerto Rican productivity would eventually create the necessary economic opportunities to overcome the problem.

As commonwealth status unfolded, federal intervention and influence in internal Puerto Rican affairs receded. Tutelage was now replaced by collaboration, a collaboration manifested in two spheres: The commonwealth offered itself as a strong partner in the Point Four and other U.S. international assistance programs. It became an active hub of inter-American meetings. By 1960, more than 10,000 leaders of opinion, experts, and trainees had come to Puerto Rico from the developing world. Muñoz Marín became a leader of the democratic left in Latin America, a close friend of Romulo Betancourt, José Figueres, Victor Raul Haya de la Torre, Eduardo Frei, and other democratic figures. Puerto Rico influenced some of the thinking that went into the recommendations made to the Eisenhower administration on inter-American relations. Puerto Ricans took an active part in the conception and management of John F. Kennedy's Alliance for Progress.

Opposition to commonwealth status continued on the island. The Pro-Independence party (PIP), which had been the second strongest political group from 1952 to 1956, lost considerable ground, largely because of internal bickering. The Republican Statehood party (PER) recouped under new leadership. The admission of both Alaska and Hawaii into the Union was a psychological lift for it. Also, the party's links with the Republican establishment increased its Washington influence. Commonwealth leaders, on the other hand, pushed for clear definition of the terms of the U.S.–Puerto Rican association. But while there was good will in Congress, no action was taken. The prostatehood groups had strong allies among the Republicans to help thwart the initiatives. The PPD, however, under Muñoz's leadership, retained its strength. In November 1960, the PPD obtained 457,800 votes compared with 252,000 for the PER, while the Pro-Independence Party received only 24,000.

Puerto Rican cooperation with the United States reached its zenith during the Kennedy era. A strong personal friendship developed between the young president and Muñoz. Kennedy paid a special visit to Puerto Rico in 1961; he received the greatest welcome awarded to any U.S. president. A tremendous outpouring of people cheered him as he entered

San Juan. His visit evidenced a spirit of partnership, not tutelage. Puerto Rico had traveled a long way since the Reily and Winship days.

Letters exchanged between Muñoz and Kennedy further clarified Kennedy's support for a fully developed commonwealth in permanent association with the United States and showed agreement for a consultation so that the people could "express any other preference, including independence, if that should be their wish." The way was open for another expression of the people's will. Efforts to get congressional action however failed. Congressional powers, still rooted in the Treaty of Paris and the territorial clause, continued to make negotiations extremely difficult. Finally, after Kennedy's death, Congress agreed in 1964 to create a U.S.–Puerto Rican commission on the status of the political relationship between the United States and Puerto Rico but without a mandate for Congress to act or provision for a plebiscite.

Muñoz Marín decided to resign as governor to marshal support for commonwealth status in the plebiscite. He handpicked Secretary of State Roberto Sánchez Vilella as his successor. In retrospect, it was a damaging decision for the PPD's future. Sánchez Vilella was an able administrator but lacked Muñoz's political skills. In trying to build an independent political base, he clashed with the legislative leaders and eventually estranged himself from Muñoz and the party. In this difficult situation for the PPD the plebiscite was held. Of 702,500 voters, 425,000 or 60.5 percent favored commonwealth whereas 273,000 or 38.9 percent voted for statehood. Encouraged by this showing, the statehooders registered a new party, the New Progressive party (PNP) and went on to defeat the divided PPD. When Sánchez led a splinter party of the PPD in the 1968 elections, the PNP candidate, Luis A. Ferré, was able to squeeze through with a 23,000 vote plurality. Although the procommonwealth forces were a majority, the party split had brought the statehooders into power. The Pro-Independence party continued to be a very distant third force.

The last years of the PPD democratic hegemony were accompanied by great social and economic strides. In his 1963 State of the Commonwealth message, Muñoz had many reasons to be optimistic. Every economic index showed undeniable progress. Investment in construction reached $443 million; net income from manufacturing was $381 million with an increase in investment by local capital. Grazing and poultry added new impetus to farm production. The coffee crop was the highest since the 1929 storm. In 1963, Puerto Rican trade reached $1,098 million, and the island was the second largest market for U.S. products in the hemisphere, right after Canada and ahead of either Brazil or Argentina. Trade with other nations was also rising. To Muñoz, Puerto Rico was now the industrial workshop of the Caribbean.

In his last 1964 message, the governor observed that Puerto Rico's rate of economic growth was one of the fastest in the world, that the workers' share in net income has risen to 68 percent of the total, and that more factories were opening with Puerto Rican capital and management. The governor expected net income to reach $5 billion in 1975. This was certainly not the picture of a weak, dependent, welfare economy. The dynamic growth had been the result of wise policies and increased productivity. The policies that had been adopted within the framework of commonwealth status had clearly worked.

The End of Consensus

But the signs of imminent disarray were evident. Political morale was deeply affected by the split between the legislature and the executive, foreshadowing a period of alternating governments and increased ideological polarization. Divisions were not caused simply by status issues; they involved personalities, the unity or disunity of parties, and the strength of electoral organizations, as well as policy issues.

The consensus of the 1967 plebiscite led nowhere. Under Ferré, an ad hoc advisory group simply explored the desirability of extending the presidential vote to Puerto Rico, an issue of great importance to statehooders but one on which commonwealth partisans were sharply divided. The group recommended that the presidential vote be accorded to the people of Puerto Rico and the issue submitted to a referendum.

By 1972, the PPD had regrouped and was ready to face Ferré and the PNP. Under the leadership of Rafael Hernández Colón, a young attorney, and with Muñoz's strong support, the PPD defeated the PNP, 609,600 votes to 524,000. Efforts were made then to revive the ad hoc advisory group and implement the 1967 plebiscite. The group, now cochaired by Muñoz and Senator Marlow W. Cook, concluded after years of study that a new compact of permanent union should be adopted to replace the Puerto Rican Federal Relations Act included in Public Law 600. The draft proposal reaffirmed the principle of compact grounded upon common citizenship, currency, defense, and markets, with the U.S. Supreme Court as the final arbiter. The Nixon-Ford administration took little interest in the report. The same held true for an indifferent Congress. President Ford totally disregarded it; instead, before leaving office in January 1977, he made a proposal to Congress in favor of statehood.

By that time, another political change had taken place in Puerto Rico. Hit by the world recession that forced the government to undertake unpalatable tax policies to preserve fiscal integrity, and rocked by inflationary pressures, the Hernández Colón administration was defeated in its bid for reelection. Carlos Romero Barceló, the mayor of San Juan, became governor by 40,000 votes. The PIP still remained a distant third. Romero's first administration was characterized by an intense drive for statehood and by an effort to involve Puerto Rican politics in the national mainstream by holding presidential primaries and establishing close contacts with both the Republican and Democratic parties. While Ferré worked with the Republican leadership, the governor established himself as a pro-Carter man among the Democrats. The strategy produced dividends in the control of local patronage and in a rash of statements by leading Americans in support of statehood. "Statehood now!" was the cry of presidential candidate George Bush, echoed by Senator Howard Baker, as well as by the Carter representatives in the 1980 primary fight against Ted Kennedy, in spite of the fact that Carter had promised to respect all options in a 1978 message to Puerto Rico.

Economic policies now favored the gradual reduction of tax incentives and fuller integration into the U.S. economy by a higher dependence on federal funds. The extension to Puerto Rico of many features of President Johnson's Great Society had increased the flow of federal assistance to the island. More and more federal transfer payments bolstered family incomes. Net federal disbursements increased about fourfold, from $608 million in fiscal year 1970 to $2,381 million in fiscal 1977. These disbursements reflected federal, rather than commonwealth, priorities. Little comprehensive planning was behind the aid.

It was evident, as Puerto Rico faced the 1980s, that the political and economic consensus that had characterized the Muñoz era had dissipated and been replaced by harsh polarizations. In spite of federal patronage, in spite of prostatehood support from politicians in both U.S. parties, including Ronald Reagan, Governor Romero was unable to obtain the sweeping victory he envisioned. In 1980, the PNP maintained its strength in metropolitan areas but in a stiff battle lost fifty-five of seventy-seven municipalities. The governor was able to squeeze through with a mere 3,000 vote plurality, leaving many voters with the impression that his victory was largely the result of his control of the electoral machinery. The PPD eventually prevailed in the Legislative Assembly. The statehood drive that promised to be a juggernaut and had so impressed many sectors of American opinion had been stopped in its tracks. Instead, a stalemate prevails.

Conclusion

A new trend has emerged of late. Since Puerto Ricans cannot create their own consensus—the argument goes—the United States should create it for them. Congress should act according to its paramount powers, derived from the Treaty of Paris and the territorial clause. Some policy analysts argue that it should promote Puerto Rican independence; others, that it should bring about a decision between statehood and independence. Commonwealth and its emphasis on free association are declared obsolete. The principles of compact and government by consent are conveniently shelved. In spite of the fact that judicial opinion has not invalidated the compact, that decisions of the First Circuit Court in Boston have affirmed its validity and existence, the issue is simply eliminated from consideration. Puerto Rico is returned to the status of a possession and dependency, and the doors are shut to any further analysis of the validity and potentialities of further commonwealth growth.

While this happens, support for commonwealth is far from disappearing in Puerto Rico. All political parties are suffering from severe internal strains, but the ailment is particularly strong within the prostatehood forces, while divisionism is also found in the small proindependence movements.

This internal political situation, which has brought the procommonwealth forces to full power in 1984, exists at a time when the Reagan administration is proceeding in the rapid remilitarization of the island. The strategic imperative looms again as a key factor in U.S. policies.

Unless tact, prudence, and political sensitivity prevail, particularly in presidential decisions, the Puerto Rico situation can become explosive. Abandonment of self-determination, annulment of the principles of compact and government by consent, to be replaced by congressional decision and executive pressure through the manipulation of federal funds, can bring about a very tense situation in the island. Violence has been limited to a small fringe; it could become more general if a new status is seen as resulting from external imposition, not internal consensus. The delicate pattern of economic interdependence can suffer grave damage, to the mutual loss of the Puerto Rican economy and of American investments now totaling more than $10 billion.

If there is a lesson of this historical retrospective, it is that a meeting of the minds between Puerto Rico and the United States is a very difficult, but not impossible, task. The United States has emerged since 1898 as a world superpower; Puerto Rico is but a small link in the chain that forged the rise to U.S. globalism. And yet it has struggled for its own identity under the shadow of the mightiest industrial power on earth. During the period 1944 to 1968, there were a convergence and a consensus that yielded mutual benefits. Federal power receded in some key areas to be replaced by a fruitful collaboration in others.

How to restructure a new consensus is a delicate, crucial challenge for both the United States and Puerto Rico. But it certainly cannot be attained by U.S. unilateral action, by the use of overwhelming pressures, or by shelving principles and concepts that have become rooted in the historical experience. If there is to be a way out of the present predicament, if a new encounter is to be achieved, wise and informed counsel should prevail.

Notes

1. Alfred T. Mahan, *Lessons of the War with Spain* (Boston, 1918), p. 29.

2. Murat Halstead, *Pictoral History of America's New Possessions* (Chicago, 1899), p. 511.

3. Elihu Root, "The Principles of Colonial Policy," *The Military and Colonial Policy of the United States* (Cambridge, 1916), pp. 163–165.

4. Quoted in Arturo Morales Carrión, *Puerto Rico: A Political and Cultural History* (New York, 1983), p. 160.

5. Theodore Roosevelt, Jr., *Colonial Policies of the United States* (New York, 1937), pp. 117–118.

6. Typical views on this point have been expressed by Juan M. García-Passalacqua, "Decolonization in the Caribbean: The U.S. and Puerto Rico" (Paper submitted to the First Conference on International Relations held in San Germán, Puerto Rico, April 22–23, 1983). See also Alfred Stepan, "The United States and Latin America: Vital Interests and the Instruments of Power," *Foreign Affairs*, 58, 3 (1980):675–679.

7. Little use has been made by recent analysts of a key book for understanding the commonwealth process, written by Puerto Rico's resident commissioner, Antonio Fernós Isern, *Estado Libre Asociado. Antecedentes, Creación y Desarrollo hasta la Epoca Presente* (University of Puerto Rico Press, 1974), particularly pp. 99–112.

THE ECONOMY: FROM BOOTSTRAP TO FOOD STAMPS

Introduction

The most immediate, indeed urgent, problem in Puerto Rico is not political status, but the economy. A few statistics suffice. Unemployment has been running between 20 and 30 percent for the past several years. Fifty percent of the inhabitants of the island receive food stamps. Federal transfer payments represent one-third of the island's gross national product.

Moreover, this economic dependence rests on precarious foundations, as Bertram Finn shows in his chapter. The rapid economic growth of Puerto Rico in the 1950s and 1960s was due in part to governmental manipulation of factor prices by tax exemptions, wage differentials, administrative quotas, and so on. Changing conditions made these policy tools obsolete, but nothing was put in their place. Finn argues for a new approach to stimulate growth, based on developing indigenous resources, especially the island's trained labor force.

The heart of Puerto Rico's industrialization policy, however, continues to be the exemption from federal taxation enjoyed by subsidiaries of U.S. corporations located on the island. Yet these tax privileges are under increasing attack in Congress as affording large tax shelters to mainland firms without a corresponding increase in jobs in Puerto Rico. In 1982, the Congress came close to reducing drastically these exemptions and did cut them back, although much less than the original legislative proposals envisioned. The remaining tax credits are an obvious target for future congressional efforts to reduce the federal deficit.

As for federal transfer payments, which one author in this book says have become "a way of life in Puerto Rico," they too depend on the most ephemeral of congressional moods. Puerto Rico often has been included in federal welfare programs as an afterthought. Puerto Rico was included in the food stamp program, for example, when Senator George McGovern decided it would be unfair to leave the island out. Yet Puerto Rico's GNP is 70 percent of that of the poorest state in the Union, with the result that almost every second person on the island became eligible for the program. In these circumstances, the food stamp program in Puerto Rico inevitably came under attack from those in Congress who saw it as a flagrant giveaway or were concerned about the moral implications of the program as it was administered in Puerto Rico.

The struggle over these two programs in Congress is described in the case studies recorded in Chapter 4 by some of the protagonists. The point is not that Congress can giveth and taketh away—that is true for all Americans—but in Puerto Rico's case, the Congress is often legislating only or primarily on matters peculiar to Puerto Rico, yet—and this is the crux of the matter—with objectives other than Puerto Rico's economic development or the welfare of its inhabitants. Without voting representation in the Congress or presidential elections, Puerto Rico is reduced to lobbying when these legislative initiatives threaten. In this sense, the island's relationship to the federal government is more analogous to that of Chrysler, Lockheed, or Penn Central than to a state of the Union. In these case studies, there is no villain (both sides have valid arguments) unless it is the absence of any mechanism by which the national interests and the specific Puerto Rican interests can be reconciled when they seem to clash.

Randolph Mye argues that the need for such a mechanism transcends questions of legislative efficiency. In Mye's view, a special federal body exclusively devoted to assisting Congress and the executive to support Puerto Rico's economic growth is essential for healthy development. Moreover, says Mye, the emphasis in Puerto Rican political discourse on the status question puts the cart before the horse: Without economic development Congress will never have the confidence in Puerto Rico's ability to manage its affairs to consider seriously any status option. A central complement to a federal commission, in Mye's view, would be a development planning body in Puerto Rico representing the major public and private interests in the economy. What Mye is calling for is nothing less than a major act of political will by both the federal government and Puerto Rican leaders. The latter would have to put aside their bitter political differences for the sake of a new economic development effort that would have major support on the island. The federal government would have to suppress its penchant for letting sleeping dogs lie and tackle the thorny problem of federal-commonwealth relations, at least economic ones.

3

Puerto Rico's Economic Development: The Old Formula No Longer Works —A New Strategy Is Needed

Bertram P. Finn

Introduction

For many years, Puerto Rico's economic development program and its supporting institutions were held up by experts as the model for other developing countries, and rightly so. Puerto Rico's economy had built a solid record of performance. Year after year the economy had grown in real terms in excess of 5 percent a year. Regardless of what was happening to the U.S. economy or in the world's markets, the Puerto Rican growth machine consistently produced superior results.

No longer do the experts hold up Puerto Rico's economy as a model to emulate. Something happened in 1974. Forces that had been building in the obscurity of the shadows emerged on center stage and manifested their presence with two consecutive years of negative economic growth. Since that sharp setback, the Puerto Rican economy has stagnated and has not provided the economic resources to deal effectively with Puerto Rico's social problems.

Between 1948 and 1973, the Puerto Rican economy averaged a real growth rate of 6.96 percent per year. Indeed, the growth rates of Puerto Rico's gross domestic product (GDP) in those twenty-six years were roughly double those of the United States. In contrast, during the last ten years the Puerto Rican GDP has grown by only 1.86 percent per annum, or roughly at the same rate as the U.S. economy.

In this chapter, we will try to analyze the underlying changes that brought about the inability of Puerto Rico's traditional growth strategy to continue to produce the high levels of economic expansion that the island needs. We will attempt to show that Puerto Rico's problems are not caused by cyclical factors as some allege, but are structural in nature. Finally, we will suggest measures that can be taken by the federal government and the commonwealth government itself to broaden and diversify Puerto Rico's development.

Factors Contributing to Puerto Rico's Growth

Our analysis of what went wrong with Puerto Rico's growth strategy will focus on seven factors—wages, tariffs, taxes, public administration, geographic location, infrastructure, and labor—that combined in the postwar era to promote a high growth rate. Some of these factors, like taxes, were susceptible to policy, whereas some, like geography, were fortuitous. We will see why after the mid-1970s these factors failed to produce results. Before we begin our analysis, however, one point deserves emphasis. Since the 1950s, the Puerto Rican economy has been progressively more integrated into the world economy and thereby exposed to those same forces that positively or negatively affect the system as a whole. Unfortunately, the decade of the 1970s was not the most propitious time for greater economic integration into the rest of the world. In the last thirteen years, two major recessions, a period of high inflation, stagflation, and an energy crisis have slowed growth worldwide. These outside events have clearly contributed to Puerto Rico's economic problems since 1974. Such changes in the economic climate demanded new policies, a new strategy of economic development. Efforts at policy innovation, however, were not responsive to this new environment.

The Wage Advantage

When Puerto Rico's development strategy shifted to the promotion of private sector manufacturing enterprises in 1948, Puerto Rico had a very sizeable wage advantage over the U.S. mainland. In 1950, manufacturing wages on the island were 28 percent of manufacturing wages on the mainland, indeed, the average manufacturing wage on the island was 56 percent of the mainland minimum wage.

In the ensuing thirty-five years, wages in Puerto Rico have grown at a much faster rate than on the mainland. The relative wage increase can be easily seen by examining the ratio of the average Puerto Rican hourly manufacturing wage to the average hourly manufacturing wage for the nation as a whole for selected years since 1950 (Table 3.1). Beginning at a ratio of 28 percent in 1950, the wage creep began slowly; the ratio only increased to 29 percent in 1955. However, after 1955 the ratio's growth began to accelerate, indicating that wages in Puerto Rico were rising more sharply than those on the mainland. In 1960 the ratio rose to 41 percent, then to 48 percent in 1965, and to 53 percent in 1970. The ratio continued to rise slowly through 1977 to 56 percent and has since remained constant. (As an aside, the constant ratio since

Table 3.1

**Comparative Average Hourly Wage in Manufacturing in the
U.S. Versus Puerto Rico for Selected Years, 1950-1982**

| Years | Average Hourly Manufacturing Wage | | Ratio of P.R. Average to U.S. Average (%) |
	U.S. ($)	Puerto Rico ($)	
1950	1.50	0.42	28
1955	1.91	0.56	29
1960	2.30	0.94	41
1965	2.64	1.26	48
1970	3.37	1.78	53
1975	4.83	2.59	54
1976	5.28	2.86	54
1977	5.60	3.11	56
1978	6.17	3.44	56
1979	6.70	3.75	56
1980	7.27	4.10	56
1981	7.99	4.45	56
1982	8.50	4.75	56

Sources: 1. U.S. Commerce Department, *Economic Study of Puerto Rico, Vol. 2* (Washington: GPO, December 1979), p. 56.

2. Puerto Rico Labor Department, *Annual Census of Manufacturers*, various years.

1977 tends to discount the allegations that the whole problem is due to the imposition of the full federal minimum wage after 1977.)

Even while wages in Puerto Rico were rising faster than those on the mainland, it was not until 1965 that the average hourly wage on the island exceeded the mainland's minimum wage. Thus all through these early years of Puerto Rico's development program, the island enjoyed very significant wage advantages compared to the mainland, when the entire manufacturing sector's averages are concerned. However, such a wage comparison does not reflect the differing compositions of manufacturing in Puerto Rico and the mainland. For example, Puerto Rico's manufacturing sector does not contain major automotive, aircraft, or primary metals manufacturing facilities. The differing composition may obscure some of the trends in specific industrial sectors.

For that reason, seven industrial sectors that exist in both economies have been selected for relative wage comparisons from 1955 to 1982 (Table 3.2). Five of the sectors—food and kindred products, tobacco, textiles, apparel, and leather products—are labor intensive, and therefore wage sensitive. Two sectors—chemicals and electrical equipment—are moderate to heavy users of capital. In 1955, wages in these industries

Table 3.2

**Average Hourly Earnings in Puerto Rico as a Percentage
of Those Earned in U.S. in Specific Manufacturing Sectors
for Selected Years, 1955-1982**

Industry	1955	1960	1966	1971	1975	1980	1982
Food & Kindred Products	38	45	56	57	55	59	61
Tobacco	30	39	50	52	52	48	49
Textiles	39	60	62	66	61	68	70
Apparel	35	54	61	68	66	72	73
Chemicals	36	47	54	59	66	64	63
Leather Products	34	45	55	60	62	72	72
Electrical Equipment	34	52	55	57	61	59	58

Sources: 1. U.S. Dept. of the Treasury, *The Operation and Effect of the Possessions Corporation System of Taxation* (Washington: GPO, 1983), p. 44.
2. Unpublished data, Office of Economic Research-Fomento Económico.

were generally 60 to 70 percent less in Puerto Rico than they were in the United States. During the next twenty-seven years, Puerto Rican wages more than doubled in relative terms: From earning between 30 and 40 percent of their compatriots' wages on the mainland in the 1950s, workers in Puerto Rico by the 1980s were generally earning between 60 and 70 percent. The only exception to this trend was in the tobacco industry, where wages increased to about half those paid comparable laborers in the United States. In general, the labor-intensive industries—textiles, apparel, and leather products—experienced the most rapid relative wage growth during this period.

Although this analysis indicates that wages in labor-intensive industries on the island are approaching the national average for their respective industries on the mainland, it excludes two important elements. First, the average wages for any mainland industry include the wages from all regions aggregated into one figure. There actually may be wide geographical variations among the wages in any industry. Wages in Puerto Rico may be 70 percent of those for the mainland as a whole, but could also be equal to those paid in Alabama, rural Georgia, Mississippi, or North Carolina. A prospective investor does not look at the wages represented by the national average or even the national average for a specific industrial sector. What is relevant is the wage that must be paid in a given plant in Cidra, Puerto Rico, versus that in Plains, Georgia.

Second, this analysis omits consideration of the average wage paid in foreign locations. In many third world countries, workers in the apparel industry are paid significantly lower wages than in Puerto Rico. In Haiti, for example, workers are paid $2.50 per day. In other Caribbean locations wages are higher, but the $0.85 per hour in the Dominican Republic, for example, is still 23 percent of the wage paid in Puerto Rico. Even assuming that the productivity of foreign workers is lower than that of Puerto Rican workers, the sheer size of the wage differential can compensate for large differences in relative output and still provide a wage incentive to locate in the third world.

In conclusion, the very large wage advantage that Puerto Rico once held compared with the mainland has narrowed considerably over the last thirty-five years. Relative wages have climbed from 28 to 56 percent of the mainland's for the entire manufacturing sector and have increased to more than 70 percent for most of the labor-intensive industries. Furthermore, the wages prevailing in third world countries are significantly less than wages paid in Puerto Rico. Thus, Puerto Rico's comparative advantages in wages vis-à-vis both the mainland and the third world have declined significantly in the last thirty-five years.

The Protective Tariff Advantage

Puerto Rico is included within U.S. customs territory and is therefore protected from foreign competition by U.S. tariffs and nontariff barriers. During the years following World War II, the United States has taken an overtly free-trade policy toward manufactured goods and services, but has taken a protectionist attitude toward agricultural trade. This philosophy has been reflected in three major tariff negotiations under the auspices of the General Agreement on Tariffs and Trade (GATT).

The first of these negotiations, the Dillon Round in the late 1950s, dealt with the tariffs on products produced by and traded among the industrialized countries. Therefore, the labor-intensive goods produced in Puerto Rico retained their protection from low-cost foreign imports from the less developed countries.

The second major round was the Kennedy Round, which began in 1963. These negotiations resulted in a reduction of approximately 33 ⅓ percent on a wide range of products, including labor-intensive ones. As a result, Puerto Rico's tariff protection on apparel, textiles, shoes, and so on, was reduced by one-third over a five-year period beginning in 1967. The third round of GATT tariff negotiations, the Tokyo Round, reduced tariffs by 30 to 40 percent depending on the origin of the product. These reductions will be gradually implemented over an eight-year period ending in 1988. Once again labor-intensive products from the less developed countries were included in the tariff reductions. The general effect of these three tariff negotiations has been to open the U.S. market to higher levels of imports. Labor-intensive industries in both Puerto Rico and the United States were seriously affected by this increase in imports. For example, in 1967 the imports of apparel outerwear controlled 13.6 percent of the U.S. market; this percentage increased to 30.8 percent in 1971, 35.6 percent in 1977, and is now estimated to be 50 percent.

In Puerto Rico, the effect of the increased flow of foreign import competition was just as dramatic. The footwear industry was the most severely affected. In 1968 it employed 11,300 workers in fifty-three establishments. After the Kennedy Round tariff reductions were fully implemented in 1974, there were 6,100 workers in forty-one establishments. That represents a loss of more than 5,000 jobs, or about 46 percent of the total employment in the industry.

The reduction in tariff protection during the past thirty years has limited Puerto Rico's ability to expand its labor-intensive sectors. There has been a slow atrophy within this area. Every year a few more jobs are lost. The rate of decline has been slowed by the multifiber agreement that has limited the growth of foreign apparel imports. However, since this agreement allows for the positive growth of imports, the island's labor-intensive industries may slowly decline.

Taxes

In 1948, when the Puerto Rican government decided to utilize tax exemption as a tool to attract U.S. businesses to locate on the island, U.S. corporations were paying an average tax rate of 37 percent on every dollar of profit; by 1951 the effective tax rate had increased to 54.2 percent. The Puerto Rican government offered firms the opportunity, in conjunction with the possessions system of corporate taxation at the federal level, to avoid all corporate taxes—local, state, and federal. Firms that located in Puerto Rico retained their gross profits instead of paying half to various levels of government. By 1952 roughly seventy new plants were opening in Puerto Rico every year.

Over time, however, there has been a tendency for the U.S. effective corporate tax rate to decline. From its highest level in 1951, 54.2 percent, the rate gradually fell to the 48 percent range for 1954–1961, then, following President Kennedy's tax reductions, to 41 to 43 percent through 1972. It then began to decline more rapidly, falling to a level of 34 percent before the passage of the 1981 Economic Recovery Tax Act. This act further reduced the effective level of corporate taxes to below 30 percent.

Concurrent with this reduction in the effective level of U.S. corporate taxes, the government of Puerto Rico began to impose corporate taxes. In 1976 the Puerto Rican government imposed a dividends repatriations tax upon the formerly exempt profits earned by firms with industrial tax exemption grants on the island. More specifically, when a firm's profits were to be repatriated before a full liquidation of the island subsidiary, the dividends were to be subject to a 10 percent withholding tax.

In 1978 a new industrial incentive act was legislated that eliminated the 100 percent tax exemption for firms; imposed a low partial income tax upon profits ranging from 4.5 percent in the first five years, 11.25 percent in the second five-year period, 15.75 percent in the third five-year period, and 20.25 percent in the fourth five-year period; integrated several alternatives for firms to reduce the dividend repatriations tax from 10 percent to 7 percent, 5 percent, or 3.5 percent; and introduced a method for firms operating under the 1963 incentives act to avail themselves of the benefits under the new act. The 1978 Industrial Incentives Act was only applicable to new firms or new expansions after the date of its enactment. Companies that held grants under the 1963 act could continue operating under that act with 100 percent exemption from corporate income tax—but they were still subject to the 10 percent, or 7 percent, tollgate tax when their dividends were repatriated.

The 1978 act imposed an effective tax—which combined the income tax with the tollgate tax—of approximately 9.28 percent for firms' first five years of operation. Assuming that the effective federal corporate tax rate was 29.7 percent in 1982, we can subtract the Puerto Rican effective rate, 9.28 percent, to obtain the tax advantage of firms locating on the island. This calculation gives us a tax advantage in 1982 of 20.42 percent. The very substantial tax advantage that Puerto Rico was able to offer firms, some 54.2 cents on every dollar of profit in 1954, has gradually been eroded.

The Administrative Advantage

At various times Puerto Rico has been able to use federal administrative procedures to attract new firms and to stimulate economic growth. These administrative actions by the president or legislated by Congress have occasionally been powerful enough to be overriding determinants for industrial location—even when the basic or underlying economic criteria could not otherwise support such a decision. However, utilizing this type of action to generate economic growth is a two-edged sword.

The petrochemical industry in Puerto Rico was built upon special provisions contained in the import quotas set by the Federal Oil Import Administration in 1959, and then modified by Presidential Proclamation

3693 in 1965. These federal actions allowed firms located in Puerto Rico special access to cheap sources of foreign crude oil and feedstocks. Because of this very significant price advantage, many firms located in Puerto Rico. As long as the provisions remained in effect, the industry expanded and prospered. Once the system changed, however, the basic underlying economics of the industry would not support the established operations.

The second and definitely more important administrative instrument for development in Puerto Rico has been federal tax legislation—the possessions system of corporate taxation—upon which Puerto Rico has built its industrial sector. Many modern, high-technology firms on the island did not choose to locate there because of its natural economic attributes. Puerto Rico is neither the source of their raw materials nor the market for their final products. These firms nonetheless purchase raw materials, ship them 1,500 miles to Puerto Rico, process them on the island, and ship them 1,500 miles back to their customers. Firms go to this trouble because of the benefits they receive from locating on the island—a skilled, productive, readily available labor force and very significant tax benefits.

The skilled labor force is one of Puerto Rico's strongest natural economic underpinnings for industrialization. The tax benefits, however, are not native to Puerto Rico. They are granted by the interaction of Puerto Rican legislation and legislation of the federal government—over which Puerto Rico has limited influence. (See Chapter 4.)

Even Puerto Rico's tariff advantage is vulnerable to the vagaries of administrative manipulation. President Reagan has recently tightened the quota system, implemented through the multifiber agreement, that will force greater production of apparel goods in the United States. With the benefits that Puerto Rico's location offers, the island can obtain a significant share of this new domestic production. Protectionist policies, however, move in and out of favor. Jobs created by taking advantage of these new quotas will exist only as long as the quotas remain in effect.

During the last ten years, the boost to the Puerto Rican economy from various administrative measures has been weakened by changes in the measures themselves and in exogenous factors. The petrochemical industry on the island was damaged in part by the removal of the quota system and was finished off by the oil crisis, which turned Puerto Rico's administrative advantage into an insurmountable disadvantage. The recent threats in Congress to the island's special tax status have caused the loss of significant numbers of projects and investments.

Territorial Advantage

As part of the United States, Puerto Rico has been able to offer prospective investors safety for their investments, a similar legal and court system to protect their rights, freedom from exchange rate problems, and protection within the U.S. tariff area. These benefits have become less important over the past thirty-five years. Other areas have demonstrated political stability and fairness in their court system for non-resident investors. In addition, the potential investors themselves have become more sophisticated in evaluating political risk and in minimizing such risk through diversification.

With passage of the administration's Caribbean Basin Initiative, duty-free access on a limited basis is being extended to Puerto Rico's neighbors. Participating countries will be able to ship goods produced in their countries—with the exception of apparel products, rums, and canned tuna—into the United States on a duty-free basis for a period of eight years.

Infrastructure

The physical and social infrastructure of Puerto Rico has been expanded and improved since 1950 to meet the needs of a modern industrial society. Although in some respects inferior to that of the mainland, Puerto Rico's infrastructure is far superior to that of its Caribbean neighbors and can be expanded to meet the island's future needs. In this regard, the island has maintained its position relative to the mainland and has even increased its advantage over foreign countries.

Labor Force Advantage

In the early years of Puerto Rico's program to attract private firms to the island, the labor force offered several advantages for employers. Many workers had skills suited for the apparel industry that they had acquired in the home-sewing industry. Second, two or three workers were available for every new job. And, third, workers were paid considerably less than their mainland counterparts for the same job.

However, the vocational school system at that time had not been equipping students with higher level skills. Although willing and enthusiastic, the labor force could not be called highly skilled.

Today the situation has changed. Vocational schools have been equipping large numbers of students with saleable skills; there is room for improvement, but relative to 1948 great advances have been made. In addition to the vocational system, Puerto Rican workers have learned special skills on the jobs through in-house training by employers. Thirty years of on-the-job training tends to build a large reservoir of skills in the labor force.

The Puerto Rican Economic Development Corporation (*Fomento*) has established, in cooperation with the Department of Education, several specialized schools for the electronics industry. These schools are run to equip workers with the skills and knowledge required to perform tasks in the electronics sector. *Fomento* has also run a specialized school for metal work that has successfully provided highly skilled and sought after graduates, who work for wages below those paid to their mainland counterparts. There is still a readily available supply of workers for potential investors, but now the labor force is considerably more skilled than that found in Puerto Rico's Caribbean neighbors or in foreign competitors. The skill gap that existed between Puerto Rico and the mainland in 1950 has been closed; this will be a positive factor in Puerto Rico's ability to attract the high-technology industries that are expanding within today's economy.

Summary

The ability of Puerto Rico's traditional strategy to provide the levels of economic growth required has been cast into doubt by its performance since 1974. Although this system used to produce a real growth rate of 5 percent year after year, since 1974 it has been hard pressed to produce even a 3 percent annual rate of growth.

The very success of Puerto Rico's export-oriented manufacturing and tourism development strategy has exposed ever-growing proportions of the economy to the forces prevailing in the U.S. mainland and world economies. The Puerto Rican economy will therefore move more closely in unison with these other economies, and economic policy will have to adapt to this new circumstance. In many cases, old techniques, such as the manipulation of factor prices administratively or by law, will not work.

The analysis of the seven factors that have contributed significantly to Puerto Rico's growth has clearly indicated where policy needs to be altered. Five of the factors—the wage advantage, the tariff advantage, the tax advantage, the administrative advantage, and the territorial advantage—have all become constraints to economic growth on the island. The infrastructural advantage has remained neutral to positive, and the labor force advantage has become a more positive factor in Puerto Rico's growth.

Unfortunately, none of the relative changes in these factors can be deemed cyclical; they will not suddenly revert to their original position at some other point in the business cycle. They are long-term structural changes. This means that spending more money, or doing more of the same thing, will not be enough; the system has been made obsolete by changes in the environment in which it must perform.

Actions to Accelerate Economic Growth

Puerto Rico can and should build a more dynamic economy within the existing economic system. What is required is not starting from scratch but making modifications and creating new emphases to reflect the changed economic environment. Many, if not most, of the required policy changes can be undertaken by the commonwealth government; yet the federal government ultimately has both the power and the capacity to stifle or encourage economic growth, and federal policies are therefore an essential part of the recommended strategy.

The policy prescriptions offered here are specifically designed to create the appropriate environment and stimulus for growth, based on expansion of the private sector. Indeed, the experiences of the last thirty-five years confirm that the government should not become directly involved in the economy, but rather should attempt to create the appropriate environment for businesses to maximize their potential for growth.

Although Puerto Rico may not have many easily exploitable mineral resources on which to base an extractive or processing industry, its other attributes could serve as a basis for a new period of economic development. The Puerto Rican people are the island's greatest economic asset. During the past thirty-five years of industrialization, the labor force has become skilled and productive. Puerto Rican labor has the necessary skills to operate and manage production, to market products, and to provide the professional services required to make the system work. In addition, the island's educational facilities, both at the university and vocational levels, are continually producing new workers with modern industrial skills.

Puerto Rico has the necessary infrastructure preconditions for building a strong economy. The island's roads, bridges, airports, port facilities, electrical system, water supply, and industrial waste disposal plants are in place.

Puerto Rico enjoys a sunny tropical climate where the visitor is always assured warm temperatures. The natural beauty of the island is highlighted by a tropical rain forest, breathtaking views of the oceans, historical wonders left by the Indians and Spanish settlers, clear waters, and magnificent beaches.

The governmental structure, democratic in form, and the relationship to the United States (for example, inclusion within the U.S. tariff area) also provide Puerto Rico with advantages that can be used in a development strategy.

Building upon and utilizing these inherent advantages, Puerto Rico can broaden the scope of its historical development strategy to stimulate additional economic activity. One lesson drawn from the 1960s, the decade of 7 percent real growth, is that many components of the economy must be expanding simultaneously if high levels of growth are to be achieved. During the 1960s, there was a continuing expansion in the labor-intensive manufacturing sectors, expansion in the capital-intensive petrochemical sector, expansion of tourist hotel facilities, expansion of the local government's capital improvement program, and expansion in residential construction. All these sectors expanding concurrently pulled along the commerce and service sectors and produced the phenomenal growth of the 1960s; any new strategy must broaden growth into several sectors and into several components of these sectors.

Tourism

The tourist industry in Puerto Rico still has abundant potential for growth. It should try to broaden its appeal in the United States (especially in the West and Midwest), Europe, Canada, and South America. To achieve this goal the advertising budget for the Tourism Development Company should be increased so that Puerto Rico can compete with the substantial television advertising of Jamaica and the Bahamas. Puerto Rico cannot continue to depend on the high-income tourist; a greater attempt must be made to attract middle-income tourists by promoting the development of middle- to low-cost tourist facilities outside San Juan. Furthermore, special deals should be worked out to lengthen the very short tourist season and increase occupancy during the eight-month "off-season."

These aggressive marketing strategies should be supported by the government. Vocational schools should place greater emphasis on training service industry employees. New or expanded hotels should be included in the industrial incentives program in the same manner as manufacturing plants and qualify for fuel benefits under the act. Industrial bond financing through the Puerto Rico Industrial, Medical, and Environmental Pollution Control Facilities Financing Authority (AFICA) should be allowed for hotel facilities. Finally, the federal government should permit foreign cruise lines to carry passengers between Puerto Rico and the mainland.

If these policies were adopted, the tourist industry in Puerto Rico could become one of the leading sectors in the island's economic recovery.

Agriculture

1. More research and development programs should be formed to produce new crops and farming techniques to improve the return per acre. Attempts should be made to utilize federal agricultural research

more fully, and federal research should focus on the agricultural problems of Puerto Rico.

2. The system that transfers new agricultural techniques to farmers should be improved.

3. The educational program to improve the quality of agricultural techniques, marketing ability, and farm finances should be enlarged.

4. A program should be developed to utilize government farm land currently unused, or being used for sugar cane, for new crops. Governmental lands can be leased for agricultural purposes at very low rates to attract new farming activity.

5. New agricultural enterprises should be promoted in the same manner as new manufacturing plants are. We should seek out new farming operations among firms with adequate technology, markets, and financial strength.

6. Governmental assistance programs should be oriented to output and production. The partial tax exemption program recently enacted for this sector is an example of this philosophy. Rather than subsidize parts of the whole, e.g., fertilizers, farm labor, farm machinery purchased, we should provide a guaranteed price program for locally produced farm products. We should leave the agricultural process to the farmer but ensure that he can earn a reasonable income by selling produce in the private market or to the government at the guaranteed price. This type of assistance would not smother the farmer with government paper work, nor would the farmer's ingenuity be smothered by a well-meaning government.

7. The governmental sugar corporation should be critically analyzed on a cost-benefit basis. The publicly owned corporation running Puerto Rico's sugar industry incurs annual losses approaching $100 million per year. Much of this loss now comes from the interest payments on the accumulated deficits and may have reached such dimensions that the corporation can never be profitable. The sugar industry's debts are its legacy to future generations of Puerto Ricans. There is no justification for the continuation of losses this size. All personnel engaged in the sector could be retired at the same pay for a considerably smaller sum than $100 million. The funds lost each year could easily be put to more productive purposes.

Manufacturing

1. The single most important action to stimulate investment and production in the manufacturing sector is the elimination of the uncertainty surrounding section 936 of the U.S. Internal Revenue Code. The U.S. Congress and its individual members are responsible for virtually halting new manufacturing investment on the island. The events leading

up to the inclusion of revisions to section 936 in the Tax Equalization and Fiscal Responsibility Act of 1982, the continued comments of certain legislators concerning the need to "revisit" section 936, and the inability of the U.S. Treasury to implement regulations for the revisions have combined to create a deep-seated uncertainty about what benefits will actually be obtained by firms locating on the island and, more importantly, how long these benefits will last.

The U.S. Congress and the U.S. Treasury have done immeasurable damage to Puerto Rico's economic development program. Their actions have accentuated the depth of the current recession and have directly affected thousands of Puerto Rican workers who quite possibly would have been employed by now if these unsound actions had not been taken.

The damage already done cannot be eliminated; however, there is no reason why the federal government should allow this situation to continue. Action must be taken to ensure that regulations are written and issued for section 936; these regulations will form the heart of Puerto Rico's development program. However, the regulations cannot—repeat, cannot—be written only from the perspective of the tax collector; they must have a broader scope. Two basic policy questions must be addressed: Should Puerto Rico have the ability to develop a viable economic base that provides for the needs of its people? Or will the United States ensure that Puerto Rico always remains a ward of the social welfare system?

2. Because of the continued decline in the U.S. effective corporate income tax, the tax advantage that Puerto Rico once offered has been substantially reduced. Puerto Rico will have to compensate for this loss by giving up some of its taxes. The partial tax exemption program should be revised to provide for higher rates of exemption following the fifth year in a firm's tax exemption grant. This could be accomplished directly by increasing the percentage exemption from 75 percent in the fifth to tenth years to perhaps 85 percent, or could be accomplished indirectly by providing for a credit based upon the production worker payroll paid by the firm on the island.

3. Research and development activities on the island should be increased. This goal requires actions by both federal and commonwealth governments. The federal government should make a resolution to stimulate R&D activity either through grants to universities on the island or through the establishment of a federal research laboratory or facility on the island. The federal government could also stimulate private R&D on the island by allowing this expenditure to qualify for the R&D provisions under the tax act of 1981, or through some other provisions giving preference to R&D conducted in Puerto Rico.

The commonwealth government must provide even greater incentives than partial tax exemption at the corporate level. For example, for R&D facilities entailing either some investment levels or some level of technical employment, the commonwealth government could provide a subsidy through the Puerto Rico Industrial Development Company (PRIDCO) building leases; low-cost financing for private investment; and individual tax exemption for the technical employees in the qualified facility.

4. The locally owned manufacturing sector should be expanded as a proportion of the total sector. Existing government programs should be expanded to focus on the problems of small, locally owned firms. Marketing services and export assistance should be made available on either a free or subsidized basis.

Incentives should be included in the tax code to encourage local investors to provide risk capital for the start up of new businesses or the expansion of existing firms. One possibility would be to allow an investor in such a firm to write off or deduct up to half his original investment on his individual income tax return over the three-year period following such investment, regardless of what actually happens to the investment. Should the investment succeed, the capital gains derived from its sale at some later date should be exempt from tax; if the firm failed, the investor should be allowed to deduct up to 200 percent of his original investment from his individual tax return as an ordinary and necessary business expense. In this manner, the cost of investment failure is reduced and the potential gain is accentuated. The expected value for investments in new "start ups" can be significantly increased.

Export-Oriented Services

1. Puerto Rico should provide export-oriented service firms with full and equal treatment under the provisions of the industrial incentives act of 1978 equivalent to those offered to manufacturing firms.

2. The concept of the international banking center should be restudied, and we should provide the incentives necessary to attract these firms. Time, however, is important; every day that passes with no movement in this area makes it more difficult to accomplish. We must provide incentives equivalent to those available in other locations, even if that effectively means granting full tax exemption on all non–Puerto Rican source income. This would be the quid pro quo required for the generation of professional employment opportunities on the island.

International Trade Center

The government has been attempting for some time to develop an international trade center. Budgetary problems have hampered progress. The government should turn over implementation of this project to the

Puerto Rico Chamber of Commerce, which would then organize and implement the project with governmental assistance.

Construction

1. The long delays encountered in the approval process for a construction project should be reduced. The delays discourage builders because their costs can increase considerably during the long approval process. We should consider a one-stop approval process that includes a fixed time limit for the bureaucracy to render a decision. Any time a project is denied, a reason must be provided, and an appeals procedure established.

2. Limited partnership legislation, similar to that contained in the U.S. Tax Code, should be adopted and enacted. Now a partnership in Puerto Rico is taxed as a corporation, and there is no pass-through of the gains or losses to the individual partners. Modifying partnership legislation to allow the pass-through concept would enable investors to pool their resources to construct buildings and get the benefits that very well-to-do individual investors already enjoy.

Tax Policy

In the economic statistics for Puerto Rico over the last ten years, one very serious problem stands out. Private capital investment has been falling rapidly and has now reached unacceptable levels. Economic expansion requires investment by the private sector. Unfortunately private investment has not been happening at sufficient levels to offset realistic losses resulting from obsolescence. We are disinvesting. This slow process leads to economic atrophy. New measures are needed to provide greater incentives for private investment.

1. The depreciation schedules contained in the Puerto Rican tax code should be revised to equal the new U.S. accelerated cost recovery system (ACRS) benefits enacted in 1981. In the U.S. Tax Code vehicles are depreciated in three years, machinery in five years, and buildings over fifteen years. The Puerto Rican code requires significantly longer depreciation periods that actually discourage new investment.

2. The investment tax credit (ITC) concept should be incorporated into the Puerto Rican tax structure. The ITC lowers the cost of an investment in qualifying machinery or in the rehabilitation of old buildings by providing an immediate tax credit that effectively reduces the firm's actual outlay by the amount of the credit. As such the ITC is a strong incentive for investment.

3. The taxes for individuals in Puerto Rico should continue to be reduced gradually to the point where no one would have to pay more

than 50 percent of any earnings to the treasury as individual income taxes.

4. At some future time the general corporate tax rate of 45 percent should be gradually reduced, by 1 percentage point a year, to 35 percent. At this level, along with the ACRS and ITC, the companies under the industrial tax exemption program should not have to suffer "shock" once they become fully taxable, and other nonexempt firms should be able to create more business activity resulting from the lower level of corporate taxes.

Federal Programs

Puerto Rico's 3.3 million U.S. citizens should receive full and equal treatment in all federal programs. Today many federal programs either deny or limit benefits to U.S. citizens residing in Puerto Rico.

Full participation in federal programs does not inhibit or exclude growth within the private sector. Measures can be taken to promote production within the private sector of the economy at the same time that the federal programs provide a minimum living standard for those less fortunate residents of Puerto Rico. As the private sector expands and creates new opportunities, there will be a corresponding reduction in the need for federal social welfare programs.

Public Corporations

Puerto Rico has an extensive system of public corporations that provide infrastructural services such as electricity, water, sewage disposal, communications, and transportation. In each service there is room for significant improvement in the reliability, diversity, quality, and cost of service. These corporations must begin to operate as individual private enterprises seeking to improve their efficiency, provide a reliable service at the lowest cost possible, and earn an adequate return on their capital investment. The goal should be to make these firms self-sustaining.

Education

The primary and secondary school system on the island must be improved to equip students with the basic abilities to read, write, and perform mathematical operations. A modern society requires workers with more complex skills, and these three skills are the starting point upon which others can be added.

The vocational system must also improve the quality of its training to ensure (1) that it is equipping students with skills appropriate for the modern marketplace, and (2) that the skills taught are up-to-date in terms of the jobs actually performed.

Conclusion

These measures are by no means all encompassing; yet they point the policymaker in the direction of a diversified economy with several sectors making positive contributions toward economic growth. Certainly not all these measures can be undertaken at the same time: Government fiscal and human resources are too limited. Nonetheless, policymakers must take steps to broaden and diversify the directions for future economic growth.

4
The Social Pathology of Dependence

Luis Nieves Falcón

Economic institutions are dominant in Western societies; they have a pervasive effect that conditions the rest of the institutional structure. No doubt there is a reciprocal effect, flowing from social and political institutions to economic ones, but the influence of economic institutions is clearly predominant. This differentiated impact accounts for many of the social processes generated in a society and prompts the need to examine the social consequences of economically induced changes. This chapter attempts to examine the social impact of economic processes in Puerto Rico between 1898 and the present.

This chapter is divided into four interrelated sections: a brief description of the principal phases of economic development in Puerto Rico; an appraisal of this development in terms of aggregate data; a discussion of the social impact of economic strategies; and, finally, a summation of the interrelationship of economics with political alternatives for the solution of the status issue in Puerto Rico.

Principal Phases of Economic Development

The military conquest of Puerto Rico, as a result of the Spanish-American War, brought North American control to the island in 1898. This military success epitomized the culmination of Manifest Destiny, which since 1783 had prompted North American officials to make public statements on the intentions of the United States to expand its political and economic control to the Hispanic Caribbean.[1]

The arrival of a new colonial power in Puerto Rico was followed promptly by a new strategy for colonial economic planning. The new metropolis—the United States—assigned Puerto Rico to a new economic role; the island's economy became oriented toward creating primary products for export and serving as an expanded consumer market for excess North American goods. The administrative and judiciary apparatus was designed to buttress this economic strategy. In less than thirty years, Puerto Rico was incorporated into the U.S. tariff system, which led to complete U.S. control of the island's foreign trade. The diversified nature of the economy was destroyed. Sugar barons dispossessed small farmers. Furthermore, the emergence of sugar plantations led to the brutal exploitation of natural and human resources, as well as the impoverishment of the population.

These conditions led to increasing social tensions, dissatisfaction with the colonial regime, and growing support for independence. The colonial power responded by creating supplementary social services, elevating local collaborators into the colonial administration, enforcing repressive policies against supporters of independence, and designing a new economic program. "Operation Bootstrap," as it was called, relied heavily on tax-exempt, light industries. During this phase, agriculture was greatly deemphasized, labor unionism was heavily controlled by the government to ensure an adequate industrial climate, and the public sector became the largest employer in the economy. Because of the heavy investment of North American capital into this new industrial framework, Puerto Rico became exceedingly dependent on U.S. capital, North American interests gained control of most of the island's economic sectors, and the island experienced an unprecedented increase in the national and personal debt, which still accounts for the continuing rates of negative savings. The economy became externally oriented—it consumed what it did not produce and produced what it did not consume. As a result, most goods, even agricultural products, needed to be imported from the United States.

This economic policy was coupled with a new political strategy: Commonwealth status was designed to increase local participation in colonial administration without altering the overarching control of the United States.[2] In psychological terms the status can be referred to as the solution of ambivalence, overtly claimed to be a significant political stride, but really intended to preserve the status quo and the privileged position of the United States over Puerto Rico. Efforts to increase the margin of local power within this political structure have been continually rebuffed by North Americans.[3]

Although during this economic period improvements were made in socioeconomic conditions on the island, gross national product (GNP) per capita of Puerto Rico did not rise above that of the poorest state on the mainland, Mississippi. The relative income gap between social classes increased, and structural problems like unemployment persisted. The decline of the tax-exempt factories forced unprecedentedly heavy investment in social services on the part of the U.S. government to avoid increasing levels of social conflict, particularly the ever-threatened menace of movements for independence. Social conditions worsened with increasing malaise and one of the highest rates of criminal pathology in a Western society.

The failure of Operation Bootstrap to solve the structural problems of Puerto Rican society led to still another strategy of economic development for the island: a promotional policy designed to attract heavy industries, particularly petrochemicals and pharmaceuticals. These capital-intensive endeavors required low levels of employment and did very little to solve chronic unemployment. Ironically, many of the highly skilled positions opened by the new transnational subsidiaries could not be filled from local manpower and the employees had to be imported. Most of the islanders were relegated to the limited number of low-skilled jobs made available by these new economic concerns. Although the petrochemicals and pharmaceuticals industries had an insignificant impact in terms of increasing jobs, they became the principal polluters on the island, bringing environmental contamination to unprecedented levels.[4] In short, these new economic policies did not succeed in ameliorating the socioeconomic problems facing Puerto Rico; instead, coupled with the international oil crises and Reaganomics, these policies magnified the structural problems facing the island's dependent economy. Given this present situation, there seem to be no viable solutions to the problems, and independence, despite the fears it raises, is put forward by some sectors of the island's elite as the only way out.

The failure of these new economic policies has been mitigated somewhat by two parallel modes of social action: continuous stimulation of emigration and massive sterilization of the female poor. The former has led to the biggest displacement of people in modern times, mostly to the urban ghettos of the United States.[5] Although during the late 1960s and early 1970s the flow of net emigration decreased and return migration was on the increase, the trend has been reversed and new emigratory movements continue to characterize the island. Ironically, while emigration is seen as an escape valve, a steady flow of immigrants, particularly ultraconservative persons fleeing the liberal revolutionary movements in Latin America, account for most of the natural population growth.[6] The other strategy, massive sterilization, has been responsible for the sterilization of one-third of the female population in their reproductive years. In fact Puerto Rico has the highest female sterilization rate in the world. Some local social scientists have labeled the sterilization policy an incipient genocidal policy.[7] Neither of these two measures has resulted in significant improvements for the mass of the population. The beneficiaries of the development in Puerto Rico have been the privileged sectors of society.

Selected Indicators to Appraise
Puerto Rican Development

The aggregate data at the macro level of society reveal gains in personal income, health, and school enrollment. Personal per capita income has increased from $118 in 1940 to $2,472 in 1977. Life expectancy has increased significantly and mortality rates are lower. Infant mortality has decreased from 200 deaths per 1,000 live births in 1900 to 20 in 1975. University enrollment has increased from 5,000 in 1940 to more than 50,000 today.

Construction of roads has expanded tremendously, and water and electricity are available to the majority of the population. The possession of durable goods shows a generalized diffusion of radio, television, and refrigerators. Ownership of motor vehicles, particularly automobiles, has also increased significantly.

Despite these significant material gains, critical problems persist. The main social and economic problem is poverty. Sixty percent of the population have incomes below the poverty level.[8] Since the cost of living in Puerto Rico is higher than in the United States, actual poverty is really greater. The underlying causes of poverty are an unequal distribution of income and the persistently high unemployment rate.

The illiteracy rate is around 11 percent (compared to less than 2 percent in the United States), but recent research shows rates as high as 25 percent in poor areas. The rates of functional illiteracy are still much higher.[9] Contrary to current opinion the problem is not limited to the elderly population but is found increasingly among adolescents and young adults.

Average number of years of school completed is seven. School facilities are overcrowded, supplies are inadequate, and teachers are hampered by poor training. These factors are progressively more acute among the poor sectors. The whole educational system has been unable to increase its holding power, and only about one of every ten students entering first grade is able to finish high school.[10] Although the number of college graduates has increased, many cannot find jobs. This situation accounts to a large extent for the increasing rates of emigration among college graduates and other professionals. The "brain drain" impedes future recuperative efforts of the society.[11]

In terms of social stability the Puerto Rican society shows some other disturbing signs. It has one of the highest rates of divorce, despite its Catholic background. Indeed, more than 15 percent of its families are headed by single parents.[12] Puerto Rico has one of the highest rates of alcoholism.[13] In addition, it has some of the highest rates of suicide, mental disorder, death from automobile accidents, homicide, and drug addiction.[14] In fact, the extent of criminality on the island is particularly ominous. A violent act occurs every 34.9 minutes, a person is gravely assaulted every 1.4 hours, a theft is committed every 1.1 hours, a person is killed every 18.1 hours, and a female is raped every 18.3 hours. Furthermore, property is broken into or stolen every 14.9 minutes, and a car is stolen every 39.5 minutes.[15]

This level of social pathology is compounded by political corruption, which is pervasive. Corruption seems to be growing out of control. Officials themselves have stated that "the amount of public wastage continues to increase every year . . . and the sad thing is that there is very little we can do to solve this situation which bleeds public monies."[16]

As can be surmised from this description, Puerto Rico has a social pathology characterized by what could be described, on the one hand, as escapism from reality (mental disorders, alcoholism, drug addiction) and, on the other, as self-destruction (suicides, homicides, automobile accidents). This condition, which reflects a generalized societal violence, is typical of colonial societies where extensive social violence is directed toward the colonized individual rather than the oppressive social structures. Some social theoreticians, like Frantz Fanon, see in those indicators a prelude to a revolutionary struggle. Therefore, the major question is how long can destabilizing strategies function to keep Puerto Rico away from a boiling point of social unrest and revolution.

The Impact of a Dependent Economy

The most significant manifestations of Puerto Rico's status as a dependent economy are its high unemployment rates and its poverty. Historically, unemployment rates have been high in Puerto Rico. For 1973 average unemployment was estimated at 12 percent. For fiscal years 1981 and 1982 it went up to 20 and 30 percent, respectively. The official unemployment figure for January 1983 was 25.3 percent.[17] For persons eighteen to twenty-four the figure was 48 percent.[18]

This inability to participate in an activity essential to the human being, which dignifies the person and offers an opportunity for self-realization and freedom, becomes a social tragedy and helps to explain both why the median age for a drug user in Puerto Rico is eighteen years and why drug abuse is most common in the age groups most severely impacted by unemployment.[19]

This high rate of unemployment has other repercussions. It means that the rate of participation—the percentage of the population over sixteen years included in the labor force—is decreasing; that the number of dependents per productive person is extremely high; and that an ever-increasing percentage of the population earns income without engaging in productive work. Let us take an illustration: In Puerto Rico 60 percent of the families engage in productive work. In personal terms this figure means that among the poor in Puerto Rico, twelve persons depend on the productive efforts of a single worker. Under such circumstances it is not strange to find that 63.4 percent of family income among poor families originates in transfer payments from the U.S. government (social security, public assistance, and food stamps) and that only 24.7 percent originates from productive labor.[20] Furthermore, the importance of federal transfer payments in the Puerto Rican economy is growing; in 1969–1970 the ratio of federal disbursements to the gross product was 10.4 percent; by 1982 the ratio had risen to 28 percent.[21]

The government of Puerto Rico has tried to cope with this situation by borrowing from foreign sources. As a result it pays 37.4 percent of its gross product to foreign businesses as income on investments (investments increased from $593 million in fiscal year 1970 to $4.7 billion in fiscal year 1982). This accounts for a dependency index of 28 percent for the Puerto Rican economy.[22] It also helps to explain the persistent trend in negative savings, an indication of a society that spends much more than it earns.

The intermingling of these factors—unemployment, low participation in the labor force, U.S. transfer payments, and foreign investment—is the principal economic factor promoting and enforcing a collective feeling of self-inadequacy. It has served to deflate social unrest and protest because people are afraid of the impact that such behavior may have on their immediate material condition. This situation reflects a colonial mentality forced on the islanders where they fear any change in the status quo. They know that to a large extent their present material survival is dependent on the United States, and they have been taught in no uncertain terms that material assistance will be cut in the event that the present power structure controlled by the U.S. government is threatened. In fact, they know that any concrete manifestation of objection to the regime can and will set in motion the forces of institutionalized repression existing in the colony.

Maintaining a state of dependency in Puerto Rico depends on a socialization process, buttressed by the manipulation of the fundamental needs of the population, designed to ensure the subservience of the islanders to the exercise of colonial domination by the United States. At present, the U.S. government has no desire to take practical steps that could lead to economic self-sufficiency and restored feelings of adequacy because it perceives such goals as contradictory to the economic and political interests of the United States. Furthermore, the inaction of the U.S. government is reinforced by a cultural stereotype of Puerto Ricans, which characterizes them as inadequate and thus the cause of their own problems. Obviously, this stereotype fails to consider the lack of power that Puerto Ricans have to solve the basic problems of their society and the institutionalized threat of reprisals that Americans have built into the colonial situation.

Social and Political Impact of Economics

It is quite obvious from the foregoing discussion that feelings of dependency and inadequacy will be reflected in fundamental areas of behavior. In trying to diagnose Puerto Ricans collectively, a Puerto Rican psychiatrist put forward the following profile:

> Notwithstanding the extent to which he may attempt to rationalize his situation, the Puerto Rican passively experiences his dependency with a sense of shame, while doubting his own capacity for autonomous survival. . . . There is in the Puerto Rican a fear of exercising initiative, a conviction that, if exercised, his efforts will be futile. . . . The present state of Puerto Rican society is one of identity diffusion and identity confusion. . . . There is a prevalence of negative identity elements in his self-definition. Dependency on the economic grant leads the Puerto Rican to view himself as "basically lazy," "inefficient," "passive" (or at best "passive-aggressive"), "unenterprising," and "noncompetitive."[23]

Because of this identity diffusion, the Puerto Rican perceives the colonial situation as "a picture of progress and economic development which tends to perpetuate the notion that any change in the condition of dependency is predestined to bring about economic havoc and mass starvation."[24] As a result of this psychological impact of colonialism, "political discussion related to political status remains at the level of which alternative is likely to provide the highest net yield in Federal subsidies, rather than what measures can the society undertake to increase its level of productivity and self-sufficiency. The basic premises thus assume that continued dependency is unavoidable."[25]

This psychological structure of dependency, common to colonized people the world over, has also made the Puerto Rican feel that he is unable to control the social forces that impact his daily life. Since they are outside his own control there is a strong tendency to depend on external forces for the solution to problems. Consequently, the majority of the population thinks that the best thing to do with a problem is to place it in God's hands, that the best way to solve a problem is by praying, and that some things in one's life are predestined and cannot be changed regardless of what the individual does.[26] These attitudes not only affect personal issues but also influence the social structure.

They are indicative of an ideology cultivated to ensure conformity and passivity—an ideology that best suits the persistence of the colonial condition.

The mentality of dependence or subordination is the result of the colonial condition that has exerted a normative effect on Puerto Rico during both Spanish and American colonialism. Its present behavioral manifestations are the net product of foreign control of the economic and social foundations of the society. This almost absolute control of the institutional settings has been used to develop and further a cultural imperialism aimed at creating the ideology, attitudes, and beliefs needed for the persistence of economic subordination.

Cultural imperialism in Puerto Rico has tended to erode basic elements of the culture, e.g., language, customs, and traditions; to disconnect Puerto Ricans from their historical roots, particularly those supporting a libertarian tradition; to depreciate historical figures associated with the struggle for independence; to develop negative associations with linguistic categories associated with liberation and social justice; to project negative attributes to the Puerto Rican as an individual, to the land, and to the culture; and to appraise positively the native collaborator, the Americans, and the colonial conditions.[27] Common examples of these factors include the following:

- Puerto Ricans ignore basic episodes of their country's history though generally recognize historical episodes of the metropolis as their own.
- Puerto Ricans perceive figures associated with their own liberation as insane and call local collaborators "patriots."
- Puerto Ricans believe that the widespread social inequality and poverty prevailing on the island are due to their own inherent deficiencies, particularly their laziness.
- Puerto Ricans believe that whatever material progress is found on the island is due to the United States and if the United States left the island they would starve.
- Puerto Ricans believe that the American presence is necessary in Puerto Rico to prevent them from killing each other.
- Puerto Ricans tend to define themselves in terms of American concepts of aesthetics, which are contradictory in a mestizo society.
- Puerto Ricans associate the terms *independence* and *republic* with chaos, anarchy, disorder, and "Communist" control.

All these ideological constructs have been developed for no other reason than to ensure U.S. economic supremacy in Puerto Rico.

There is no doubt that within the collective ideological makeup that dependence and cultural imperialism have embedded in the Puerto Rican, political alternatives only appear meaningful as long as they are nonthreatening to the status quo; as long as they do not disturb the conduits of material provisions that support the conditions of dependency.

The political status of independence is seen as the principal threat to the status quo. This fear has led, since the late 1930s, to establishing official policies to erode support for independence and develop negative attitudes and associations toward this political alternative. The success of such policies on Puerto Ricans can be gauged from three different sources: (1) In a follow-up to a successful cancer detection campaign, a population sample was asked to identify what each respondent feared most in life. The expected answer was "cancer" but instead "independence" emerged as the principal response. (2) A survey among public school teachers revealed that a majority expressed fears toward independence and supported their fears on the basis of Puerto Rico's inability to support itself economically; the chaos that would follow the departure of the United States from Puerto Rico since the North American presence prevents Puerto Ricans from "devouring" each other; and lastly, the threat of a communist takeover after independence. (3) Field work among fifty-nine poor communities in 1982 showed that poor people do not see independence as a viable alternative and expressed negative associations with that alternative.[28]

The formal institutional controls of the colonial society have systematically imbued Puerto Ricans with a fear of freedom. When the population was asked in 1983 to ascribe fourteen positive and fourteen negative attributes to each of the prevailing political alternatives, only one positive attribute—preservation of the culture—was ascribed to independence by a significant proportion (43 percent) of respondents. On the other hand, thirteen negative attributes were associated by the majority with the independence alternative; they included shutting down churches, loss of private property, loss of liberty, lack of food, death, violence, poverty, and indiscriminate death.[29]

Conclusion

Our analysis has shown how the colonial system of domination conditions the process of socialization and the popular support for undefined status categories. Given these conditions, Puerto Ricans must be provided with clear definitions of the various status alternatives. A concrete description of the different status possibilities would tend to alleviate the generalized fears attached to the various options. Indeed, in the public opinion poll described, only 8 percent supported the undefined option of independence, but the proportion increased to 25 percent when this status alternative was connected with the phrase "with economic assistance from the United States."

Up to this point, the U.S. government has demanded that Puerto Ricans decide which of the undefined status options is preferable. To insist on this approach is to require from them a meaningless exercise in self-determination.

Without a decolonization process that addresses both the economic and cultural aspects of colonialism, the Puerto Rican people will be unable to exercise freely their right to self-determination. Furthermore, each status option must be clearly defined in specific and concrete terms.

These two initial steps would provide a context in which the process of economic and psychological decolonization could take place. These steps must be initiated by those who ultimately control the destiny of Puerto Rico, namely the U.S. Congress. If the U.S. government insists that Puerto Ricans must resolve their problem of subordination, within the present context of constraints, the result will either be a mockery of self-determination or lead to armed struggle as the only available channel for psychological decolonization.

Notes

1. For a chronology of U.S. interests in the Caribbean, particularly in Cuba and Puerto Rico, from 1783 to 1898, see "Apuntes Para la Historia del Imperialismo Norteamericano en el Carribe: El Caso de Puerto Rico," *Libre*, September 1982, pp. 10–11.

2. During the congressional hearings debating the new status, Governor Luis Muñoz Marín affirmed: "This bill does not change the fundamental situation of non-incorporation in which Puerto Rico is now, but it allows Puerto Rico to develop along the lines of self-government in a parallel line with a Territory that attains statehood. That would be the situation under this bill. In other words, it is development into self-government on the part of a non-incorporated area of the United States, without virtually changing its position relative to the United States." House of Representatives, *Hearings Before the Committee on Public Lands*, H.R. 7674, March 14, 1950.

3. The first effort to increase the level of autonomy within the commonwealth dates back to 1959 and is known as the Fernós-Murray Bill. It was rejected by the U.S. Congress. Subsequent efforts to expand local autonomy have also been rejected.

4. See Thomas Morales Cardona, "El Uso de la Ciencia y la Tecnología en Puerto Rico Con Fines Coloniales," in *La Agresión Cultural Norteamericana en Puerto Rico*, ed. José Luis Méndez (Mexico, D.F.: Editorial Grijalbo, 1978). Also *El Nuevo Día*, February 25, 1983, p. 4, and May 5, 1983, pp. 1–3.

5. See Luis Nieves Falcón, *El Emigrante Puertorriqueño* (Río Piedras: Editorial Edil, 1975); and "The Impact of Migration on Puerto Ricans," *Sourcebook on the New Immigrations: Implications for the United States and the International Community*, Research Institute on Immigration and Ethnic Studies, Smithsonian Institution (Washington, D.C., 1980). Also, U.S. Commission on Civil Rights, *Puerto Ricans in the United States: An Uncertain Future* (1976).

6. See José L. Vázquez Calzada and Zoraiida Morales del Valle, "Características de la Población Extranjera Residente en Puerto Rico," *Revista de Ciencias Sociales* 3–4 (September-December 1979).

7. See Saúl Pratts Ponce de León, "La Esterilización Femenina en los Sectores Pobres en Puerto Rico," *Revista Puertorriqueña de Ciencias Sociales* 1, 1 (July-December 1976): 30–40.

8. Luis Nieves Falcón, "La Pobreza en Puerto Rico: Demitología de la Virtrina," *Diagnóstico de Puerto Rico* (Río Piedras: Editorial Edil, 1978); idem, "Perfil Sociológico de los Puertorriqueños Pobres," MS, 1976; idem, "Los Pobres de Puerto Rico: su Condición Material," MS, 1976; idem, *Perfiles de la Pobreza en Puerto Rico* (San Juan: Office of Economic Opportunity, 1976).

9. Ibid.

10. Ibid.

11. It has been reported that 80 percent of engineering graduates emigrate to the United States. Other occupations showing high emigration rates are medical doctors, dentists, chemists, pharmacists, accountants, and nurses. See *El Nuevo Día*, May 31, 1983, pp. 1–3.

12. Puerto Rico Planning Board, *Socio-Economic Statistics of Puerto Rico, 1963–1976* and *Puerto Rico Health System Plan, 1978–82*, MS.

13. Ibid.

14. Ibid.

15. "El Reloj del Crimen," Police Statistics (January to December, 1982).

16. See *El Nuevo Día*, February 27, 1983, pp. 1–3; January 8, 1983, pp. 1–2; January 13, 1983, pp. 1–3; February 25, 1983, pp. 1–2; May 23, 1983, p. 3.

17. See *El Nuevo Día*, February 2, 1983, pp. 1–3.

18. See *El Nuevo Día*, February 22, 1983, pp. 1–2.

19. Ecumenical Committee on the Future of Puerto Rico, "Hearings on Puerto Rican Self-Determination" (September 26–October 1, 1982).

20. Nieves Falcón, "Perfil Sociológico"; idem, "Los Pobres de Puerto Rico."

21. Francisco A. Catalá, "General Overview of the Economy of Puerto Rico," MS, 1982.

22. Ibid.

23. Héctor R. Bird, "The Cultural Dichotomy of Colonial People," *Journal of the American Academy of Psychoanalysis* 10, 2(1982):203–205.

24. Ibid., p. 206.

25. Ibid.

26. Luis Nieves Falcón, "Pobreza e Ideologia," *Revista Puertorriqueña de Investigaciones Sociales* 1, 1 (July-December 1976):15–25.

27. Luis Nieves Falcón, "Imperialismo Cultural y Resistencia Cultural en Puerto Rico," *Comunicación y Cultura*, no. 6, February 1979; idem, "The Oppressive

Function of Values, Concepts and Images in Children's Books," *The Slant of the Pen.*

28. More detailed information is provided in Luis Nieves Falcón, "La desestabilización de la Independencia y la Estrategia Colonial en Puerto Rico," *Libre*, February-March 1983.

29. This research was conducted in 1983 among a representative sample of middle-class sectors in the island (n = 375). The proportion of the sampled population who ascribed each of the negative attributes to independence was as follows: violence (64 percent), breaking family union (45 percent), anarchy (47 percent), shutting down churches (84 percent), death (64 percent), violence against women (48 percent), indiscriminate death (59 percent), poverty (60 percent), lack of food (70 percent), loss of private property (81 percent), loss of liberty (72 percent), loss of culture (22 percent), unemployment (34 percent), and increase in vices (29 percent).

5

Trains Passing in the Night: Legislating for Puerto Rico

A. THE TAX CREDIT CONTROVERSY

The Possessions Tax Credit and Puerto Rican Economic Development

Peter R. Merrill

Introduction

When the special tax exemption for income earned in the possessions was first enacted in 1921, the primary beneficiaries were U.S. companies operating in the Phillipines. By 1980, however, more than 99 percent of the benefit from this tax provision went to companies in Puerto Rico. The Puerto Rican economy now depends on affiliates of U.S. mainland companies operating with U.S. and Puerto Rican tax preferences for three-fourths of its manufacturing employment. In 1981, the possessions tax credit cost the U.S. Treasury more than $1.3 billion or about 18 percent of Puerto Rico's gross national product.

As a result of perceived abuses and inefficiencies in the possessions tax preferences, Congress considered repealing these provisions in 1973 and ultimately amended them in 1976 and again in 1982. The most recent amendment, enacted in the Tax Equity and Fiscal Responsibility Act of 1982, provoked considerable controversy and threatened the administration's relationship with the government of Puerto Rico. Nevertheless, the future of the possessions tax credit, in its current form, may not be secure. Large projected budget deficits put pressure on all preferences in the U.S. Tax Code, and some members of Congress continue to be concerned that the credit is not an efficient mechanism for promoting balanced growth in the possessions.

Ultimately, the future of the credit is closely tied to the question of Puerto Rico's political status. A change in status, whether to statehood or independence, would exclude U.S. companies operating in Puerto Rico from the possessions tax credit. The potential loss of these tax benefits inevitably influences Puerto Rico's political choices.

Taxation of Possessions Income Before 1982

Special provisions for the taxation of possessions source income were first enacted in section 262 of the revenue act of 1921. The provisions were adopted primarily to help U.S. corporations compete with foreign firms in the Philippines (then a U.S. possession). Under the act, corporations deriving 80 percent or more of their income from U.S. possessions were exempted from income tax on their foreign source income. To qualify for the exemption, at least 50 percent of the corporation's income had to be derived from the conduct of an active trade or business (as opposed to passive investment income). Dividends paid to a U.S. mainland parent from a qualified possessions subsidiary were taxable whereas liquidating distributions were tax exempt. Since the Puerto Rican Industrial Incentives Act of 1948, most possessions subsidiaries have operated under a complete or partial exemption from Puerto Rican taxes. Thus, a U.S. subsidiary in Puerto Rico could avoid both federal and local tax by accumulating operating income until its grant of local exemption expired and then liquidating into the mainland parent.

Although the Phillipines ceased to be a U.S. possession in 1946, the special tax treatment of possessions corporations remained unchanged until the Tax Reform Act of 1976.[1] At that time, Congress recognized that federal tax exemption had played an important role in Puerto Rican economic development. In the Finance Committee report accompanying the 1976 act, the purpose of the special tax treatment of possessions source income was explained as "[to] assist the U.S. possessions in obtaining employment-producing investments by U.S. corporations."[2] The need for special tax incentives was attributed, in part, to the additional costs imposed by a possessions status, such as the U.S. minimum wage standards and the requirement to use U.S. flagships.

Several features of the possessions tax system, however, had a high revenue cost with little corresponding benefit to employment or investment in the possessions. To avoid U.S. tax on dividends paid to a mainland parent, possession subsidiaries invested accumulated earnings from operations in foreign countries, either directly or through the Puerto Rican banking system. Thus, the benefits of the possessions tax exemptions were not limited to investments in the possessions.[3]

The 1976 act added section 936 to the Internal Revenue Code, which altered the taxation of U.S.-chartered possessions corporations. To conform the tax treatment of possessions income with the taxation of a foreign source income, the exemption was converted to a credit. Thus, possessions source income was included in the definition of the parent company's worldwide income. However, in lieu of the ordinary foreign tax credit (for income taxes paid to foreign governments) a tax credit was enacted (the possessions tax credit) for the full amount of U.S. tax liability on possessions source income. Dividends repatriated from a possessions subsidiary (i.e., a 936 corporation) qualified for the dividend received deduction, which generally allowed tax-free repatriation of possessions income.

The 1976 act defined qualified possessions source investment income (QPSII) to include only income attributable to the investment of funds derived from the conduct of an active trade or business in the possessions. Income from investments in financial intermediaries, such as possessions banks, was eligible for the credit only if the intermediary reinvested the funds within the possessions. Also, Congress instructed the Treasury Department to publish an annual report on the operation and effect of the possessions tax credit.

Treasury Reports on the Possessions Tax Credit

The annual Treasury reports, based primarily on tax return information, were influential in shaping congressional views on the efficacy of the possessions tax credit after the 1976 act. The four reports issued since 1976, for tax years 1977–1980, pointed out several controversial features of the possessions tax credit in Puerto Rico, including the following:

- A disproportionate share of the possessions tax credit is claimed by capital-intensive relative to labor-intensive industries.
- In some cases, income from intangibles developed on the mainland (such as patents, formulas, and processes) is shifted to possessions subsidiaries to increase tax benefits.
- The possessions credit is a costly mechanism for increasing employment: In 1980 the average revenue cost per job ($17,186) was 44 percent more than the typical possessions company employee earned.
- The restrictions imposed on qualified possessions source investment income by the 1976 act fail to ensure that the income retained by possessions corporations is invested in the possessions.

Table 5.1

Sectoral Distribution of Sec. 936 Tax Benefits in Puerto Rico

Sector	Labor Intensity 1977[a]	Percentage of Tax Benefit 1980	Percentage of Payroll 1980
All Manufacturing	24.3	100.0	100.0
Food & Kindred Products	30.7	3.4	8.9
Textile Mill Products	20.1	*	.7
Apparel	27.1	3.4	15.0
Chemicals	11.0	54.4	27.0
Pharmaceuticals		48.1	19.1
Other		6.3	7.9
Rubber and Plastics	29.4	.7	1.0
Leather	52.6	.5	3.3
Stone, Clay, & Glass	38.8	*	*
Fabricated Metal	40.0	1.3	2.8
Nonelectric Machinery	20.3	1.4	1.5
Electronic Equipment	26.5	19.3	22.1
Transportation Equipment	29.2	.6	1.3
Instruments	20.2	3.5	4.8
Other Manufacturing	40.3	11.1	11.1

*Less than 0.5 percent.
[a] Payroll as a percentage of value added in Puerto Rico, based on 1977 census data.

Source: U.S. Department of the Treasury, *The Operation and Effect of the Possessions Corporation System of Taxation, Fourth Report,* February 1983, pp. 54, 112.

The legislative history of the Tax Equity and Fiscal Responsibility Act of 1982 shows that these features of the possessions credit influenced Congress's decision to amend section 936.

Factor Proportions

Table 5.1, based on Treasury data, shows that the largest portion of the possessions credit is claimed by industries with the least labor-intensive operations. For example, the capital-intensive pharmaceuticals industry garnered 48.1 percent of the total tax benefit but paid just 19.1 percent of the compensation received by possessions corporation employees in Puerto Rico. On the other hand, the labor-intensive apparel industry received just 3.4 percent of the total tax benefit but paid 15 percent of the wage bill of section 936 corporations in Puerto Rico.

The uneven distribution of tax benefits between capital and labor-intensive industries results from the design of the possessions credit tax incentive. According to the economic theory of the firm, companies maximize profits by utilizing capital and labor inputs in proportion to their relative prices. In response to an increase in the ratio of labor's wage rate to capital's rental rate, managers attempt to substitute capital for labor. Taxes on capital income tend to raise the cost of using capital. Since the possessions credit reduces the corporate tax on capital income, it effectively lowers the price of capital relative to labor and encourages greater capital intensity. The low labor utilization of section 936 companies can also be attributed to the rapid growth of wages in Puerto Rico, which has increased the cost of labor relative to the mainland. This incentive for capital utilization is especially strong for intangible capital.

Allocation of Income from Intangibles

Before the Tax Equity and Fiscal Responsibility Act of 1982 was inacted, some taxpayers took the position that valuable intangibles developed by a parent corporation, such as patents, could be transferred to a possession subsidiary on a tax-free basis. For example, a pharmaceutical company could develop a patentable drug in its U.S. mainland laboratory and transfer the patent, without charge, to its possessions subsidiary. This maneuver could result in a double tax benefit since the research and development (R&D) costs would be deducted on the parent's tax return, and the gross income from the drug would be free of U.S. corporate income tax because of the possessions credit. The company would obtain a triple tax benefit if it claimed the 25 percent R&D credit on its development costs.

In July 1980, the Internal Revenue Service issued Technical Advisory Memorandum 8040019 that stated that intangibles transferred to a possessions subsidiary at less than a reasonable arm's length price did not belong to the subsidiary, and the income derived from the use of such intangibles was allocable to the parent corporation rather than the subsidiary. In 1982, representatives of the pharmaceuticals industry estimated that the Internal Revenue Service would propose tax assessments totaling $3 billion as a result of this memorandum.

In Table 5.2 a hypothetical pharmaceutical company's tax liability under three scenarios is shown: (1) development and manufacture of a drug by the parent corporation, (2) development and manufacture by a possession subsidiary, and (3) development by the parent and manufacture by the subsidiary. It is assumed that the R&D costs are $10 million, that the drug generates $12 million of income in the year it is developed, and that there is no income in subsequent years. The corporate income tax rate is taken to be 50 percent.

In the first case, the parent develops and manufactures the drug so that its net income after R&D expense is $2 million ($12−$10 million), and its corporate tax liability is $1 million. In the second case, the subsidiary develops and manufactures the drug in its Puerto Rican facility so that its net income is $2 million, and there is no U.S. corporate tax

Table 5.2

**Transfer of Income from Intangibles:
A Pharmaceutical Company Example
(millions of dollars)**

Income Statement Items	Location of Drug Development & Manufacture		
	Developed & Manufactured by Parent	Developed & Manufactured by Subsidiary	Developed by Parent and Manufactured by Subsidiary
Parent Corporation			
Operating Income	$12	—	$0
R&D Expense	10	—	10
Net Income	2	—	−10
U.S. Tax	1	—	−5
Subsidiary Corp.			
Operating Income	—	$12	12
R&D Expense	—	10	0
Net Income	—	2	12
Precredit Tax	—	1	6
Tax Credit	—	1	6
Tax After Credit	—	0	0
Total			
Operating Income	12	12	12
R&D Expense	10	10	10
Net Income	2	2	2
U.S. Tax	1	0	−5
Effective Tax Rate (U.S. Tax/Net Income)	50%	0%	−250%

liability because of the possession credit. In the third case, the parent develops the drug and deducts the $10 million R&D expense, which reduces its tax liability by $5 million. The patent is then transferred, without charge, to the possession subsidiary, which grosses $12 million on the drug and pays no U.S. corporate income tax. In this case, the total tax liability is −$5 million; in other words, the tax-free transfer of the patent reduces the pharmaceutical company's income tax by $5 million.

In this example, the transfer of intangibles to a possessions subsidiary dramatically lowers the effective rate of U.S. corporate income tax from zero, the case of development and manufacture by the subsidiary, to −250 percent when the patent is developed by the parent and transferred tax-free to the possessions subsidiary. Thus a tax-free transfer of intangibles to a possessions subsidiary can generate a substantial tax shelter with a high revenue cost to the Treasury relative to the employment created in Puerto Rico.

Table 5.3

Revenue Cost per Employee in Puerto Rico, 1980

Sector	Tax Benefits per Employee	Average Employee Compensation[a]	Tax Benefits as a Percentage of Compensation
	($)	($)	(%)
All Manufacturing	17,186	11,915	144.2
Food & Kindred Products	6,194	10,792	57.4
Textile Mill Products	5,299	9,530	55.6
Apparel	2,887	8,545	33.8
Chemicals	50,571	16,833	300.4
Pharmaceuticals	58,743	15,644	375.5
Other	24,523	20,621	118.9
Rubber and Plastics	12,935	12,140	106.6
Leather	1,980	8,873	22.3
Stone, Clay, & Glass	7,860	22,607	34.8
Fabricated Metal	9,426	13,704	68.8
Nonelectric Machinery	16,824	12,495	134.6
Electronic Equipment	14,628	11,236	130.2
Transportation Equipment	8,036	11,068	72.6
Instruments	12,097	11,331	106.8
Other Manufacturing	20,203	13,654	148.0

[a] Treasury computes compensation by multiplying payroll by 1.232 to reflect the employer-paid portion of Social Security, unemployment insurance, and other nonpayroll costs.

Source: U.S. Department of the Treasury, *The Operation and Effect of the Possessions Corporation System of Taxation, Fourth Report,* February 1983, p. 112.

Job Creation

One of the consequences of the tax credit's bias toward capital-intensive sectors is that, on average, it is an expensive mechanism for increasing employment in the possessions. In 1980 the tax credit cost the U.S. Treasury $17,186 per employee in Puerto Rico, 44 percent more than the average employee's compensation of $11,915 (see Table 5.3). Industries with substantial intangible assets generate the least employment per dollar of possessions tax benefit. For example, in the pharmaceuticals industry, the revenue cost per employee was $58,743, more than 200 percent more than the average compensation of $15,644 in this sector.

The unemployment rate in Puerto Rico has trended upward over the last four decades. The act imposing U.S. mainland minimum wage standards in 1938 "produced massive closing of farms and businesses" and was amended in 1940 to allow a differential between the mainland

and Puerto Rico.[4] However, the differential was phased out in the 1970s, and the unemployment rate has exceeded 17 percent in every year since 1975, rising to 24.1 percent in August 1982.[5] The high rate of unemployment is one of the most serious economic problems confronting Puerto Rico. The governor's committee to study Puerto Rico's finances concluded in 1975 that the tax incentive programs should be restructured to encourage greater utilization of labor relative to capital in order to increase the number of jobs created per dollar of tax expenditure.[6]

Investment Income

Under the 1976 act, half of a corporation's income in a possession could be derived from qualified investments in financial assets. The 1976 act sought to encourage the repatriation of possessions source operating income by eliminating the tax on dividends paid to a mainland parent. Instead there was a huge inflow of capital into the Puerto Rican banking system. At the end of 1981, $5.3 billion of possessions corporation assets were deposited in Puerto Rican banks, making up about one-third of commercial bank liabilities. The accumulation of operating income in Puerto Rico has significantly distorted the balance sheets of possessions subsidiaries: In 1980, real fixed assets (plant, equipment, and land) constituted only 12.4 percent of possessions corporation assets, whereas on the mainland 36.6 percent of the assets owned by manufacturing corporations were real assets.

This accumulation of income is primarily attributable to two changes in the Puerto Rican tax system enacted in the 1970s: (1) the imposition of a 10 percent tollgate tax on dividends paid to the mainland, and (2) the expansion of the Industrial Tax Exemption Act to include income derived from investments in Puerto Rican certificates of deposit and other eligible instruments. Thus the 1976 act was not entirely successful in reducing the accumulation of possessions source income, and much of the influx of capital into the Puerto Rican banking system appeared to be flowing out of the island to find higher rates of return. The most recent (fourth) Treasury report concludes:

> The overall picture . . . is that, at least between June 30, 1976, and June 30, 1981, section 936 and the related Puerto Rican regulations did not lead to any substantial growth in the net inflow of capital into Puerto Rico. Section 936 did bring substantial funds back to Puerto Rico, but these appear to have flowed out again through the banking system, switches in ownership of Puerto Rican public debt, and investments abroad by Puerto Rican public corporations. (p. 85)

Thus, before the Tax Equity and Fiscal Responsibility Act of 1982, a sizable portion of the possessions tax credit, attributable to passive investments, did not appear to directly encourage investment in plant and equipment in the possessions.

The Tax Equity and Fiscal Responsibility Act of 1982

The first congressional budget resolution for fiscal year 1983 provided for revenue increases totaling $98.3 billion over the three-year period 1983–1985. This unprecedented revenue target was adopted in response to a projected 1985 budget deficit of 5.6 percent of GNP (the largest peacetime deficit in U.S. history), high real interest rates, and the most severe recession in fifty years. The Tax Equity and Fiscal Responsibility Act (TEFRA) of 1982 achieved the $98.3 billion revenue target, although 1982 was an election year and neither political party controlled both houses of Congress. The Senate Finance Committee used a minor, House-passed revenue bill (H.R. 4961) as the vehicle for marking up the TEFRA on the first two days of July 1982. The Senate adopted the Finance Committee bill three weeks later and a conference committee was convened on August 3. After two weeks, the conference report was filed, and two days later the legislation passed both houses of Congress. Most provisions of the TEFRA, including those pertaining to the possessions tax credit, were marked up only once (in the Senate bill). As a result of the single markup, the absence of a public hearing, and the rapid legislative pace, the Puerto Rican government expressed concern that it had not been adequately consulted.

The Finance Committee bill would have cut the revenue cost of the possessions credit by $2.7 billion over the 1983–1985 period, or 57 percent of the estimated three-year revenue cost of $4.7 billion under the previous law.[7] The bill contained two principal provisions that reduced the amount of investment and intangible income eligible for the possessions tax credit: (1) The credit was limited to possessions corporations deriving at least 90 percent, rather than 50 percent, of gross income from the active conduct of a trade or business in the possessions, and (2) the credit was denied to possessions corporation income allocable to manufacturing intangibles (such as patents) and marketing intangibles (such as trademarks) not developed by the possessions corporation itself. The committee's decision to reduce the credits allowable on investment and intangible income was based on the annual Treasury reports. According to the Finance Committee report, "Treasury's three reports to date have confirmed the existence of two problems in that system: (1) unduly high revenue loss attributable to certain industries due to positions taken by certain taxpayers with respect to the allocations of intangible income among related parties, and (2) continued tax exemption of increased possession source investment income" (p. 157).

The Senate bill sent shock waves through the Puerto Rican government. Governor Romero wrote President Reagan and personally lobbied in the Treasury Department and the congressional tax-writing committees, arguing that without the credit U.S. firms would cancel plans to start or expand Puerto Rican subsidiaries and that existing facilities might be shut down. Governor Romero maintained that the new Puerto Rican banking regulations would prevent section 936 bank deposits from flowing out of Puerto Rico, and that the Treasury reports underestimated the contribution of intangibles-intensive industries, such as pharmaceuticals and electronics, to the Puerto Rican economy. The Puerto Rican treasury secretary argued that the Senate bill could "cause serious damage to Puerto Rico's industrial production, leading to lower than estimated Federal tax revenue, decreased imports from the U.S., excessive migration of unemployed Puerto Ricans to the mainland, and generally increased Federal expenditures both on the mainland and in Puerto Rico."[8]

Some viewed Governor Romero's position as ironic since he represented the prostatehood party; if Puerto Rico became a state it would be ineligible for the possessions tax credit. This lack of consistency is understandable in view of Puerto Rico's dependency on the credit: In 1981, possessions corporations claimed $1.3 billion in tax credits, an amount equal to about 18 percent of Puerto Rico's gross national product. The governor succeeded in convincing the Treasury Department to support a compromise that restored more than half of the possessions credit cutback adopted in the Senate bill. Concern about Puerto Rico's support for the Caribbean Basin Initiative apparently was one of the factors that influenced the administration's decision to oppose the possessions tax credit provisions of the Senate bill.[9] President Reagan wrote to the chairman of the House Ways and Means Committee and urged him "to make changes in the Senate Bill which would limit the abuses of section 936 without causing severe economic distress in Puerto Rico."

The possessions credit was the last item resolved by the conference on H.R. 4961. On the final day of the conference, Senator Dole (chairman of the Senate Finance Committee) and Congressman Rostenkowski (chairman of the House Ways and Means Committee) announced that they had agreed to drop the possessions credit provisions of the bill in favor of a substitute. This substitute proposal sought to increase employment in the possessions by replacing the tax credit with a "wage credit" based on payroll expense in the possessions. Congressman Rangel, a strong supporter of the possessions tax credit, objected to the substitute proposal. After a subsequent caucus, the conference committee adopted the Treasury/Puerto Rico compromise instead of the wage credit proposal or the original provisions of the Senate bill.

The compromise enacted in the TEFRA reduced the estimated revenue cost of the possessions tax credit by 24 percent over the three-year period (1983–1985), compared to a 57 percent reduction in the Senate bill. Eligibility for the credit was limited to possessions corporations deriving at least 65 percent (increased from 50 percent in 1982 over three years) of their gross income from the active conduct of a trade or business in the possessions. The compromise allowed a credit for U.S. tax liability on possessions corporation income allocable to intangibles subject to certain new rules designed to limit the tax benefit.

The Future of the Possessions Tax Credit

Despite the amendments to section 936 enacted by Congress in 1976 and 1982, the future of the possession tax credit remains uncertain. Modification of the credit might occur for a number of reasons. First, the large projected deficits in the 1985 budget will put substantial pressure on all special credits, deductions, and exemptions in the U.S. Tax Code. Second, it remains to be seen whether the 1982 act will resolve continuing congressional concern about the efficacy of the credit in promoting employment in the possessions. The proposed regulations implementing the intangible income provisions are generally agreed to be quite generous, and some taxpayers will obtain more benefit than under the previous law. If the revenue cost of the credit continues to exceed $100,000 per job in certain possessions corporations, as was the case for nine companies in 1978, then there is reason to believe that Congress would, once again, amend section 936.

Wage Credit Proposal

The risks of another cutback in section 936 might be minimized if the Puerto Rican government developed an alternative to the possessions tax credit that would provide more of an incentive to increase employment in the possessions. A wage credit or similar tax system would be far simpler to administer than the current section 936 intangible income provisions and would prevent a company from claiming credits far in excess of its payroll in the possessions. An additional advantage of a wage credit or similar tax system is that it would stimulate a more balanced pattern of industrial development. The current possessions tax credit is unbalanced in that it promotes industries that have no natural comparative advantage and consequently are completely dependent on continued subsidization. The main comparative advantage of the Puerto Rican economy is its ample labor supply; yet the current tax incentive system encourages capital, relative to labor utilization. This point was emphasized by the governor's committee to study Puerto Rico's finances,

> In the past, U.S. investment flowed to the island to take advantage of both tax exemption and low wage rates. Investments were predominantly in industries with low capital-output and low capital-labor ratios, such as textiles and apparels, and thus provided relatively high levels of economic growth and employment. However, more recently Puerto Rican wage rates have increased relatively faster than skill levels, thus making Puerto Rico less attractive to investors. The result is that recent Puerto Rican investment is concentrated more heavily in high capital-output and high capital-labor ratio industries, such as chemicals and pharmaceuticals, and thus provides less economic growth and employment. Hence tax exemption is increasingly the main reason for outside investment on the island, and the resulting investment is providing reduced benefits to the island.[10]

To promote a more balanced program of economic development, the governor's committee recommended a major restructuring of the tax exemption programs to treat labor and capital-intensive industries on a more equal basis.

Long-Run Economic Development

The growth rate of Puerto Rican income has slowed substantially since 1973, and unemployment has increased to more than 20 percent. The Puerto Rican government employs one-fourth of the island's work force, and dependence on the U.S. government is extremely high: Tax benefits, transfer payments, and grants from the mainland were $4.5 billion in 1981 or 60 percent of Puerto Rico's gross national product.[11] The future economic growth of Puerto Rico depends on the exploitation of its comparative advantages. This will require better utilization of its ample labor supply, further development of trade and tourism, and improved productivity in agriculture. Additional investments in the island's infrastructure will also be essential for development.[12] Although the tax exemption program has played an important role in Puerto Rico's development, the disappointing performance over the last decade suggests that incentives for development must be more efficiently targeted toward offsetting the impediments to growth.

Notes

The views expressed in this paper are those of the author alone and are not attributable to the Joint Committee on Taxation or any member of Congress.

1. In 1954, these provisions were incorporated in section 931 of the Internal Revenue Code. The special tax rules currently apply to Puerto Rico, Guam, American Samoa, and the territories of Wake, Midway, and the Northern Mariana Islands. Separate but similar tax treatment applies to the U.S. Virgin Islands.

2. Senate Committee on Finance, *Tax Reform Act of 1976*, 94–938 on H.R. 10612 (Washington, D.C., June 10, 1976), p. 279.

3. U.S. General Accounting Office, *Puerto Rico's Political Future: A Divisive Issue With Many Dimensions* (Washington, D.C., March 1981), p. 69.

4. U.S. Treasury Department, *The Operation and Effect of the Possessions Corporation System of Taxation, Fourth Report* (Washington, D.C.: Government Printing Office, February 1983), p. 43.

5. Ibid., p. 37.

6. Committee to Study Puerto Rico's Finances, *Report to the Governor* (December 11, 1975). The Puerto Rican Industrial Incentives Act of 1978 implemented this suggestion by allowing a special tax deduction for 5 percent of wages.

7. Senate Committee on Finance, *Tax Equity and Fiscal Responsibility Act of 1982*, Report 97–494 on H.R. 4961 (Washington, D.C., July 12, 1982), p. 85.

8. Secretary of the Treasury, Commonwealth of Puerto Rico, "Puerto Rican Treasury Department Position Paper on Effects of Legislative Amendments to Sec. 936 of the I.R.C. Approved by the Senate Finance Committee" (July 14, 1982), p. 2.

9. Resident Commissioner Corrada reportedly threatened to withdraw Puerto Rico's support for the administration's Caribbean Basin Initiative if the Senate bill was not modified. *Tax Notes*, September 20, 1982, pp. 1094–1095.

10. Committee to Study Puerto Rico's Finances, *Report to the Governor*, p. 43.

11. U.S. Treasury Department, *The Operation and Effect of the Possessions Corporation System of Taxation, Fourth Report*, p. 112.

12. For a discussion of these issues, see Bertram P. Finn, "The Economic Implications of Statehood for Puerto Rico: A Preliminary Analysis," Workshop on the United States and Puerto Rico, Woodrow Wilson International Center for Scholars (Washington, D.C., April 1980).

Section 936: Myths and Realities

Nelson Famadas

The possessions system of taxation (section 936 of the Internal Revenue Code of the United States) provides for 100 percent tax credits on profits earned by a mainland affiliate in a possession of the United States.

Section 936 had its precursors, beginning with section 621 of the code enacted in the early 1920s. The original purpose was to provide U.S. business operations in the Philippines with the same tax advantages that British firms enjoyed in their Asian colonies. Thus, the original intent of Congress was not to provide an instrument for economic development in unincorporated U.S. territories, but rather to stimulate investments in those territories for the benefit of U.S. companies.

Puerto Rico's participation in section 936 or its predecessors has nothing to do with the congressional legislation of 1952 that changed the nomenclature of the possession from *territory* to *commonwealth* (Public Law 600). In fact, technically speaking, it is not the possession that qualifies for the tax credit benefit, but rather the U.S. mainland company, and then only with the permission of the U.S. Internal Revenue Service. Moreover, the tax benefit has been available to mainland affiliates operating in Puerto Rico since the initial enactment of section 621. However, not until 1942, when the legislature of Puerto Rico enacted the first industrial incentives act and created the Industrial Development Corporation, did the federal tax credits begin to serve as an attraction for investments to Puerto Rico.

Had Congress intended to make this tax benefit a part of the tax structure of the unincorporated territory of Puerto Rico, it would have made this section a part of P.L. 600 (the Puerto Rico Federal Relations Act of 1950), instead of leaving it in the Internal Revenue Code.

In discussing the whole issue of the possessions system of taxation, one must clearly establish a few background facts to dispel a mythology invented and widely disseminated by commonwealthers.

1. Federal tax benefits for mainland investments in the possession are not related to the designation of Puerto Rico as a *commonwealth* nor to its continued existence under that name.
2. Regardless of the great importance that federal tax exemption may have, or may have had, for Puerto Rico's economic growth, the original intention of Congress was to benefit mainland corporations.
3. Section 936 is part of the U.S. Internal Revenue Code, and like it or not, Congress has absolute power to modify or eliminate it unilaterally, without regard to the impact on the economy of Puerto Rico.
4. This is exactly what Congress attempted to do in 1976 when it almost eliminated section 931 and in 1982 when it almost eliminated section 936.
5. The U.S. citizens of the possessions have only the power of persuasion to prevent congressional actions that adversely affect their economies. When the power of persuasion fails, as it may

in the future, the mythology that Puerto Rico is somehow *entitled* to special tax benefits will be shattered.

The future of Puerto Rico's industrial and financial development program remained in doubt during most of 1982 because of debate over proposed changes in section 936 legislation. Investors who had been considering entering the Puerto Rican manufacturing sector postponed their decisions until they could determine how the Senate Finance Committee's suggested amendments to section 936 might affect their operations. The island's financial community, with some 40 percent of its deposits consisting of funds generated by section 936 revenue, nearly lapsed into a state of panic.

During June 1982, the Senate Finance Committee unilaterally—without consulting either the government of Puerto Rico or the corporations involved—moved to approve an amendment to section 936 (the Dole amendment) that, if it had become law, would probably have shut down more than 60 percent of the manufacturing operations on the island. The government of Puerto Rico, with the assistance of many public and private organizations, mounted what may have been the most massive lobbying campaign ever undertaken by the island. In the predawn hours of the last day on which the conference committee met, Puerto Rico's arguments prevailed and section 936 (h) was approved instead of the Dole amendment. The final version was the result of eleven months of negotiations between the government of Puerto Rico and the U.S. Treasury Department, with input from the affected corporations.

Puerto Rico's leaders learned several lessons from the section 936 battle:

1. The legislative foundation of the economy of Puerto Rico is extremely fragile and the people of Puerto Rico lack any tangible political power to influence decisions that threaten this foundation.
2. What Congress giveth, Congress can taketh away, not only in terms of tax benefits, but in terms of economic benefits. This principle was clearly established in the Supreme Court case of *Harris* v. *Rosario* (446 U.S. 651) and in congressional decisions affecting the residents of Puerto Rico, with regard to food stamps, aid to families with dependent children, and Medicaid.

The Internal Revenue Service's (IRS) and the joint committee's biased views on section 936 stem from the congressionally mandated annual reports prepared by the U.S. Treasury Department. These reports have invariably overstated the costs and understated the benefits of section

936 to Puerto Rico and the United States. These reports do not fully take into account qualitative changes in the development of the Puerto Rican manufacturing sector and thus the consequent benefits to other sectors of the economy. For example, the increasing quality of Puerto Rican manufacturing employment is reflected in the burgeoning role that dynamic, high-technology industries play in the island's employment and output. Since 1976, high-technology employment in Puerto Rico has been increasing at a 6.6 percent annual rate, despite the severe national recession. Employment in the computer industry has been growing at a rate of 20 percent per annum. Furthermore, section 936 also benefits the national economy: in a study done by *Fomento*, it was estimated that the purchase of raw materials and intermediate goods by corporations in Puerto Rico created or maintained 153,000 jobs on the mainland. In addition, because of local tax law changes enacted by the Puerto Rican government, section 936 companies have paid more than $700 million in Puerto Rican taxes since 1978.

Therefore, any balanced attempt to weigh the benefits of section 936 must include an analysis of the links between the Puerto Rican and national economies. Also, qualitative improvements in the island's manufacturing sector must be taken into account. Unfortunately, the yearly Treasury report does not consider these factors in detail; on the contrary, not only does it understate the benefits, but it overstates the costs of section 936. Both the IRS's and the joint committee's cost estimates are misleading: They assume that the data represent taxes that actually would be collected in the absence of a tax credit. For example, their calculations of tax savings ignore entirely the losses to the Federal Treasury that repeal of section 936 would cause through reduced economic activity overseas. The genuine issue is *not* IRS revenue losses (real or imagined): The genuine issue is the desirability of offering corporations an incentive to conduct their operations within U.S. jurisdictions.

In summary, section 936 is not the answer to Puerto Rico's economic development requirements over the long term, but until the questions of investment security and political equality are resolved once and for all, the government of Puerto Rico intends to make the section 936 system work for both Puerto Rico and the rest of the nation. Meanwhile, the experiences of 1982 should serve as a clear signal that Puerto Rico remains what it has always been: an unincorporated territory with almost no direct control over the enactment or repeal of laws that can significantly affect its economic future. Thus, under its present territorial status, Puerto Rico lacks the power that can only be guaranteed by political equality: What Congress giveth, Congress can taketh away.

How Section 936
Can Be Made More Effective

Miguel Lausell

Present Status of the 936 Program

During the past six years, both the U.S. Treasury and Congress have been paying closer attention to the 936 program. Although the periodic Treasury reports provide some background, they present an unbalanced view of the program.

In this context two points must be made. First, the Treasury reports tend to view the legislation simply in budgetary terms. The reports fail to take into account the importance of Puerto Rico to the United States in terms of foreign policy and national security. Second, the Puerto Rican government has not devoted enough energy toward convincing the Treasury and Congress that the 936 program must be viewed in a wider context, not simply as a budgetary issue.

The Budgetary Process

The tendency to view the 936 program in budgetary terms is not a new one. The program has historically been considered by the Congress in that manner. This fact would suggest that the Puerto Rican government should attempt to establish a close working relationship with those members of the U.S. Congress that have a direct role in the budgetary process. The goal of such a relationship should be to ensure that the strategic importance of Puerto Rico in U.S. foreign policy is clearly understood by Congress. Puerto Rico's position at the gateway to the Caribbean cannot be overemphasized. Puerto Rico is also the United States' best ally in Latin America. At present, Puerto Rican politicians should emphasize the island's position as a staging ground for the Caribbean Basin Initiative and its position as a stable political entity in the region.

Such efforts to affect the budgetary process should be undertaken by the Puerto Rican government in a rational and coordinated fashion.

For example, the lack of preparedness and the degree of improvisation that Puerto Rican representatives displayed during their defense of the 936 program when it was amended by the Tax Equity and Fiscal Responsibility Act of 1982 (TEFRA) were clearly counterproductive to the island's interests. That experience demonstrated that a new legislative strategy should be followed by Puerto Rico. The 936 program can no longer be justified solely in terms of its beneficial effects in creating jobs and assisting with capital formation.

For the Puerto Rican government to alter the manner in which Congress deals with the 936 program (and other matters affecting Puerto Rico) a clearer definition of, and commitment to, a long-term political relationship with the United States would be required. Yet, given the reality of local political conflicts, a clear definition of this relationship may be difficult to achieve. In the meantime, the Puerto Rican government should attempt to influence Congress on the 936 program by hiring a well-qualified lobbyist. There is still time for such a representative of the Puerto Rican government to establish the necessary credibility and contacts in Congress because the Treasury Department will not review the TEFRA amendments until 1986.

Promotion Under the Puerto Rican Industrial Incentives Act

Two points should be made concerning promotion under the Puerto Rican Industrial Incentives Act (PRIA). First, the PRIA specified that the application for tax exemption grants would be characterized by negotiations. These negotiations were superficially justified on the grounds that they were aimed at obtaining for Puerto Rico a fair quid pro quo in exchange for tax exemption. Yet, even though the negotiations of specific grants were successful, as a governmental process the negotiation of tax exemption grants has generally failed because of a lack of clearly articulated criteria on which to judge individual cases. Furthermore, the negotiations are too exposed to political pressures.

Second, the vast majority of potential investors see the TEFRA amendments as clear evidence of the willingness of the U.S. Congress to treat the 936 program as simply an item in the budgetary process, devoid of any long-term policy implications. In other words, the TEFRA amendments have been perceived by potential investors as an indication of the inherent instability of the 936 program. This perception has made them extremely cautious about investing in Puerto Rico.

The Passive Income Component

The passive income component of the 936 program has attracted the most attention, especially since the conversion process allowed under the 1978 Industrial Incentives Act concluded. From the U.S. point of view the changes to bear in mind are those introduced by TEFRA.

The passive income component has resulted in the accumulation of nearly U.S. $7 billion in Puerto Rico in the 936 funds market. That market is defined by the limitations imposed on the utilization of those funds by section 936 of the U.S. Internal Revenue Code. From the operational viewpoint, however, the local regulation of those funds most directly and dramatically affects their movement, in large part because the U.S. Treasury has not taken a stronger hand. Since 1976, the U.S. Treasury has de facto extended the benefit of a tax holiday to the passive income earned by participants in the 936 program, whenever such income has been earned in compliance with the local regulatory scheme. Given this situation the Puerto Rican government should quickly develop a data base to help understand and effectively regulate the 936 funds market to channel these funds into priority investments for the island's economic development.

Suggestions for Utilization

Two factors limit the possibilities for using the passive income component of the 936 program. The most important of these factors is the policy embodied in the legislation; stated in the simplest terms, that policy calls for (1) the accumulation of tax holiday funds in Puerto Rico only to the extent that the local economy can absorb them, and (2) the prompt repatriation to the United States of all funds that the local economy cannot absorb.

The need for funds in Puerto Rico is obvious. Statistics on housing needs, unemployment, and deterioration of infrastructure do not have to be elaborated. Yet the need for funds is distinct from the capacity of the economy to absorb funds. The capacity to absorb funds is first and foremost a function of Puerto Rico's credit rating. Yet paradoxically, the relatively high credit ratings enjoyed by Puerto Rico are maintained by not attempting to borrow all the funds needed to deal with the critical problems facing the economy.

However, the fact that alternative ways of attracting funds for the private sector have not been effectively developed can and must be criticized. The opportunity afforded by the 936 funds market calls for a concerted effort under a government coordinator in which a working committee for *each sector of the economy* will develop specific programs for attracting funds *to the private sector,* without forgetting that to attract the needed funds for the programs must result in investment instruments with a suitable credit rating.

An illustration of how this could work can be found in a program recently developed by the private sector with the Federal Home Loan Bank of New York (FHLB/NY), a program that has recently been accepted by the Puerto Rican Savings and Loan League. In essence, the program involves placing obligations of the FHLB/NY in the 936 funds market; the placement will be handled by the private sector. The proceeds of the placement will be earmarked for the savings and loan industry in Puerto Rico, with that industry receiving the benefit of the lower cost funding.

By imaginatively designing a program to invest 936 funds and by working closely with the United States, Puerto Rico can use 936 funds as a powerful economic development tool. It should be noted that the 936 program is possible because of Puerto Rico's present political status; it would be impossible under statehood. Thus the solution to Puerto Rico's economic problems is not to change its political status, but rather to influence more effectively the Congress within the context of the present political relationship.

B. CASHING-OUT FOOD STAMPS

Tinkering with Hunger: Puerto Rico's Food Stamp Saga

Guy F. Smith

In 1981, the Reagan administration endorsed an attempt to remove Puerto Rico from the federal food stamp program. At that time, roughly 56 percent of the population of Puerto Rico received benefits from the program. The vicissitudes of the food stamp program in Puerto Rico provide a telling—and painful—demonstration of how congressional legislation designed to achieve budgetary or other public policy objectives can ignore what should be the central consideration in legislation concerning Puerto Rico—the welfare of the island's inhabitants.

One result of the Reagan administration's budget-cutting triumphs in 1981 was a new program for Puerto Rico: The food stamp program became the Nutritional Assistance Block Grant. The new program was part of a Republican budget that systematically cut social spending across the board. This budget bill, which finally passed the U.S. House of Representatives on June 26, 1981, was known as the Gramm-Latta substitute. It was strongly supported by Republicans and was hailed as a major victory for the administration.

The budget contained a special provision, supported by Office of Management and Budget (OMB) officials and advocates of cutbacks in the food stamp program (particularly Senator Jesse Helms in the Senate Agriculture Committee), that cut the food stamp program in Puerto Rico by 25 percent. In spite of vigorous informal lobbying by the governor of Puerto Rico and others, the legislative process was virtually closed to Puerto Rican participation. No hearings were held to determine the effects that the cutback would have on the U.S. citizens living in Puerto Rico, and no formal consultations were sought with either the governor or the resident commissioner of the island.

Of course the Gramm-Latta substitute directly affected every U.S. citizen, but in the case of Puerto Rico, the effect of the bill was discriminatory. No other U.S. citizens were singled out for reductions in the food stamp program above and beyond the across-the-board cuts.

The high level of participation in the food stamp program on the island—Puerto Rico received 10 percent of the total federal benefits—was the major reason cited for proposing cutbacks. Yet one must understand that the island has a per capita income approximately one-half that of the poorest U.S. state, Mississippi. Furthermore, U.S. citizens in Puerto Rico already had been subjected to unequal treatment in other social welfare programs. For example, they are excluded from the Supplementary Security Income Program (SSI). And for other federal programs, Puerto Ricans must have a lower income than mainland residents to qualify. Although both the governor and the resident commissioner raised these points before the Senate and House Agricultural Committee, their efforts were to no avail. The administration had already made its decision to lower nutritional benefits for the people of Puerto Rico.

The government of Puerto Rico was told to come up with a new food stamp program at a level of $825 million a year for three years. This represented a cut of almost $200 million compared to the total disbursement ($1.04 billion) of food stamps in the three years prior to the new budget. Fortunately, the new legislation permitted considerable flexibility in devising a new system to deliver nutritional benefits. Guidelines, endorsed and approved by the U.S. Department of Agriculture's food and nutrition service, specifically supported developing a program chosen from several alternatives. These guidelines provided the basis for the decision of the administration of Governor Romero to "cash-out" the nutritional benefits in the form of checks to participating individuals.

When it became clear that the USDA would endorse the Romero administration's cash-out plan, opposition developed in the House led by Congressman E. Thomas Coleman (R.-Mo.). He introduced a "sense of Congress" resolution on April 1, 1982, opposing the cash-out concept and asking Puerto Rico to amend its plan so that the program would "provide assurance that any assistance provided under such plan will be used only to purchase food." In addition, Congressman Coleman held hearings on April 29, 1982. The USDA appeared in support of the governor's decision to cash-out the program whereas the food wholesalers and retailers were the most vocal critics of the cash-out concept. Despite Congressman Coleman's opposition, the island's plan went into effect on July 1, 1982. A total of 90,838 families were no longer eligible for assistance under the new income ceilings. Yet the new program disbursed benefits to 1,582,524 individuals out of a total of 3.2 million citizens on the island.

Congressman Coleman pursued another course of action to require Puerto Rico to change the cash-out delivery system of its nutritional assistance program. The House Agriculture Committee adopted an amendment presented by Congressman Coleman that mandated that the island should change the cash-out delivery system to a noncash one by October 1, 1983. This action by the House created a furor in Puerto Rico. Another lobbying effort was set into motion, again led by Governor Romero, Resident Commissioner Corrada, and Secretary of Social Sciences Collazo. They asked for a hearing on the island, which, after several months of delay, was held on June 21, 1983. Congressmen Jim Olin (D.-Va.) and Sid Morrison (R.-Wash.) chaired the hearings. Governor Romero defended his cash-out delivery system and requested that Congress either rescind the Coleman amendment or postpone any action for two years while data could be collected to determine the present system's effectiveness. Meanwhile, the Senate Appropriations Committee passed an amendment that would extend the deadline to propose a new program until January 1, 1984.

Public Law 98-204, signed by President Reagan on December 2, 1983, suspended the noncash benefit requirement for the Puerto Rico Nutrition Assistance Program and continued the program until September 30, 1985. The signing of this law was the culmination of a congressional effort to maintain the existing program in Puerto Rico.

This brief chronology of events has demonstrated several aspects of the political relationship between the U.S. and Puerto Rico. The manner in which the U.S. government changed the food stamp program to the Nutritional Assistance Block Grant seemed, from a Puerto Rican perspective, to be a unilateral decision taken without due consideration of the effect on the Puerto Rican economy or the welfare of its citizens. In addition, the unequal treatment accorded to U.S. citizens in Puerto Rico underlined, once again, their status as second-class citizens.

Cashing-Out Food Stamps: A Bad Idea

Congressman E. Thomas Coleman

Since 1982, Puerto Rico has participated in the food stamp program through an annual block grant set at $825 million. The block grant was designed specifically to allow Puerto Rico to formulate its own food assistance program in accordance with the needs of the island's low-income people.

There were several reasons for providing Puerto Rico with a block grant for food assistance. The food stamp program as designed for the states had changed Puerto Rico, affecting profoundly the island's people and their economic status. Before the block grant, about 58 percent of the Puerto Rican population received food stamps. Fully 10 percent of the entire U.S. food stamp budget went to Puerto Rico, and 10 percent of the personal income of the people of Puerto Rico was derived from the food stamp program. It seemed to me that the old food stamp program was inappropriate for the island, and a majority of the Congress agreed with this. Food stamps were no longer a way to respond to the food needs of the low-income and unemployed people of Puerto Rico. Instead they were part of the economy of the island—a big part—and a way of life for many.

The food stamp program also changed the island's economic base. Less land was used for farming, and the amount of cultivated cropland decreased. The people of Puerto Rico had to rely more and more upon imported (and therefore more expensive) foods. For all these reasons I believed that Puerto Rico should have the ability to design its own food assistance program.

Legislation was enacted to provide food stamp funds to the government of Puerto Rico in a block grant, and by July 1, 1982, Puerto Rico had designed a food program for its low-income population and began issuing benefits. Unfortunately, these benefits were dispersed in cash. Checks were issued that could be cashed and spent on any product; for the first time recipients were not limited to buying foodstuffs. Instead of an $825 million food stamp program, Puerto Rico now had an $825 million cash assistance program.

The conversion from the food stamp program went smoothly, without disruption of benefits and with a minimum of administrative problems. The basic design of the program more than satisfied the Department of Agriculture.

A fatal flaw, however, is the delivery system chosen by the Puerto Rican government. The Reagan administration also deserves criticism for approving such a system: By accepting the cash-out system, the administration is virtually washing its hands of responsibility for millions of dollars of taxpayers' money. In this case, the administration appears to be more concerned with form than substance. Simply turning over the implementation of a federal program to a state, a territory, or a commonwealth is not New Federalism. The administration is passing the buck, and in this case, passing millions of bucks.

During the debate on the food assistance program in the agricultural committee in 1982, there was no indication that the block grant would be used to support the cashing-out of the food stamp program in Puerto Rico. The committee's clear intention was to provide $825 million for food assistance to the commonwealth. When the Puerto Rican plan was implemented as a cash-out program, it changed from a food assistance program to a guaranteed income program, with—ironically—absolutely no guarantee that these millions of dollars would be used for food.

Obviously, many, if not most, people in Puerto Rico will buy food with their cash grants. True, the old program, which relied on coupons, had serious flaws: Coupons were easily available at discount prices in exchange for cash. Yet progress was being made to combat these irregularities. Moreover, the fact that serious abuses exist in the food stamp program is not a valid reason to abandon it. Fraud in the food stamp program will not be eliminated through changing the delivery system to cash-out. Instead, cashing-out will eliminate the ability to find out where the fraud exists.

Have we surrendered in the battle against fraud in the food stamp program so easily? Do we really want to forfeit any assurances that the poor will receive food assistance? Cashing-out the food stamp program in Puerto Rico may be the first step toward cashing-out the entire program on a national basis. Furthermore, if Reagan's New Federalism ideas gain more currency, several other programs may also turn into cash giveaways. For example, if the delivery system for the school lunch program is changed to cash-out, children would be given money to purchase their lunches with the naive assumption that they would spend it on meals in the school cafeteria. The crux of my criticism against the cashing-out of the food stamp program is that, at some future date, it may serve to open the door to the national repudiation of feeding the American poor.

Cashing-out the food stamp program is not a new idea; it has been debated in the halls of Congress for years. What is surprising is that this administration would carry out the liberal philosophy offered by others, in the past, under the guise of states' rights. Whatever happens to the concept of New Federalism the Congress must not give up the goals and purposes for which programs are established. Policy decisions on program goals must not be blurred because of the type of delivery system used. Certainly this course is the converse of that in the recent past when many goals of programs were lost because of faulty administration. Closer scrutiny by the White House of what happens to these block-grant programs once they are given to the states would ensure that the New Federalism truly will be an improvement on the old federalism.

The food assistance program in Puerto Rico should both meet the needs of the low-income population and ensure that the goals of the program are met. Neither can be achieved when cash is distributed. The government of Puerto Rico is capable of designing a workable program that assures that the $825 million authorized and appropriated each year by the U.S. Congress is spent on food by eligible individuals and families.

6

Puerto Rico: Economic Development Should Come First

Randolph Mye

In this century, changes in the Puerto Rican economy have been profound; yet one of the fundamental problems of underdevelopment has remained—Puerto Rico continues to be an exposed economy, vulnerable to the vagaries of U.S. and world business cycles and to shifting comparative advantage. At present, the Puerto Rican economy is suffering from the most recent severe cyclical downturn in the U.S. economy, as well as from long-term stagnation reflecting deeper structural problems. The endless debate over the island's political status has diverted attention and energy from a consideration of the urgent need to do something about its economic crisis. Indeed, the debates have, by and large, missed the connection between the economy and future political status or have put the cart before the horse.

Each faction increasingly argues that only its preferred status option will provide a suitable environment for economic progress. Yet none of the proponents has faced the fact that the present economic stagnation makes the achievement of any alternative status problematic at best. This chapter takes a different tack. It argues that the establishment of a sustainable and viable economic growth process is a prerequisite to addressing Puerto Rico's status problem. The basic thesis is that Puerto Rico's "welfare" image jeopardizes any opportunity for success in the status debate. On one hand, leaders on the mainland appear resigned to the fact that the island's economy cannot function without large amounts of federal financial resources, and on the other, they seem unable to recognize the limitations of a programmatic approach in the disbursement of these resources on the growth and development process. The need to carefully control federal resources gives little or no flexibility or responsibility to the island leadership. The economic crisis on the island promotes reliance on federal funds and reduces the vitality of the island's people. Hence, there is a vicious circle: Heavy dependence on federal transfer payments reduces confidence in the island's leadership and in its people's self-reliance. The weakness of local savings and entrepreneurship confirms the view on the island that federal handouts are indispensable and that Puerto Ricans are helpless. The pessimistic expectations for Puerto Rico's economy among both islanders and mainlanders must be reversed, and the paralysis of the status debate must not be permitted to interfere with the need to transform the Puerto Rican economy.

The Growth of Dependence

The Puerto Rican economy is experiencing a serious crisis: Real investment has declined in the last decade; future economic growth is uncertain; the changes in federal tax policy have reduced the advantages to plants that locate in Puerto Rico; and recent changes in U.S. trade policy may further dampen the potential growth of the economy. Most significantly, the primary source for even the limited economic growth of the past decade has been federal funds.

Not since the 1940s and the late Governor Muñoz Marín's Operation Bootstrap has a development strategy been debated, let alone formulated. The success of Operation Bootstrap was accepted as a given and no further discussion was thought necessary. Some observers warned that the treadmill of tax-exempt, off-island investment could not be perpetuated and that income and employment would not automatically continue upward. These gloomy predictions were ignored. The oil shock of 1973 pointed up to some the fallacy of a strategy that neglected internal savings and investment while encouraging consumption. Decisionmakers, however, continued to ignore these signs; no one came forward with a development program to substitute or supplement the past strategy; instead, increasing federal expenditures were sought to fill the vacuum.

Meanwhile, the federal government, in developing its budgetary priorities for the mainland, extended off handedly many welfare programs and policies to the island. In some instances the programs were applied exactly as they were on the mainland, in others, only partially or not at all. With few exceptions, the programs were generally geared to maintain incomes and therefore consumption. They were not designed to promote Puerto Rican development. For example, the food stamp program was extended to Puerto Rico without thought about the reasonableness of applying U.S. poverty standards to an island where per capita income was only one-half that of the mainland. Revenue-sharing and supplemental security income programs were not extended to Puerto

Table 6.1

**Federal Expenditures, by Major Category
in Puerto Rico, 1965-1981**

Category	1965	1970	1975	1980	1981
Federal Transfer Payments	136.7	303.3	1,167.1	2,359.5	2,858
Rebate of Customs and Excises	60.9	118.6	136.1	240.2	316.7
Federal Agency Expenditures	110.8	160.8	188.0	302.8	545
Aid to State and Local Governments	126.0	256.5	650.6	1,348.4	1,151.3
Total Gross Receipt	434.4	839.2	2,141.8	4,250.9	4,871
Less Payments to U.S.	109.4	231.1	591.2	834.8	949
Net Federal Funds Receipt	325.0	608.1	1,550.6	3,416.1	3,922.0

Source: Alan Udall, "The Reagan Administration and Federal Funding to Puerto Rico," *Puerto Rico Business Review,* Vol. 6, No. 10, October 1981 (Government Development Bank of Puerto Rico), pp. 2-3.

Rico, presumably because the islanders pay no federal taxes. Some programs—Medicaid, Medicare, and highway trust funding among others—included Puerto Rico but with special funding.

Federal economic and social policies with their varying standards for Puerto Rico reflected the needs of the United States, whereas the island's needs were haphazardly addressed, if at all. The results were ambiguous except in one respect—the dependence of the island on federal transfers increased enormously. Between 1965 and 1981 net federal funds transferred to the island increased more than tenfold. In the five years between 1975 and 1980 they more than doubled (Table 6.1). Federal outlays represented 10 percent of the island's gross product in 1970 and more than 32 percent by 1982. There is no way that federal outlays can be expected to sustain this growth rate in the 1980s nor is there economic development, under any definition of the concept, when the principal source of growth is transfer payments.

The U.S. Treasury Department in its annual report to Congress on section 936 of the IRS code has raised the question of an appropriate federal economic policy toward Puerto Rico. The Treasury Department indicated that federal revenue losses are increasing rapidly, but the investments generated by the corporate federal tax exemption are not providing the desired employment levels on Puerto Rico. In the view of the Treasury Department, the cost per job created on the island is excessive, and a better strategy is necessary. Yet there is no federal institutional structure that can address the broader issue implicitly raised by the Treasury Department—what is a viable development strategy that relies less on special federal treatment? Neither the Congress nor the executive branch is prepared currently to deal with substantive economic issues in Puerto Rico, and, therefore, Puerto Ricans will view their problems as increasingly political phenomena.

Dependency and the Status Debate

In terms of the fundamental political issues, Congress is not ready to grant statehood or make any "status" changes when Puerto Ricans themselves cannot agree on a solution. In the meantime, the island's economy should not be permitted to sink into a welfare dependency even more exaggerated than that today. Federalization of the Puerto Rican economy is inconsistent with any status that aspires to a minimal degree of viability, including that enjoyed by a state of the Union. Federalization of the Puerto Rican economy over the past decade (federal disbursements relative to Puerto Rican GNP, for example) has made the economy's growth a function of federal budget and tax policy decisions.

As the federal role has increased, Puerto Ricans have had more and more difficulty determining their own growth policies, nor are they able to influence federal budget priorities to make them more reasonably related to their long-term economic needs. Puerto Ricans on the island cannot express their political views in the same ways that U.S. citizens do on the mainland. Without votes in presidential elections and with hardly any voice in Congress, Puerto Ricans must seek to influence federal decisions through whatever means they can. Yet heavy reliance on informal, ad hoc lobbying that Puerto Rico's lack of political clout makes necessary has high costs. The acrimony over changes in welfare programs (like food stamps) and in federal tax policies that affect the island's traditional investment strategy, as well as the controversy engendered in Puerto Rico by the Caribbean Basin Initiative, reflect the powerlessness felt by the U.S. citizens on the island. In most instances, whether changes in federal policy adversely affect the economy or not, the perception that Puerto Rico was taken for granted in the process only heightens political tensions.

The security interests of the United States are adversely affected by the present political and economic impasse. Continued economic stagnation on the island will necessarily produce a high level of frustration directed at the mainland. Threats and attacks against military installations are an extreme manifestation of that psychological malaise, but it manifests itself in other harmful ways, such as almost continual criticism of Washington from all parts of the political spectrum. This criticism in turn produces congressional resentment toward Puerto Rico, which is increasingly viewed as an ungrateful ward. In this way, the underlying economic problems of the island result in a political atmosphere in

Washington that is inhospitable to any discussion of the status issue. Priority attention needs to be given to solving the economic problems of Puerto Rico instead of concentrating on the endless debate over the status issue. Congress is "turned off," the Puerto Rican people are undecided, and the American public is embarrassed by the island's image. Puerto Rico and the United States should seek to establish a less dependent island economy, relying more on domestic savings and investment for capital formation and on greater local entrepreneurship. Then, and only then, will there be an atmosphere conducive to action on political status.

A Proposal

A discussion between decisionmakers on the mainland and the island should be undertaken about the future direction of the island's economy. Not only the direction, but the strategy to be followed must be formulated. Economic decisions made in Puerto Rico have to be coordinated with federal policies. This coordination will require major changes in the decision-making process in both federal executive and legislative branches and on the island.

The three crucial elements for the success of this proposal are (1) that the Puerto Ricans develop a viable development strategy with attendant self-help measures; (2) that the federal government create an institutional structure that will provide a focal point for policies affecting the island; and (3) that the federal government reorganize its budgetary process for the island. Without these changes the island's leaders will continue to wander through the policy thickets created by Washington.

The Elements of a Development Strategy

The objectives of a development strategy for Puerto Rico should be to increase domestic capital formation, promote exports to nonmainland markets (to minimize the possible adverse effects of mainland business cycles), create adequate employment opportunities, promote industries that use island inputs, further develop island financial and service industries, and revive agriculture by moving toward truck farming for the local markets. This is a formidable set of goals for Puerto Ricans to sort through if development on the island is to take place not merely at the mercy of events and decisions on the mainland.

As an initial step, the Puerto Rican governor, legislature, and other decisionmakers should join together to create a development commission to define the economic development strategy best suited to meet these objectives. The commission would have one year in which to make recommendations. It would work with island leaders to try to achieve a consensus on a development strategy. Once that has been accomplished, Puerto Rican representatives would undertake a dialogue with mainland political leaders to develop a joint approach to the island's development.

What might be some of the techniques of an economic development strategy in Puerto Rico? A strategy would continue to give priority to attracting off-island investment, but the objective should be to maximize these industries' links to the local economy. The "deepening" process would provide greater entrepreneurial opportunities for Puerto Ricans. Existing high-technology industries, for example, might be encouraged to set up research facilities in Puerto Rico in conjunction with special educational programs in local universities. A partnership between the engineering and science faculties and the private sector could be encouraged to develop new industries. Risk capital could be made available through the government development bank as a means of encouraging local entrepreneurship and local capital formation. For example, industries based on research in renewable-energy technologies might be created on the basis of an existing activity at the University of Puerto Rico.

Unlike the experiment of vertical deepening carried out with the petrochemical industry (which was induced to locate on Puerto Rico because of federal tax exemption and the privileged access for refined products granted by the oil quota program), this deepening process would maximize the use of local inputs. Because the petrochemical industry was not formed on the basis of a comparative advantage, but rather reflected the operation of an administrative system whose eventual undermining could be predicted, the new industries would have stronger ties to the local economy.

A future strategy would presumably be more flexible, less energy intensive, and less dependent on tax exemptions and special administrative treatment. Puerto Rican tax policy should be changed to increase savings and investment to enhance the development strategy. For example, in the agriculture sector an implicit income tax could apply to land use: Underutilized land would be taxed at a rate inversely related to its productivity, rewarding efficient activities, while taxing at a maximum rate unutilized or low-productivity activities. These new agricultural activities, stimulated by policies to increase production and productivity, could be linked to the canning and processing industries, fulfilling the desired goal of flexibility and local resource utilization.

Some institutions of the Puerto Rican government should be reshaped or made more efficient to administer these new programs. One might expect that private and public institutions on the mainland would participate in providing technical assistance for the process of economic transformation.

Institutional Changes

Whatever strategy the Puerto Rican leadership chooses—and the foregoing are only sketchy suggestions—it will be essential that the federal government change the way it does business with Puerto Rico. This change will require an overhaul of federal budgetary practices and innovation in federal institutions.

Over the last three decades, the federal government has lacked a focal point for economic policy toward the island. Federal funds were disbursed to Puerto Rico on the basis of programmatic goals unconnected to the magnitude of other programs or the long-term needs of the population. The fairly recent substantial expansion in federal disbursements to Puerto Rico reflected at least partly the island's desires to obtain federal funds on the same basis as other political entities and the lack of alternative sources of financing sufficiently large to meet growing problems. Because of the island's relative poverty, federal expenditures have become so important to the economy that their abrupt reduction or elimination would create an economic crisis of immense proportions.

Congress must now reassert control over the expenditure process and transform federal assistance to Puerto Rico into a mechanism for promoting economic development. The automatic extension of federal programs to Puerto Rico makes no sense when it only fuels "welfarism."

The responsibility of the federal government to support this approach might be carried out through a federal commission composed equally of representatives from the executive and the Congress, staffed by a small secretariat to work out procedures and legislation for unifying federal programs that apply to Puerto Rico. The commission would also review federal policies and regulations affecting the island to minimize any adverse impact they might have on development efforts. Close consultation would be essential between the Puerto Rican development commission and the federal commission.

The federal commission should be a permanent body able to deal with Puerto Rican problems as a whole. The commission would report in a timely fashion to the executive and legislative branches on the progress, changes, and implementation of the development strategy. It would not act on behalf of Puerto Rican interests to change federal policies that have primarily mainland application. But obviously it could act to advise both branches of the federal government on the potential impact of federal policies and legislation on the island's economy. The commission would consult and advise the appropriate Puerto Rican political bodies without constraint, but in no way interfere with Puerto Rico's responsibilities to carry out the programs and projects. Administration of the funds and programs would fall specifically on the political structures of Puerto Rico—the governor and legislature. A budgeting process should require a joint decision of these two bodies.

Changes in Federal Budgeting Process and Tax Policy

In 1982 federal budget gross disbursements to Puerto Rico amounted to about $4.8 billion of which about $1.8 to $2.0 billion were entitlement programs—social security, veterans' payments, and education. With the exception of social security and veterans' programs, which result from contributions in money or kind, the budget can be altered by congressional action to consolidate and reshape funds applied to Puerto Rico.

Over the years Congress has accorded special treatment to Puerto Rico by applying dollar limitations for certain programs or excluding it from other programs. The Supreme Court sanctioned differential treatment for Puerto Rico on various occasions, the most recent (1978) involving health and human resources programs. The pattern of treating Puerto Rico distinctly does not appear to follow any prescribed path. For example, Puerto Rico was excluded from the Supplemental Security Income Program, but essentially was given unlimited access to food stamps (before 1982). The rationales behind these disparities do not appear to reflect any global view of Puerto Rico's economic problems.

By contrast, what is envisioned in this proposal is either a series of block grant programs or a single grant program. Congress would act to pull various expenditure programs together into a more centralized financing package that could be more easily channeled by federal and Puerto Rican authorities to meet economic development needs.

Conditions applied to funds that now go to the island under various federal programs could be replaced by generalized conditions on timing and use. To satisfy concern over the possible maladministration of funds, the proposed federal commission would review and evaluate their use. The commission would advise the Puerto Rican authorities on their findings, as well as the federal branches of government. There will be concern that the Puerto Rican government lacks the administrative capacity to administer funds without tight federal control. Yet unless the island's government is trained to administer programs and funds, the Congress may never be willing to agree to the various political status alternatives, all of which envisage greater local autonomy.

The New Federalism offered by the administration in 1981 provides a useful conceptual framework. At the heart of the plan would be a transfer of responsibility and financial resources to the local government to permit it to restructure programs in accord with local priorities and to provide a strong financial foundation for the island's economic development.

The Congress should not only restructure the programmatic approach used to disburse federal funds to the island but also tax policy. Tax credits and exemptions for Puerto Rico should be reexamined to ensure that they are effectively promoting economic development and not serving merely as tax shelters for mainland corporations. However, the continuation of federal corporate tax exemption for repatriated earnings of possession corporations is necessary for a fixed period to allow island policies to stimulate local savings. Island tax exemption policies should be gradually modified along with existing island corporate taxation policies to induce increased corporate links with the Puerto Rican economy. Firms using the island as an export platform to nonmainland markets could be given special tax treatment. In other words, the island's administration should undertake to evaluate and modify corporate tax laws to make them consistent with its long-term economic development strategy. Over time, successful economic development should reduce the economy's dependence on section 936 of the U.S. Tax Code.

With a long-term commitment from the federal government, projects in both public and private sectors could be carried out with certainty and consistency. The efficient use of financial resources by the Puerto Ricans would demonstrate their ability to develop and carry out a strategy of sustainable growth.

Conclusion

The federalization of the Puerto Rican economy over the past decade, whether planned or inadvertent, has thrust on the federal government a major responsibility to take an active role in supporting a development strategy that would apply these federal funds to projects and programs contributive to the process of sustainable growth. Puerto Ricans, for their part, should do more than point to the seriousness of their economic plight; they should take the initiative in developing the consensus required for the formulation of a development strategy.

The ability of the late Governor Muñoz Marín to define a development strategy and mobilize popular support was the key to the island's initial economic transformation. His strong will and leadership are not easily duplicated. Nevertheless, today's Puerto Ricans must strive to repeat the Muñoz Marín feat. Without popular consensus, no government can alter the structure of its economy. Without question, the development strategy will involve risks, yet the alternatives offer little or no hope that Puerto Rico's condition will change.

THE STATUS ISSUE:
THE WAY AHEAD

Introduction

The official U.S. position notwithstanding, the issue of Puerto Rico's political status is an international issue. As Robert Pastor details in his chapter, keeping Puerto Rico off the agenda of the UN General Assembly is a perennial chore for U.S. diplomats. From time to time, it requires the mobilization of senior U.S. officials and the cashing in of political chits with friends and adversaries. Moreover, as Pastor notes, the Puerto Rico issue has tended in recent years to spread to other international forums.

Yet, when all is said and done, he finds that the chief argument for a change in U.S. policy on the issue in the international arena is one of tactics, rather than of substance. Pastor argues that by taking a less defensive approach to the question in the United Nations, the United States could more easily defend itself from criticism from abroad and diminish outside interference with its efforts to deal with Puerto Rico's future. However, the real need for a change in policy, says Pastor, stems from national interests of a more profound kind.

Pastor sees the political inferiority of Puerto Rico—its second-class juridical status—as contradicting American ideals and belying American values. If the United States holds self-determination as an important principle, basic to the kind of society we say we are, then it must do more than give lip service to the principle in the Puerto Rico case. To be faithful to self-determination, the United States, says Pastor, must take the initiative to implement a process by which Puerto Ricans have the practical possibility of determining their future. Pastor notes that self-determination and independence are no longer automatically complementary; the former may not necessarily produce the latter.

Why is it so difficult for official Washington to undertake a process of self-determination for Puerto Rico? After all, numerous governmental study commissions over the past twenty years have recommended action. Juan Manuel García-Passalacqua believes that bureaucratic politics can explain the inertia in Washington. He concludes that only leadership from the top of the U.S. government can provide the momentum to break the issue loose from parochial interests of the departments and agencies. García-Passalacqua sets forth a series of steps in both Washington and San Juan that would culminate in an act of self-determination by Puerto Rico.

An essential feature of the process that García-Passalacqua suggests is a definition of what each of the status outcomes (statehood, "perfected" commonwealth, and independence) means in specific terms. What would Congress be asked to provide in financial resources? What exceptions from federal policy on language and education would be expected? What about U.S. military installations? How long a transition? For Puerto Ricans to make a meaningful choice, they must know how far Congress would be willing to go to make each status outcome viable. Likewise, Congressmen would want to know what they are voting for. This implies negotiations, and García-Passalacqua sets forth the possibilities for that process.

In an attempt to begin the task of defining status specifics, representatives of each of the four principal Puerto Rican political parties were asked to describe what they would ask the federal government to do to make their preferred outcome possible. (Although there was an attempt to leapfrog the usual effort by Puerto Rican political leaders to put forward the case for their status, it was impossible for the authors to avoid entirely the temptation.) Although they disagree on the outcome, all four spokesmen seem to agree on the need for a process to permit Puerto Ricans to decide their future status, and on the necessity of federal initiative to get the process rolling.

7

Puerto Rico as an International Issue: A Motive for Movement?

Robert A. Pastor

Estragon: Wait! I sometimes wonder if we wouldn't have been better off alone, each one for himself. We weren't made for the same road.
Vladimir: It's not certain.
Estragon: No, nothing is certain.
Vladimir: We can still part, if you think it would be better.
Estragon: It's not worthwhile now.
Vladimir: No, it's not worthwhile now.
Estragon: Well, shall we go?
Vladimir: Yes, let's go.

> *They do not move.*
> *Curtain.*

—Samuel Beckett, *Waiting for Godot* (1948)

Introduction: The Summer Ritual

Every summer since 1972, just as surely as humidity descends on Washington with the tourists and scatters the natives, a small group of officials in the State Department and, from time to time, in the White House become anxious about Puerto Rico. These officials know that the Cubans are already ahead of them, conspiring mercilessly to ruin their summer by gathering support to condemn the United States for colonialism in Puerto Rico at the UN Special Committee on De-Colonization, which meets every August or September. So these officials scurry around to gain the necessary clearances for cables to be sent to U.S. ambassadors all over the world to try to stop this nefarious Cuban plot.

Invariably, our ambassadors are instructed to call in their chips or offer new ones, using pretty much the same arguments, year after year:

- Puerto Rico is a democracy (which is more than can be said for Cuba et al.). The political parties in Puerto Rico that favor independence have always obtained a small percentage of the total vote.[1]
- The United States recognizes Puerto Rico's right to determine its own future free of external interference (meaning the UN). The U.S. president will respect and support whatever the people of Puerto Rico decide.
- The issue of Puerto Rico's political status was settled when the UN General Assembly removed Puerto Rico from the list of non-self-governing territories in 1953. It is now an *internal matter.* The United States feels strongly that it is inappropriate for the UN to debate the question of Puerto Rico's political status, and we are offended at it being described as a colonial or even an international issue. A vote with Cuba and against the United States cannot help our relations, and (depending on how harsh the summer, how new and assertive the U.S. ambassador to the UN, and how strong the support for Cuba) it could really hurt our relations.

Each year, U.S. arguments grow more strident, but more nations are not convinced. The United States has to use more pressure and offer more incentives to gain a nation's vote. And it is harder to elude the ironies. While insisting that Puerto Rico is an internal matter, high-level officials in each administration spend as much, if not more, time on Puerto Rico as an international issue than as a domestic one.[2] While refusing to debate the issue directly in the UN committee, the United States is probably more engaged on the issue of Puerto Rico than on most others in which it directly participates.

The U.S. government's position on Puerto Rico incurs an annual diplomatic fee, and some would argue that the price is steadily rising. *Should the United States continue to pay the price, or should it reconsider its position?*

This paper has three purposes. First, I will review the evolution of the international debate on Puerto Rico. Which institutions and organizations debate the issue? How has the debate changed over time? Is opposition to U.S. policies increasing? Which Latin American governments take this issue most seriously, and why? How would they view a decision by the people of Puerto Rico to become a state in the Union? Second, I will evaluate the costs of maintaining the status quo—both the position of the U.S. government in the UN that Puerto Rico is an internal, not an international matter, and the current political status of Puerto Rico. Although primarily concerned with the international costs of maintaining the status quo, I will also assess whether other reasons would justify changing the U.S. position and beginning a process that would lead to a decision on political status. In short, what are the motives for movement? Finally, I will propose a process that will permit both the U.S. government and the people of Puerto Rico to make a future decision on status.

Internal Matter or International Issue?

When asked whether a particular event constituted a turning point for Puerto Rico, Luis Muñoz Marín, Puerto Rico's governor from 1946 to 1964, responded that when you are traveling on a circle, every point is a turning point.[3] In examining the course of the international debate on Puerto Rico from 1945, one can identify several turning points and also some trends. To assist the reader in distinguishing between recurring arguments and discernible trends, the debate will be arbitrarily divided into the following four periods: (1) On and Off the List, 1946–1959; (2) The USSR and Cuba Repeat the Question, 1960–1970; (3) The Issue Takes Hold, 1971–1976; and (4) Converging Debates, 1977–present.

On and Off the List, 1946–1959

With hindsight, the Charter of the United Nations appears surprisingly cautious on the issue of colonialism. In the preamble, purposes, and principles of the charter, the reference closest to colonialism is a phrase suggesting that "friendly relations among nations [should be] based on respect for the principle of equal rights and self-determination." However, while collective security was the charter's main purpose, it also included a "Declaration Regarding Non-Self-Governing Territories" (Chapter 11) and a trusteeship system (Chapters 12 and 13), which described the responsibilities of member nations to ensure that these territories attain "a full measure of self-government." Until that occurs, member nations were required to transmit information annually on their territories' conditions. As a driving force behind decolonization, the United States accepted its own responsibility and included Puerto Rico—along with Alaska, Hawaii, Guam, and the Virgin Islands—on the list of seventy-four non-self-governing territories compiled by the General Assembly in its resolution of December 14, 1946.

Soon after that, discussions within Puerto Rico and between Puerto Rico and the United States on the mechanism for attaining self-government began. A constitutional convention met in Puerto Rico in 1952 and declared that when the constitution takes effect, and Puerto Rico becomes a commonwealth or *Estado Libre Asociado*, "we [the people of Puerto Rico will] attain the goal of complete self-government, the last vestiges of colonialism having disappeared."[4] On July 25, 1952, the constitution came into force, and on January 19, 1953, the United States informed the United Nations of the change in government in Puerto

Rico and requested that the island be removed from the list of non-self-governing territories. During the debate, the U.S. ambassador to the United Nations transmitted a message from President Eisenhower to the UN General Assembly that "if at any time the Legislative Assembly of Puerto Rico adopts a resolution in favor of more complete or even absolute independence, he [President Eisenhower] will immediately recommend to Congress that such independence be granted." This letter implied that the status of Puerto Rico as a commonwealth might not be permanent.

On September 30, 1953, when the UN Fourth Committee debated the U.S. proposal to remove Puerto Rico from the list of non-self-governing countries, the president of the Independence party of Puerto Rico asked to be heard. The request was denied, as had previous requests by groups from other non-self-governing territories, but the Latin American governments divided on the issue, with Argentina, Bolivia, Guatemala, and Mexico voting to hear the testimony, and Brazil, Chile, Colombia, Cuba, Dominican Republic, Ecuador, Nicaragua, Panama, and Peru opposing it. Nonetheless, the General Assembly fully debated the Puerto Rican question, and on November 27, 1953, it passed UN Resolution 748 (viii), which recognized that Puerto Rico had "achieved a new constitutional status," that the people had "effectively exercised their right to self-determination," and that the people have "attributes of political sovereignty which clearly identify the status . . . as that of an autonomous political entity."[5] In the final vote, of all the Latin American nations only Mexico and Guatemala voted against the resolution. Argentina and Venezuela abstained, but the rest of the Latin American governments voted for it. The final vote was 26 to 16 with 18 abstentions.[6]

Puerto Rico was deleted from the list, and from then on, the United States has insisted that the UN lacks jurisdiction to debate it. But the proclamation of commonwealth did not quell the debate on political status in Puerto Rico any more than Resolution 748 ended the international debate. Since 1953, Puerto Rico has requested Congress to alter its status four times, and three different commissions of U.S. and Puerto Rican leaders have also recommended changes.[7] None of these requests, however, has elicited a satisfactory response. The international debate has also continued without resolution, although it was quiescent until 1960.

The USSR and Cuba Repeat the Question, 1960–1970

The fifteenth General Assembly, which opened in September 1960, was described by one scholar as "an important turning point in the history of the Organization." In that year, the UN accepted seventeen new members, sixteen of them from Africa. Looking back to 1955, only

13 percent of the UN membership had achieved independence since 1945; by 1966, the number had increased to 45 percent. These new nations were "possessed of a compelling desire to eradicate speedily the remaining bastions of European colonialism."[8]

The Soviet Union, which had previously criticized the United States for colonialism on Puerto Rico,[9] decided to try to get in front of this new wave. On September 23, 1960, Premier Khrushchev introduced a draft declaration at the UN calling for the immediate granting of independence to all territories and remaining colonies. At the same time, the Soviet and Cuban delegates charged that commonwealth status was a disguised form of colonialism. Puerto Rican Governor Luis Muñoz Marín immediately cabled a response to the UN that Puerto Rico "has freely chosen its present relationship with the U.S." and that a new vote on status would occur whenever 10 percent of the voters requested it.[10]

The African and Asian countries wrote an alternative to the Soviet resolution that was less anti-Western; Resolution 1514 (xv) passed by a vote of 89 to 0 with 9 abstentions. The United States abstained at the last moment because of a special request from British Prime Minister MacMillan to President Eisenhower. The Declaration on the Granting of Independence to Colonial Countries and Peoples insisted that "immediate steps shall be taken in Trust and Non-Self-Governing territories or all *other territories which have not yet attained independence* to transfer all powers to the peoples of those territories, without any conditions or reservations to enable them to enjoy complete independence and freedom."[11] Advocates of independence for Puerto Rico cite this resolution to support their position.

The very next day, however, the UN General Assembly adopted Resolution 1541, which contradicted 1514 at least as it applied to Puerto Rico. Resolution 1541 indicated that a non-self-governing territory can be said to have reached a full measure of self-government by (1) emergence as a sovereign state; (2) free association with an independent state; or (3) integration with an independent state.[12] When opposing efforts to reconsider the status of Puerto Rico at the United Nations, the United States cites this resolution as well as Resolution 748 of 1953, which removed Puerto Rico from the list of non-self-governing territories.

In 1961, the UN General Assembly established the Special Committee on De-Colonialization* to review the implementation of Resolution 1514

---

*The exact name of the committee is the "Special Committee on the Situation With Regard to the Implementation of The Declaration on the Granting of Independence to Colonial Countries," but for obvious reasons, people refer to it as the Special Committee on De-Colonization, or more simply as the Committee of 24. When Venezuela rejoined the committee in 1980, it became the twenty-fifth member, but the group is still known as the Committee of 24.

and to maintain pressure on the colonial powers to move their territories toward independence. Initially composed of seventeen members, the committee added seven more in 1962, and it has since been called the Committee of 24.

The government of Cuba has used Resolution 1514 and the establishment of the Committee of 24 to force the United States and the other nations of the world to address the issue of Puerto Rico as an international one. Cuba's interest in its neighbor runs deep. Cuba and Puerto Rico were the last two Spanish colonies in the Americas, and when José Marti, the founder of the Cuban nation, began dreaming of independence for his country, he shared his dream with Puerto Rican separatists. Cuban nationalists kept alive Marti's dream of independence for both islands after the United States replaced Spain, and to no one is the dream more vivid than to the most vigorous Cuban nationalist of the twentieth century, Fidel Castro. In his student days at the University of Havana, young Castro led a pro–Puerto Rican independence group. When he came to power in 1959, Castro soon established a close working relationship with Juan Mari Bras, the leader of the proindependence movement and subsequently the Socialist party of Puerto Rico. Together, Cuba and independence leaders of Puerto Rico pressed the issue on the UN Committee of 24.

In an effort to preempt and undermine this campaign, President Kennedy asked Governor Muñoz Marín to hold a plebiscite in 1962. Muñoz decided to try to use that plebiscite as a device to "perfect" the commonwealth, but Muñoz's proposal was more than Kennedy could accept, and negotiations over a plebiscite dragged on until it was finally held in 1967.[13]

During the 1960s, the United States was reasonably successful in blocking Cuban efforts to address the Puerto Rican issue at the United Nations, and so the Cubans took the case to other forums. At the second summit of nonaligned nations in Cairo in 1964, Castro successfully persuaded the Non-Aligned Movement (NAM) to draw attention in its final declaration to the issue of colonialism in Puerto Rico.[14] Also, in November 1964, Havana hosted a conference of Latin American Communist parties, which issued a communiqué offering "resolute support to the cause of independence for Puerto Rico."[15]

The Issue Takes Hold, 1971–1976

Frustrated over its inability to get the Committee of 24 to consider "the colonial issue of Puerto Rico," Cuba brought its case directly to the UN General Assembly. On September 23, 1971, the General Committee considered the request, but rejected it by 10 votes to 5, with 8 abstentions. Still, the Cuban ambassador placed the issue before the

General Assembly the next day, where after a brief debate, the assembly overruled the Cubans and decided by 57 votes to 26 with 38 abstentions to adopt the General Committee's recommendation not to include the item on the agenda.

The United States and Great Britain, believing that decolonization had by and large run its course and weary of the endless anti-imperialistic propaganda of the Soviet bloc, withdrew from the Committee of 24 in 1971, and Cuba finally found room to make its case. On August 18, 1972, the committee passed a compromise resolution by a vote of 12 to 0 with 10 abstentions, which linked Puerto Rico for the first time explicitly to Resolution 1514, recognizing "the inalienable right of the people of Puerto Rico to self-determination and independence in accordance with General Assembly Resolution # 1514." The resolution also instructed a working group to submit a report in 1973 describing the procedure by which Resolution 1514 would be implemented for Puerto Rico.[16]

In short, 1971 was a watershed year for the internationalization of the Puerto Rico issue. Before then, Cuba and the Soviet Union would periodically try to raise the issue, but it was, by and large, ignored in the UN. In 1972, and every year since then, the UN Committee of 24 considered the issue, and as time passed, more nations and more international organizations chose to pursue it, and the resolutions became more strident. Cuba broke through in 1972.

In August 1973, the Committee of 24 voted to hear the Puerto Rican Independence party (PIP) and the Puerto Rican Socialist party (PSP). On August 30, the committee adopted a resolution that reaffirmed the 1972 resolution, asked the United States to refrain from obstructing Puerto Rico's right to independence and self-determination, and decided to keep the question under continuous review. The resolution passed 12 to 2 with 9 abstentions. After analyzing the UN's actions in 1973 and the two previous years, W. Michael Reisman concluded that: "Puerto Rico may be in the process of becoming an international issue."[17]

At the fourth summit of the nonaligned nations in Algiers on September 9, 1973, the declaration urged the UN General Assembly to approve the committee's report, and urged the committee and other official bodies "to step up and expand measures which could help the Puerto Rican people gain complete sovereignty and independence and recover its heritage."[18] On December 14, 1973, the UN General Assembly approved the special committee's report, which included the resolution on Puerto Rico by a vote of 104 to 5 with 10 abstentions. The United States opposed the resolution, along with France, Great Britain, Portugal, and South Africa.

In 1974, the committee briefly reviewed the issue, and after listening to representatives of the independence parties of Puerto Rico and to the Cuban representative, it agreed to keep the issue under review. At the end of the year, Cuba was appointed to the committee by the president of the General Assembly after consultations.

Cuba intensified its campaign outside the UN as well. A coordinating bureau meeting of NAM issued a declaration in Havana in March 1975 urging "the U.N. to recognize the Puerto Rican national liberation movement as the legitimate representative of its people and [asked] that the Committee of 24 study seriously and positively the proposal of sending a mission to visit the aforementioned territory [Puerto Rico] under colonial domination."[19]

In August 1975 as the Committee of 24 began considering a resolution along the lines of the NAM declaration, U.S. Ambassador to the United Nations Daniel Patrick Moynihan was looking for an opportunity to persuade Secretary of State Henry Kissinger to put some diplomatic muscle behind United States efforts at the UN. Moynihan persuaded Kissinger to inform members of the Committee of 24 "in their capitals that we would regard voting against us on this matter to be an 'unfriendly act.'" The United States succeeded in stopping that resolution and substituting one that recognized the "inalienable right of the people of Puerto Rico to self-determination and independence" and to postpone further consideration for another year. The vote was 11 to 9 with 2 abstentions.[20]

In September 1975, the Cubans hosted the International Conference of Solidarity with the Independence of Puerto Rico as a way to maintain the pressure. The nonaligned nations summit met in Sri Lanka in 1976 and rejected Havana's recommendation to recognize the independence movement as "the only legitimate representative of the people of Puerto Rico." Instead, the NAM summit reaffirmed previous decisions, declared support for self-determination and independence, asked the Committee of 24 to recommend to the General Assembly effective measures for the implementation of Resolution 1514, and "demanded that the government of the United States halt all political or repressive maneuvers that tend to perpetuate Puerto Rico's colonial status." The Committee of 24 discussed these issues in September 1976 and agreed by consensus to keep the issue under review.

Converging Debates, 1977–Present

While the international debate on Puerto Rico widened and intensified, it had almost no discernible impact on the United States and very little on Puerto Rico. However, in the 1970s, independent of that debate, there were several economic and political changes in Puerto Rico that increased the dissatisfaction among all political parties with the status quo, affected the relationship with the United States, and produced an unintended, but important, convergence between the internal and the international debates.

The spectacular economic growth that Puerto Rico sustained in the postwar period, averaging more than 6 percent annually from 1947 to 1973, slowed in the mid-1970s because of the recession in the United States and the sharp rise in the cost of energy. The Puerto Rican government has always played a large role in the island's economic development, and its leaders also have substantial expertise in lobbying the federal government for assistance. Therefore, when the economic downturn occurred, the government stepped in quickly to maintain the economic well-being of the island. By 1979, the commonwealth government was the principal employer on the island, federal assistance totaled 29 percent of the gross product (as compared to 9 percent in 1950), transfer payments to individuals accounted for 15 percent of personal income, and federal grants-in-aid accounted for 35 percent of commonwealth government recurrent receipts.[21]

Although commonwealth status was established with lavish praise in 1952 as a dynamic and pragmatic contribution to government, Puerto Rican attempts to revise it failed to elicit a response from Congress. By the late 1970s, there was an emerging consensus among the leaders of all the political parties that fundamental political changes in Puerto Rico's relationship with the United States were necessary, but little agreement on what these changes should be or how they could be achieved.

The heightened sense of economic and political dependence coincided with a public opinion trend in favor of statehood. From 13 percent in 1952 to 25 percent of the popular vote in 1956, statehood parties gradually increased their share of the popular vote to 48.3 percent in the 1976 election when its candidate, Carlos Romero Barceló of the New Progressive party (PNP) captured the governorship. Romero's determination to change the status impelled the Popular Democratic party (PDP) to dissociate itself from the status quo and reposition itself behind a more "perfect" and autonomous commonwealth status. And the *independendistas* also felt impelled to look for new strategies to make their case.

Thus, the 1976 election was another turning point. All the political parties concluded that the status quo was no longer desirable, and they petitioned Washington and then New York for a change. In August 1977, for the first time representatives spanning the entire political spectrum of Puerto Rico testified before the Committee of 24. This startled the committee but had little effect that year on its resolution.

Cuba again introduced a resolution, which called for self-determination and independence, the release of the five nationalists from prison, and a number of other demands, but the United States succeeded in persuading several committee members to approve an Australian proposal postponing the vote on the resolution.

On July 25, 1978, in a statement issued on the twenty-sixth anniversary of the Commonwealth of Puerto Rico, President Carter reiterated his support for self-determination "as the fundamental principle in deciding Puerto Rico's future." Carter said that if the government of Puerto Rico decided to hold a referendum, he "will support, and urge the Congress to support, whatever decision"—statehood, independence, commonwealth status, or mutually agreed modifications in that status—the people of Puerto Rico reached.[22]

Having crossed the threshold at the UN with apparent impunity in 1977, the Puerto Rican leaders became bolder in 1978. A full train of Puerto Rico's leaders including the prostatehood (PNP) governor, the autonomist (PDP) former governor, and the mayor of Miami, as well as the top *independendistas* all chugged through the committee. All—including the governor, who referred to "vestiges of colonialism" in Puerto Rico—expressed dissatisfaction with the status quo. Oreste Ramos, a pro-American conservative Senator and leader of the governor's New Progressive party told the committee: "The political inferiority inherent in Puerto Rico's present status is an insult to the national decorum of the United States and to the dignity of the people of Puerto Rico."[23] Maurice Ferré, the Puerto Rican–born mayor of Miami, explained that Puerto Rico "has not achieved a full measure of self-government." He asked the committee to return the island to the list of non-self-governing territories for a very explicit reason: "By your act, public opinion will be aroused in the U.S., and thus, will the Congress of the U.S. and the people of Puerto Rico be awakened to the reality of Puerto Rico."[24] Governor Romero, while acknowledging his commitment to change the political status of Puerto Rico, was explicit that the Committee of 24 not interfere: "So long as we continue to possess the means to determine our own destiny, we shall neither welcome nor tolerate outside interference in this ongoing process."

As before, the Cubans lobbied the committee to accept a resolution that reaffirmed Puerto Rico's right to self-determination and independence (Resolution 1514), criticized U.S. violations of the Puerto Rican people's national rights, and urged the United States to completely transfer all powers to the Puerto Rican people. This last point reflected the *independendistas'* strategy to demonstrate to the people of Puerto Rico that they were capable of independence before a plebiscite. India and a few other nations tried to seek a compromise resolution, but a number of

Puerto Rican leaders, including the leader of the Popular Democratic party, Rafael Hernández Colón, persuaded Cuba to accept language that endorsed independence *and* "any form of free association between Puerto Rico and the U.S. based on political equality and a recognition of the 'sovereignty' of the people of Puerto Rico." This resolution passed, and it symbolized the tacit alliance of the *independendistas* (PSP) and the *populares* (PDP) to stem the drift toward statehood (sponsored by PNP). However, Puerto Ricans viewed the resolution as a mistake, and Hernández Colón's position was not enhanced by his negotiations with Cuba. The resolution drew very little attention in the United States, but it proved an embarrassment for the *populares* in Puerto Rico.

In an analysis of the status issue, José Cabranes reviewed the 1978 UN debate and concluded that it was significant for two reasons. First, Puerto Rican leaders of "every political stripe" for the first time "recognized the existence of an alternative forum for efforts to resolve the prolonged Puerto Rican identity crisis." More important than their testimony, some of which was repeated from 1977, was their active role in trying to shape the resolution. Second, he felt that the debate "shattered the delusion of a generation of U.S. policy-makers that the question of Puerto Rico's political future is strictly an American domestic issue."[25] Juan Manuel García-Passalacqua argued persuasively that the trip to New York "legitimized" the issue of colonialism in the debate on Puerto Rico in the UN.[26]

On August 2, 1979, just before the debate in the Committee of 24, Congress passed a joint resolution that affirmed "its commitment to respect and support the right of the people of Puerto Rico to determine their own political future through peaceful, open, and democratic processes." This statement assured some Puerto Rican leaders but had no discernible impact on the debate, which was similar to that of 1978, except neither the PDP nor PNP tried to negotiate a resolution. The result was a resolution similar to that of 1978 but without the reference to "free association" as a legitimate outcome.

On August 18, 1980, once again driven by the special committee's debate, the U.S. mission to the UN issued a comprehensive press statement that described why the mission refused to testify—simply because the issue was settled when the General Assembly recognized in 1953 that "self-determination has occurred." The mission also repeated that the United States would support whatever the people want, and it broke new ground by stating it "would have no problem supporting a decision by the Puerto Rican people to extend an invitation to the U.N., the O.A.S., or other appropriate international body to observe such a plebiscite."[27] The statement hardly dented the committee's debate. The committee heard from representatives of twenty organizations. On August

20, the committee adopted a resolution sponsored by Cuba and Iraq that repeated the statements of many previous resolutions, but included condemnations against the United States on a number of new issues, including U.S. naval activities on the island of Vieques. The resolution was adopted 12 to 0 with 11 abstentions, but there was no further debate in the UN.

By this time, the UN debate on this issue had a life of its own. On August 17, 1981, U.S. Ambassador Lichenstein sent a letter to the chairman of the special committee restating the U.S. position and declaring any further action by the special committee to be "totally improper." The special committee ignored the letter, heard representatives of nineteen organizations, and on August 20, adopted a resolution by a vote of 11 to 2 with 11 abstentions calling for the Puerto Rican issue to be included as a separate item not on the 1981 General Assembly agenda, but on that for 1982.

This outcome reflected changes in strategy by the United States and Cuba and reduced influence in the committee by the United States. In 1980, the Cuban resolution contained a veritable laundry list of grievances against the United States. The essence of U.S. strategy in 1980, and indeed in every session since 1972, was to lobby key members of the Committee of 24 to preclude a recommendation from the committee to the General Assembly to debate the issue. Although U.S. influence had diminished, it still was sufficient to preclude a majority of the Committee of 24 from voting to inscribe Puerto Rico on the UN General Assembly agenda. In 1981, the U.S. mission issued a statement but apparently did not lobby the members of the Committee of 24 before the debate. At the same time, Cuba dropped the laundry list and focused on getting the committee's support to forward the issue to the General Assembly. The Cubans succeeded. Following the debate, the U.S. mission issued a statement: "The U.S. deplores the outcome. . . . [It] regards the resolution . . . as an inappropriate and wholly indefensible interference in the internal affairs of Puerto Rico and the U.S."

The resolution was contained in the report of the special committee, which was adopted on December 1, 1981, by the thirty-sixth General Assembly as part of the omnibus resolution. The United States was 1 of 3 votes against the resolution; 130 voted for it.[28] *For a decade, the United States had succeeded in keeping the Puerto Rican issue outside the gates of the General Assembly but that ended in September 1982.* The twenty-nine-nation steering committee debated the Cuban proposal to place the question of Puerto Rico on the assembly agenda and rejected it by a vote of 11 to 7 with 8 abstentions. Two days later, on September 24, 1982, Cuba requested that the full General Assembly disregard the decision of the steering committee and take up the question. After what a *Washington Post* correspondent called "an intense global lobbying campaign—unprecedented since the battles over Chinese representation in the early 1970s," the assembly rejected the Cuban proposal to inscribe the Puerto Rican issue on the assembly's agenda by a vote of 70 to 30 with 43 abstentions.[29]

Although the United States technically succeeded in keeping the issue off the agenda, Cuba succeeded in generating a debate on Puerto Rico. Moreover, the United States mounted a costly diplomatic effort. "They truly pulled out all the stops," noted one African ambassador, who said that Secretary of State George Shultz had personally phoned his president who then phoned him with instructions to vote with the United States. Kenneth Adelman, who was described as the U.S. "field commander," told delegations that a vote against the U.S. position "would be unfavorably met in bilateral relations and on Capitol Hill."

Cuban Ambassador Raúl Roa-Kouri argued that statements made before the Committee of 24 by a representative group of Puerto Ricans "prove unequivocally the dissatisfaction of the people of Puerto Rico with their present political status." But the most persuasive statement in the debate was made by the Mayor of San Juan Hernan Padilla, who was designated an alternate U.S. representative to the UN in order to speak before the General Assembly. Padilla spoke softly and in Spanish and reassured Latin Americans that "whatever our political relation is with the U.S., this does not change our feelings and cultural identification." He ended his statement with an eloquent plea: "Our democratic system does not need the intervention of the international community. We—the people of Puerto Rico, and we alone, will decide how and when to alter our political status. It is our responsibility. It is our right. It is our destiny."[30]

Because of the U.S. lobbying, Panama, Brazil, and Costa Rica, which were expected to vote with Cuba, voted instead with the United States. Mexico, Colombia, and Peru, which were expected to vote with Cuba, abstained. The pressure, however, left bruised feelings. One Puerto Rican leader said that the subsequent election of Nicaragua to the UN Security Council over vehement U.S. objections was in part a reaction to U.S. pressure on the Puerto Rico vote.

In annual addresses before the General Assembly, several Latin American leaders expressed their support for independence in Puerto Rico as a way to compensate for their vote against inscribing the issue. Panamanian Vice President Jorge Illueca said: "Independence for Puerto Rico is one of the deferred tasks of the liberating revolution of Latin American nations. . . . The issue of Puerto Rico has historical roots. The fact that it was not included in this year's agenda is not a solution nor is it evidence that the problem does not exist. It would be naive to think that votes cast here for reasons of state are sanctioned by Latin American public opinion. . . . Latin Americans have a feeling of kinship for the people of Puerto Rico." Mexican President José Lopez Portillo made a similar statement before the General Assembly: "We see with concern that pressures are being exerted on the members of the UN to change their votes. The favorable results thus obtained exhibit only the vulnerability of some countries."[31]

Cuba did not press the issue in the UN General Assembly in 1983 or 1984, but the debate and the resolutions passed by the Committee of 24 followed the pattern of previous years with one important difference. In August 1984, for the first time, Venezuela introduced and cosponsored with Cuba a resolution reaffirming Puerto Rico's right to "self-determination and independence." The resolution eschewed the rhetoric about U.S. colonialism and repression. Cuba evidently preferred to accept a milder resolution in exchange for having Venezuela's cosponsorship.

The United Nations has remained the central international forum for debating the issue of Puerto Rico, but it is hardly the only forum. Since 1964, the Non-Aligned Movement (NAM) has issued a statement on Puerto Rico after each meeting. The most recent NAM summit in New Delhi in 1983 issued a statement, which is typical of recent ones: "Recalling the previous decisions of the Movement and reaffirming the need to do away with colonialism in all its forms and manifestations, the Heads of State or Government reiterated their support for the Puerto Rican people's inalienable right to self-determination and independence in conformity with resolution 1514 (XV)." Cuba prefered a harsher resolution, and when it controlled the drafting, as at the NAM summit in Havana in September 1979, the declaration reflected its influence. That one included a number of critical comments against the United States, including calling on the U.S. government "to refrain from any political or repressive maneuvers that tend to perpetuate the colonial status of Puerto Rico . . . and [the NAM] demanded the transfer of powers to the people of the territory so they can freely determine their future political status."

The Socialist party (PSP) of Puerto Rico has worked closely with the Cuban government to ensure continued attention to the issue of Puerto Rico in the NAM's deliberations. Probably of greater significance in the long term, however, is the role played by the Puerto Rican Independence party (PIP) under the leadership of Ruben Berrios Martinez to develop close associations with the Social Democratic parties of Latin America and Europe. Berrios attended his first meeting of the Socialist International (SI), the group of about seventy Social Democratic parties, in 1978, and he quickly built support within the organization for Puerto Rican independence. The SI today includes the governing parties in Spain,

France, Portugal, Sweden, the Dominican Republic, Barbados, Costa Rica, Australia, and several others. Among the individuals who play an active role in the SI are former German Chancellor Willy Brandt, French President François Mitterrand, Spanish Prime Minister Felipe Gonzalez, and Swedish Prime Minister Olaf Palme.[32] At a regional meeting of the SI in Santo Domingo in March 1980, attended by former Costa Rican President Daniel Oduber, former Venezuelan President Carlos Andres Perez, and then Jamaican Prime Minister Michael Manley, Berrios won support for independence. However, the SI conference in Madrid later that year was not yet prepared to advocate independence; instead, it merely welcomed the previous resolution.

In addition, Berrios' party joined the Conferencia Permanente de Partidos Politicos de America Latina (COPPAL), a group of twenty-one Latin American Social Democratic parties from fourteen countries. Organized by the Mexican Party of Institutionalized Revolution (PRI), COPPAL monitors the Puerto Rican issue among many others, and it offers Berrios an opportunity to try to persuade other Social Democratic parties on the case for independence for Puerto Rico.

A major breakthrough occurred at the Socialist International conference in Portugal from April 7 to 10, 1983. PIP was accepted as a member with consultative status, and with the support of the eighteen Latin American and Caribbean parties, the final declaration stated: "The Socialist International supports the independence of Puerto Rico—a Latin American nation." Berrios said it was not easy to get the SI to pass this resolution since the United States was lobbying hard against it. During the debate at the conference, one representative urged the SI to change the resolution to read that the SI supports independence "if the people of Puerto Rico want it." Berrios objected, asking whether the SI would be willing to amend other resolutions in a parallel way. For example, would the SI be interested in a resolution of support for the Portuguese Socialist party "if they are elected"; or support for denuclearization of Finland "if they want it"? His argument apparently carried the day.[33]

Although the declaration represents the SI's official position, the French insisted it was reached by consensus and did not represent the position of the French Socialist party. (Because of their own overseas territories, the French are sensitive to references to colonialism.) The State Department was angered by the resolution and issued a statement protesting it since Puerto Rico had opportunities to express itself through elections: "It was therefore completely inappropriate to tell Puerto Ricans what their situation should be, and it constitutes interference in the internal affairs of the United States."[34]

Although Cuba remains the single most ardent advocate of Puerto Rican independence, Cuba's closest ally in the hemisphere, Nicaragua, supports it as did the revolutionary government of Grenada between 1979 and 1983. On her maiden speech to the Organization of American States in 1979, Ambassador Dessima Williams of the revolutionary government of Grenada expressed her government's solidarity with Puerto Rico's quest for independence.[35]

Venezuelan leaders feel a bond with Puerto Rico that extends back to Simon Bolivar, who considered liberating Puerto Rico after South America. In explaining his government's position before the UN General Assembly on September 27, 1983, Venezuelan Foreign Minister José Zambrano Velasco said Venezuela had "a deep-rooted feeling that Puerto Rico should be a member of the Latin American family." But the Venezuelan government only recently decided to express this feeling by voting for Puerto Rican independence at the UN. In 1972 and 1973, the Venezuelan government chose to abstain on the issue of Puerto Rico. Venezuela withdrew from the Committee of 24 in 1975 but returned in 1980 and subsequently voted with Cuba. Venezuela's two major political parties now support independence, and there are increasing signs—such as the declarations at Bolivar's bicentennial and their more active role in the UN—that Venezuela will play an increasingly vigorous role internationally on behalf of Puerto Rican independence.[36]

The Status Quo—How Durable?

Before judging whether the United States should change its position in the UN or its position on political status, let me briefly summarize the major events in the international debate and analyze its implications for U.S. policy.

Summarizing and Analyzing the Debate

Few domestic issues have consistently generated as much international debate as that of Puerto Rico. It has been on the UN agenda since representatives of the Puerto Rican Nationalist party went to San Francisco for the signing of the UN Charter in June 1945.[37] Although the U.S. government may have convinced itself that it removed Puerto Rico from the international agenda in 1953, few others are convinced.

The United Nations, and particularly its Special Committee on Colonialism, has remained the central international forum for reviewing the issue of colonialism in Puerto Rico, but over time, the issue has been raised in other organizations, including the nonaligned movement, the Socialist International, COPPAL, and even the Organization of American States (OAS). Until 1961, the United States kept the debate under control. There was considerable disagreement about removing Puerto Rico from the list of non-self-governing territories in 1953, but this, of course, was the beginning of decolonialization, and the case of Puerto Rico—whose people were not seeking a more independent relationship from the United States—was less compelling.

From 1961 to 1971, the Soviet Union, and especially Cuba, dogged the issue, and tried unsuccessfully to corner the United States with condemnatory resolutions in the Committee of 24. Blocked in the Committee of 24, in 1971, the Cuban government tried to take the issue directly before the General Assembly. They succeeded in provoking a debate, but the United States prevailed in the vote to keep the item off the agenda. Of greater significance was the decision made that same year by the United States (and Great Britain) to withdraw from the Committee of 24 and to discourage other western countries from replacing them. "Thereupon," as Daniel Patrick Moynihan later wrote, "the issue of Puerto Rico became a fixture of the Committee's proceedings."[38] Each year, the United States had to work through fewer nations to try to keep from being condemned for colonialism. As expected, the resolutions tended to become more stridently critical of the United States.

Beginning in 1977, members of the two major parties of Puerto Rico (one proautonomy, one prostatehood) testified before the Committee of 24 on colonialism in Puerto Rico. The decision by moderate politicians, including the governor and former governor, to participate in a debate in 1978, which the U.S. government refused to acknowledge, proved not only exceedingly awkward for the United States, but also helped to make the case for Cuba—that Puerto Rico wanted to decolonialize. The Committee of 24's resolutions naturally grew bolder, and in 1981, the committee finally voted a resolution calling for a debate in the General Assembly. Although the United States defeated the Cuban effort to have the issue of colonialism in Puerto Rico inscribed on the General Assembly agenda, it was at substantial cost. At the same time, other legitimate organizations like the Socialist International became advocates of independence.

Some conclusions emerge. First, more nations and more international organizations are considering the issue of Puerto Rico's status than ever before. Second, the United States has to work harder and expend more diplomatic resources to prevent nastier resolutions, condemning U.S. colonialism and calling for the liberation of Puerto Rico. Third, U.S. protestations to the contrary, the UN debate has frequently been an important factor in expediting major U.S. decisions on Puerto Rico's status, and it might play a similar role in the future. For example, the movement toward commonwealth was partly to stay ahead of the debate on decolonization, and after the proclamation of the new constitution, the United States quickly requested the UN to recognize self-government there. In the 1960s, when the Soviet Union and Cuba sought to exploit what they perceived as an imperialistic anomaly, the United States turned to its usual methods to prove them wrong—elections and a plebiscite. In the 1970s, the United States tried to respond to the increasing pressure by repeating its support for self-determination, but this response was inadequate, in part because the Puerto Rican political leadership was itself now calling for decolonization.

Although more nations and international organizations are engaged in the issue of Puerto Rico today than thirty years ago, this does not necessarily mean that the intensity of interest in the international community has changed. If one looks beneath the pushing and the shoving or listens to the silences behind the clamor and the screaming, one will find that almost all the pushing and shouting is done by just two nations—the United States and Cuba—following each other across the international landscape looking for new ways to irritate each other. Most other nations are simply trying to get out of the way; the consistently high number of abstentions is clear enough indication of that. Another important indicator is that the United States has made its case for Puerto Rico to many nations, but no nation has ever made a demarche to the United States on Puerto Rico. If a nation felt its real interests were at stake in the U.S. treatment of Puerto Rico, it would not hesitate to try to change U.S. policy, as several Latin American governments did about the need for a new Panama Canal treaty. Other than the United States and Cuba, and a very few others, international support for independence is wide but not deep.

The United States is unwilling to change its position or resolve the status problem in part because it is not sure it knows how, and it is also not sure what Puerto Rico wants, if anything. Besides, the principle of self-determination is unimpeachable. Cuban opposition only guarantees that the United States will never disengage from the debate. Indeed, the U.S. obsession mirrors Cuba's on this issue (and on most other issues as well).

To understand how deep is the Cuban obsession with Puerto Rico, one has only to compare the NAM resolutions on Puerto Rico that emerged from debates in Havana, which the Cubans can more effectively control, with those announced elsewhere. In discussing Puerto Rico in separate conversations with Cuba's highest officials, I found that only *one* could be said to be genuinely obsessed with the issue, and that person was Fidel Castro. He pursues the issue of Puerto Rico's independence as if Cuba's own independence depended on it, and in a sense, it does. Revolutionary Cuba has discovered that effective and repeated defiance of the United States is not the same as genuine independence. In one sense, Cuban attacks against the United States only confirm their continued dependence. George Washington described the malady best in his farewell address: "The nation which indulges toward another an habitual hatred or an habitual fondness is in some degree a slave." Puerto Rico, which not only rejects defiance but seriously ponders different forms of *permanent attachment with the United States as a way to achieve equality*, stands as a threat to revolutionary Cuba's sense of self. Although Cuban tactics on Puerto Rico may change somewhat, as long as Fidel Castro rules, Cuba will remain unyielding on this issue, and it could become dangerous if Puerto Rico moves toward statehood.[39]

Alongside Cuba and the United States as central actors in the international debate are the leaders of Puerto Rico. In the Socialist International, Puerto Rico's Independence party (PIP) is key. PIP has won credibility as a Social Democratic party searching for a fair and principled resolution of the status issue in a very significant organization that sensitizes and educates many of the world's current and future leaders.

The *independentistas* have always viewed the UN as the principal platform from which to state their case before the world and prevent the United States from any "annexationist impulse." "Without the U.N. and other international fora," Ruben Berrios told me, "Puerto Rico could become like Hawaii. No trouble. The U.S. can do whatever it wants." The *independentistas* take the long view: "The U.N. helps in the process. We didn't win last year [1982], are unlikely to win this year or next, but like China, which eventually gained admission, we will win," said Berrios. Carlos Gallisa, secretary general of the Socialist party (PSP), agrees that it is a mistake to think of the UN General Assembly debate in 1982 as a defeat. It was more like opening a new front.[40]

The *independentistas* were as surprised as the U.S. leaders when the moderate parties began using the UN to decry U.S. colonialism. *For Puerto Rico's leaders as for those of the United States and Cuba, speaking out at the United Nations has become a substitute for grappling with the real issues*. But by and large, neither the statehooders nor the *populares* are very eager to make their case internationally or even to contribute to the international debate. Although Carter administration officials encouraged non-*independentistas* to explain their positions to Latin American governments or international organizations, very few did this. Some justify this reticence by saying that their central interest is Puerto Rico and that the *independentistas* make their case abroad because no one listens at home.

Other countries and leaders are concerned about Puerto Rico, but none of them is as important as those described above. If Venezuela

Table 7.1

Vote in UN General Assembly on Puerto Rico, 1953-1982

Year	Favoring	Opposing	Abstaining	Ratio (Favor:Oppose)
1953	26	16	18	1.6:1
1971	57	26	38	2.2:1
1982	70	30	43	2.3:1

Note: A vote in favor is a vote with the U.S.

Source: Dept. of Public Information, *Yearbook of the United Nations* (New York: United Nations, 1953, 1971, 1982).

should choose to play a more active role for Puerto Rican independence, it would lend great weight to the cause. The United States can dismiss a cause led by Cuba much easier than it can dismiss one led by Venezuela. Many other countries in Latin America feel a cultural attachment to Puerto Rico and believe that it must be independent someday. Most of the most active advocates for independence tend also to be fervent nationalists or leftists, but the general support for independence in Latin America and Spain is probably quite broad.

Juan M. García-Passalacqua has suggested that Latin American votes on the issue reflect a "tension between the historical Latin American kinship with Puerto Rican independence and the interests of [and the pressure brought to bear by] U.S. hegemony."[41] There are two problems with this argument. First, although Mexican President José Lopez Portillo complained of undue pressure to change the Mexican vote, it is hard to believe that Mexico would really be swayed by the United States on an issue of principle. The United States has applied much more intense pressure more consistently over the last twenty years to change Mexico's policy on Cuba, and yet the Mexican government has not flinched or moved an inch. More likely, Mexico conceded its vote on an issue that was not important to it and where the question of principle was not at all clear cut to put the United States in its debt for a more important issue in the future. Second, although Latin American governments are increasingly assertive in international affairs and U.S. hegemony is said to be declining, the vote on Puerto Rico in the General Assembly during the last thirty years reflects very little change, as Table 7.1 demonstrates. In fact, support for the U.S. position has increased slightly over the last thirty years. In each vote, about 30 percent of the countries have abstained. The voting also increasingly reflects East-West divisions; the vast majority of those voting against the U.S. are Soviet-bloc countries. So Cuba and its Soviet bloc partners clearly see Puerto Rican independence as an issue worth exploiting. Mexico, of course, voted against the United States in 1953 and has not hesitated to vote against the United States in the UN on a wide range of issues. The same holds for Panama, Peru, Colombia, and others. How is one to explain the votes of Panama, Mexico, and other Latin American governments in 1982?

Too much attention is given to pressure and too little to the conflict of principles at the heart of the international issue of Puerto Rico. When decolonization began, most governments assumed that *self-determination* and *independence* meant that the first would lead to the second. Few thought that the international community would have to choose between these two; however, now that colonialism is ending, the remaining colonial issues—the Malvinas/Falklands, Guadeloupe and Martinique, and Puerto Rico—pose that very question.

How many countries would insist on independence even if the people of Puerto Rico choose something else? Clearly, Castro's Cuba, perhaps also Venezuela, but who else? Hernan Padilla is one of the few Puerto Rican leaders who systematically canvassed the governments of Latin America during the 1982 debate, and he concluded: "In general, the Latin Americans are confused about Puerto Rico, but if they were assured that the vote in Puerto Rico were totally free, they would abide by the Puerto Rican decision."[42] Based on other conversations, I would add that most Latin American governments definitely prefer independence but would accept, some more resentfully than others, whatever the people of Puerto Rico choose, provided that (1) the electoral turnout was high; (2) the vote was deemed fair by credible international observers; (3) the winning status received a high percentage of the vote; (4) Puerto Rico would retain their cultural and linguistic identity; (5) a good educational campaign was undertaken internationally on the nature of the vote; and (6) the United States was perceived as becoming more tolerant of Hispanics and blacks.

Nonetheless, until such a vote, it will become more difficult and costly for the United States to maintain its position in the UN that Puerto Rico is a domestic issue. More nations will speak out, if for no other reason than to support those in Puerto Rico who are arguing that the issue is colonialism. In his inaugural address for his second term as governor, in January 1981, Carlos Romero Barceló, a conservative statehooder, proclaimed the decade of the 1980s as "the decade of decolonization of Puerto Rico." This, and not so much the echo in the UN, necessitates a review of current U.S. policy.

The Costs of Maintaining Current Policies

Two policies need to be reviewed: (1) *the U.S. position at the UN* that the UN has no jurisdiction on the issue of Puerto Rico and, therefore, the United States will not even deign to testify before the Committee of 24; and (2) *the U.S. policy on status* that whenever and whatever the people of Puerto Rico decide on their political status, the U.S. president will accept. With some variation, these two policies have constituted the position of the U.S. government since President Eisenhower's administration. What is the international cost of maintaining these two policies now and in the immediate future?

The United States invests a great deal of energy, prestige, and resources—mostly diplomatic, but occasionally economic and political— each year to try to keep from being condemned as a colonial power. The president, the secretary of state, and of course, the U.S. ambassador to the UN may have to write letters, make phone calls, threaten reprisals, and offer promises of aid or attention to issues of comparable concern to those the United States is trying to influence. For example, if country X is leaning away from the United States on the Puerto Rico issue, and its president has been seeking a meeting with the U.S. president or an increase in aid, and the vote matters a good deal to the United States, then some kind of trade is likely.

Other costs may entail a change of U.S. policy on another issue to induce a change in country X's vote on Puerto Rico, or it may just mean that we incur a debt, a future obligation. If the United States "pulls out all the stops," as it apparently did in 1975 and in 1982, the tactics might be viewed as so offensive that they provoke a response, which adversely affects other U.S. interests.

Other, more intangible costs should not be overlooked in evaluating the U.S. position on Puerto Rico in the UN. U.S. influence in the UN or internationally is not enhanced when the United States appears either self-righteous or defensive—its usual posture on this issue. From the opposite perspective, U.S. public support for the UN—always too low— is reduced still further on issues such as Puerto Rico where it appears that the undemocratic third world is ganging up and accusing the United States of something preposterous, like colonialism! The United States has an important stake in the UN, and policies that reduce popular support for the organization without achieving any important international objective harm long-term U.S. national interests.

These costs are likely to increase in the future, particularly if Venezuela and the Socialist International play active roles, and if the moderate political parties of Puerto Rico participate in the international debate and themselves criticize the United States for colonialism—or "candy-coated colonialism" as Governor Carlos Romero Barceló called it.[43]

The worst part about paying this toll is that the United States has no control over the number of turn-stiles—actions in international forums—placed in its path nor over the escalating price of passage. In recent years, the United States has had to work harder in more international forums, which meet more often, just to keep from being condemned. It is hard to measure progress under such circumstances.

Besides the costs of trying to influence international debates and looking a bit foolish when it fails and sometimes if it succeeds, the United States fortunately incurs no other important costs to its bilateral relations. Even with Venezuela and Panama, countries that take Puerto Rico's ties to Latin America seriously, bilateral relations are affected not by how the United States treats Puerto Rico, but rather by how *they* vote in the UN. This partly reflects the asymmetry in the relationship, but also the different degree of importance attached to the issue—it is much more central to the United States—and their recognition that the principle of self-determination cannot be ignored.

Another reason why the issue of Puerto Rico does not adversely affect U.S. relations with Latin America is because it is still unresolved. If Puerto Rico moved toward statehood, nationalism would be aroused in Latin America, and this could affect U.S. relations with several countries. How great this effect would be depends on the process by which Puerto Rico came to a decision and the degree to which this was viewed as credible and understandable in Latin America.

In short, important costs are required to maintain the status quo—both policy in the UN and policy on status—and these costs will increase in the future. If Puerto Rico were to apply for statehood, the costs would be even greater to U.S. relations with Latin America. But just because there is a cost does not mean that it should not be paid; the relevant question is whether there are less costly alternatives. The United States would certainly pay a much higher price—to its prestige and values—if it forced Puerto Rico to accept either statehood or independence against the will of the people. There are other options.

Revising the U.S. Position at the UN

Although the United States prides itself on being pragmatic, its position at the UN on the issue of Puerto Rico is anything but. The United States works hard to influence the debate of the Committee of 24, yet it refuses to recognize UN jurisdiction or even to testify before the committee. The only obvious conclusion one can draw from the policy is that this must be part of a strategy, which the United States has pursued successfully over the last thirty years, of keeping itself on the defensive in the UN as much as possible.

The United States should change its approach in three ways. First, it should seek reelection to the Committee of 24 and should try to influence the composition of the committee so that it includes more members whose understanding of self-determination roughly corresponds to our own. In retrospect, the U.S. decision to leave the committee and the gradual change in its composition have made it more difficult to sustain the U.S. position. Instead of just responding each year to a hostile committee, the United States ought to invest some energy in transforming its composition.

Second, the United States should testify each year before the committee, either through its permanent UN representative or by inviting an alternate delegate, who is an elected Puerto Rican official, someone like San Juan Mayor Hernan Padilla or U.S. Congressman Robert Garcia. Whether the United States retains or alters its position on the status issue, it should respond to charges against it at the UN, should correct errors or distortions, and should directly defend its position, rather than issue press releases before the debate and protests after.

Third, and most important, the United States should actively try to shape the agenda of the committee and seriously debate the issues involved in the case of Puerto Rico. The principal issue is the position that the international community should adopt when the joint principles of self-determination and independence apparently conflict. When these two principles were joined in Resolution 1514 in 1960, most members assumed that self-determination would naturally lead to independence. Now with 159 members in the UN, it is clear that with the exception of Namibia, the issue of decolonization has been turned on its head. Not only are colonies not fighting for their independence, but many, like the Falklands/Malvinas, Anguilla, and Martinique, seek continued dependence. It is time for the Committee of 24 to either concentrate solely on Namibia, pack up, or debate the remaining issue of self-determination *and/or* independence. While recognizing that many nations are more interested in politics than the merits of these issues, the United States should take these questions and the committee seriously. Instead of trying to put out fires in August, the United States ought to plan for the debate the previous January. If the United States wants to try a little mischief to get the attention of the Soviets, we might consider raising the issue of the Baltic states before the committee.

What does the United States lose by adopting these three changes? In a sense, the United States implicitly accepts the jurisdiction of the UN by testifying and taking the issue seriously. But it is pure fantasy to believe that current policy has inhibited the UN debate in any way. These three changes are not likely to produce a positive statement of support for the United States in the Committee of 24 or the UN, but they will increase the ability of the United States to influence the debate.

A Clue to Breaking the Stalemate on Status:
The Psychology of U.S.–Puerto Rican Relations

> Estragon: I can't go on like this.
> Vladimir: That's what you think.

> —Samuel Beckett, *Waiting for Godot*

The question of whether to change U.S. policy on self-determination for Puerto Rico is of a different order than whether to change U.S. policy at the UN for two reasons. First, self-determination is a core value of the U.S. political creed. Second, the United States could not disregard the views of the people of Puerto Rico on an issue as fundamental as its status without jeopardizing relations with all of Latin America.

There have been, however, some important, recent changes in the U.S. policy on self-determination to Puerto Rico. On New Year's Eve, 1976, from the slopes of Vail, Colorado, President Gerald Ford endorsed statehood. President Jimmy Carter, however, refused to endorse any status and pledged to "support, and urge the Congress to support, whatever decision the people of Puerto Rico reach." With evidently unintended irony, the 1980 Republican party platform addressed the issue of Puerto Rico in the section on Latin America and unabashedly offered a strategic rationale: "Republicans recognize the special importance of Puerto Rico and the United States Virgin Islands in the defense of freedom in the Caribbean. We believe that Puerto Rico's admission to the Union would demonstrate our common purpose in the face of growing Soviet and Cuban pressure in that area."

During the campaign, on the day of the Republican presidential primary in Puerto Rico, Ronald Reagan promised to initiate statehood legislation if elected, and on September 27, 1981, Vice President George Bush ended a rousing speech at a San Juan rally as follows: "I can tell you how I feel in two words: 'Statehood Now!'" President Reagan, like his predecessor, has said he recognizes "the right of the Puerto Rican people to self-determination," and in a statement on January 12, 1982, endorsing statehood, he said: "This Administration will accept whatever choice is made by a majority of the island's population."[44] *In short, whereas President Carter said he would accept and support whatever the people of Puerto Rico decide, President Reagan said he would accept whatever they decide, but he would only support statehood.*

The distinction is not insignificant. The position of President Reagan and the Republican party diminishes the scope and meaning of the concept of self-determination since the president's active support is a critical factor in fulfilling the wishes of the people of Puerto Rico. Congress obviously will have difficulty accepting any option currently envisioned by Puerto Rico's leadership; if only one option can count on presidential support, that biases the vote. To use an analogy, a school class was told that they were free to vote for John or Frank. However, if they voted for John, they would immediately get free ice cream, and if they voted for Frank, they would have to wait in line to purchase the ice cream, and there might not be enough ice cream to go around. Obviously, the vote will be biased by the promise; self-determination would be reduced.

The Republican party position also affects the U.S. international position. If the United States is genuinely neutral on status, it is in a stronger position to argue against the stand taken by several Social Democratic parties, which support self-determination but prefer independence. One could argue that this is a contradiction; if one genuinely believes in a people's right to self-determination, one should accept and support whatever the people choose. However, the Social Democratic parties respond that their position is essentially the same, though inverted, to that of the Republicans who support self-determination but prefer statehood. And they are right.

Therefore, the U.S. government—and both political parties—ought to support self-determination and remain neutral on specific status. Second, the U.S. president and Congress should reaffirm their willingness to accept and support whatever the people of Puerto Rico decide. But, as we shall see, this too begs the question of what we mean by self-determination.

The Puerto Ricans who have trekked to the UN in recent years to tell the world about U.S. colonialism have held the full spectrum of political views and have represented some of the island's most perceptive and intelligent thinkers and leaders. Many have also talked with officials in the Carter and Reagan administrations, but with little meaningful communication. Indeed, although José Cabranes later wrote that the expedition to the Committee of 24 "shattered the delusion of a generation of U.S. policymakers, that the question of Puerto Rico's political status is strictly an American domestic issue," the delusion appears firmly intact; the policy has not changed.

The stalemate that currently inhibits any meaningful debate on the status issue between Puerto Rico and the United States can only be broken when one comprehends why the Puerto Rican and U.S. policymakers have missed each other. Let me start by describing the two perspectives as a way to begin bridging them. Of course, this distillation of the perspectives does not adequately capture the diversity of views within each position; nonetheless, I believe it captures the essential points and differences.

Puerto Rican Perspective. Those who testify before the UN see the problem facing Puerto Rico as colonialism; it may reflect colonialism by consent, and it may be sugar coated, but that is not escaping the fact that the fundamental decisions on Puerto Rico's future lie in Washington, not in Puerto Rico. Washington has neglected the problem of status and indeed most of Puerto Rico's problems because it does not take the island seriously, and because the United States is not organized to deal with Puerto Rican problems. No person in the White House or in office in the entire federal government exists to coordinate policy toward Puerto Rico.

A Puerto Rican policymaker in the UN might express the following opinions:

> The status quo may appear comfortable, but it is not viable as it is degrading; it institutionalizes inferiority. The fact that two-thirds of the people are now dependent on food stamps and that almost all food consumed by Puerto Rico is imported is symptomatic of a colonial relationship. It is *Washington's responsibility to take the first step* to resolve the stalemate on status, but since Washington is oblivious to the true nature of the problem, it is imperative to "shock" Washington out of its complacency, and the Committee of 24 hearings are one way of doing that.
>
> Washington may not view itself as colonialistic, and it certainly dislikes being called that, but it is a fact, and the more it hears that name the more likely it will be provoked into taking some action. Self-determination is a cop-out. The United States colonized Puerto Rico without asking our permission; now it should de-colonize.
>
> Washington may think the problem is distant, but we will argue that it is urgent—that the current calm in Puerto Rico is superficial and deceptive, concealing grave problems that could explode unless they are addressed now. "The days when Washington could treat Puerto Rico with benign neglect are over."[45]

U.S. Policymaker's Perspective. Those who make U.S. policy that relates to Puerto Rico believe that Puerto Rico is free and democratic, with a politically active and aware citizenry and extremely talented and capable leaders. It might be easy for Washington to begin a process to resolve the political status question, but it would be wrong, insensitive, and arrogant. The decision should come from the people of Puerto Rico, and it *will* come when they are ready. The leaders *may be* ready and seeking to end run their electorate, but deep down, they understand that the people are still more satisfied with the status quo than with available alternatives. When and if the people are ready to decide, the leadership will guide them. And at that point, the United States should support whatever the people decide.

A U.S. policymaker might describe the present U.S.–Puerto Rican relationship as follows:

> While Puerto Rican leaders imply that their fate is decided by Washington, they are among the most shrewd political manipulators that ever steered the federal government. Although they complain about being neglected, Puerto Rico gets more federal aid per capita than any state, and that is not because of Washington's largesse but because of the capabilities of Puerto Rico's leadership. Although they complain about a lack of focus in the federal government, they know it is due to Muñoz's deliberate strategy, and it has worked effectively since then: Keep Washington divided and uninformed; it's much easier to manipulate them that way. The worst thing would be to set up a single office, which would soon compete with the resident commissioner, and before too long, would become a veritable Viceroy of Puerto Rico. Puerto Ricans don't want that, and frankly, we don't either.
>
> Although we were initially angry and confused by Puerto Rico's decision to take its case to the UN, and irritated at the use of the word *colonialism*, we still argue that the issue is an internal one, and that future status should be decided by the people of Puerto Rico. The Puerto Rican leaders choose to testify before the UN because they are unable to make this key decision. *Puerto Ricans have the power to "liberate" themselves;* that they choose to testify, rather than make a decision, proves that colonialism is not a U.S. problem; it is in the minds of Puerto Rico's elite. The Puerto Ricans who testify enjoy using the word *colonialism* to shock the United States, as much as a young child uses dirty words to irritate his parents. However, after the 1978 scene at the UN, some leaders were so embarrassed that they sought a scapegoat. Washington, ever available, was criticized for its inability to seek a compromise resolution. However, we in Washington never felt that the UN was the place to solve the problem of Puerto Rico, and our view was confirmed—not changed—by the 1978 debacle.
>
> *Puerto Rico should take the first step,* and we will accept whenever and whatever they decide.

It is astounding how thoroughly these two perspectives have missed each other. Cultural differences only explain a small part of the divergence since most of the Puerto Rican leaders are extremely familiar with the United States, having excelled at the best universities and in public life, and many U.S. policymakers are familiar with Latin American customs and politics and the recurring dilemmas of inter-American relations.

The divergence, instead, is symptomatic of a *political gulf and an agonizing problem*. It is precisely because the problem is so agonizingly difficult that neither side has been willing to walk up to it, and both sides *insist that the other must take the first step*. Instead of addressing the problem, the United States smugly retreats behind the principle of self-determination, refusing to recognize that it is a major part of the reason why Puerto Ricans cannot make the decision, and Puerto Ricans lamely succumb to "Yankee-baiting" at the UN, rejecting their own responsibility for the predicament.

The core of the problem is that there is no consensus on political status in Puerto Rico, and almost everyone fears that to force the issue before its time risks instability and perhaps violence. That may be one reason why President Reagan, who walked closer to the issue than any previous president, ultimately backed away when he realized the possible consequences. With the Caribbean Basin already seething with revolutionary change and violence, President Reagan evidently decided in late 1981 that this would not be an opportune moment to initiate statehood legislation, as he had promised in 1980.[46] Why initiate a process if the outcome could create more problems than the status quo? And one should not discount the compelling quality of the principle of self-determination; the United States simply would not be comfortable at this time—or perhaps ever—imposing a decision or even a process for making a decision on the people of Puerto Rico.

That explains why the United States has been reluctant to take the first step. What about Puerto Rico? Just below the surface, Puerto Ricans are deeply ambivalent on the issue of political status—torn by psychological, political, cultural, economic, and familial ties. On the surface, statehooders want equality—the same rights and responsibilities as all U.S. citizens. *Independentistas* want dignity—the legitimacy of being a Latin American nation. And commonwealth supporters want both but accept commonwealth with greater autonomy as the best and most likely alternative since it combines elements of both. And the current status— while imperfect and defended by no one—most accurately reflects the ambivalence of all the Puerto Rican people, which explains why there is no popular groundswell on the island for change.[47]

However, below the surface, many Puerto Ricans share the passions and ambivalence, which flow from being both a Latin American and a U.S. citizen. How these passions are blended and distilled into one of the three status options ultimately depends on the individual—his values, his personal and familial ties, and his aspirations. Because each of these options pulls at so many Puerto Ricans, they are collectively incapable of making a decision, and some appeal to the United States to make it for them.

Beyond this subconscious appeal is also a genuine understanding of the distribution of power. As Maurice Ferré, the mayor of Miami, put it: "The question is not what the people of Puerto Rico want; it's what the Congress will concede."[48] Few Puerto Ricans want to commit themselves fully when they know the ultimate—if not the primary—decision rests in Washington. They have an obvious and real need to leave themselves some room, their dignity. For the United States to demand a decision first and leave questions about whether that decision will be accepted, is to leave the Puerto Ricans with no margin of error, no *dignidad*. And from a U.S. perspective, that is the worst possible procedure; if Puerto Rico made a decision and then the United States rejected it or fundamentally altered the terms, the United States would unwittingly transform a part of the family into a very resentful and angry neighbor.

To return to the initial question, the international cost of maintaining the current U.S. policy of support for self-determination is high but bearable. *Regardless of how embarrassing the UN debates get, how many hostile resolutions are passed, how much leverage and resources the United States needs to use, the United States should pay the price of defending one of its core political values, self-determination. However, self-determination is neither the point nor the issue in Puerto Rico, and the United States is mistaken in defining the issue in those terms.* It should change its policy not because the international costs are too high or will get higher; *the United States should change its position because the costs in Puerto Rico and to core values of our political creed are too high.*

The United States is founded on principles and ideals—equality before the law, freedom, justice, and social mobility—and these shape Americans' view of themselves and their behavior in the world. It runs against the grain of the American character to have either a permanent privileged class or an underclass. Puerto Rico combines both, and many Puerto Ricans feel the awkwardness of being treated generously but not equally. All Americans should share that feeling of awkwardness; it is a testament to the distance of Puerto Rico and our own insensitivity that so few feel it.

It took a very long time for white Americans to understand the discrimination that black Americans felt for decades. Once whites understood, however, the United States set about correcting that injustice. Similarly, in time Americans will come to realize that Puerto Ricans are not equal and that diminishes our freedom as much as it does theirs.

The real cost in Puerto Rico is not the food stamps, but the dependence, the feelings of inferiority. The real reason why statehood and commonwealth leaders are hesitant to travel through Latin America to explain Puerto Rico and their status preference is because they are uncomfortable; they are embarrassed. It is easier to stay home. "Latin Americans don't understand Puerto Rico," they argue, but, of course, the problem is that Latin Americans *do* understand Puerto Rico, and Puerto Ricans understand that. They understand that Puerto Rico is caught in the U.S. embrace but is neither the United States nor fighting for liberation. In the Muñoz era, when commonwealth was a fresh and creative idea, and Muñoz and other leaders of his generation had stature among the democratic left of Latin America, there was a good deal of communication between Puerto Ricans and Latin Americans. As the commonwealth arrangement became harder to defend, and the torch passed to the next generation, there was less contact.

In explaining inter-American relations, Carlos Rangel argued that although Latin America has benefited economically and politically from the example of and the proximity to the United States, it has fared poorly in a much more important way. To the extent that the "most basic need of any society is probably the ability to live with itself, and to accept its position with respect to the rest of the world," it is clear that Latin America, and especially Puerto Rico, which "suffers from an acute case of the Latin American complex," has been harmed by its relationship with the United States.[49]

The current political status may indeed be comfortable, and its inherent ambiguity may accurately reflect the ambivalence of the people, but it suspends the island between two worlds. Perhaps, in an interesting twist, only the political leadership—those whose lives are shaped by politics and governance—cannot cope with the ambiguity in the present status whereas the vast majority of the people of Puerto Rico, whose lives are filled with the mundane problems of the human condition, are neither affected nor bothered by the ambiguity. It is also possible that the current framework serves the basic needs of the majority more than a radical change toward either statehood or independence. Certainly, the people should speak and decide. The United States can either impede such a decision—as it is currently doing, however unintentionally—or facilitate it.

Ironically, the motive for movement, for changing its current policy on political status, is not the international costs but the principle of self-determination. The United States has hindered the exercise of self-determination by retaining residual powers to veto a Puerto Rican decision. Although it is comfortable for the United States to retain its current position, it damages the principle of self-determination, which it may think it is defending, because the people of Puerto Rico cannot make a decision until the United States agrees to make it *with* them.

Mutual Determination: A Proposal

"We're waiting for you," Miguel Laussell, an advisor to Governor Rafael Hernández Colón, told me recently. "And," I responded, "the U.S. Government is waiting for you." I have tried to explain the reasons for the present deadlock and the reasons why it should be broken. The time has come for the debate to shift from "who goes first?" to "how can we *both* do it?" The time has come to shift from an academic debate on the meaning of self-determination to a political process to implement "mutual determination."[50]

True to the American predisposition for elections as a political solution, the proposal of mutual determination aims at ensuring a fair and credible process for reaching a decision on the political status of Puerto Rico rather than a specific outcome. The objectives of the proposal can be defined in terms of five groups that need to be included in the process and four potential problems that need to be avoided.

For the decision to be fair and credible, the process must be shaped or monitored by (1) both Puerto Rico and the United States; (2) both Congress and the executive branch; (3) both major U.S. political parties and all the parties representing the three major options in Puerto Rico; (4) a representative cross-section of leaders, groups, and state and local actors from the mainland; and (5) the international community (representatives from the United Nations and the Organization of American States). *In short, the process should be joint, bicameral, and bipartisan, and it should touch nongovernmental U.S. groups and be monitored by appropriate representatives from the international community.*

For the decision to be sustained, the process must avoid (1) a one-sided question, which any of the political parties view as unfair; (2) a vote on three "impossibilities," three options that represent wish lists rather than feasible political outcomes;[51] (3) a rejection by the U.S. Congress or the American people and the inevitable resentment this would breed in Puerto Rico; and (4) an outcome viewed as illegitimate by Latin America and the international community.

The plan begins with a private poll of the Puerto Rican people. If a clear majority are in favor of beginning a decision process on political status, then the leaders of the United States and Puerto Rico would announce their intent to start the process. Group I, composed of leaders from the United States and Puerto Rico, would meet to sketch the status options and to gain their approval and some negotiating flexibility by the political parties of Puerto Rico. A year later Group II—an expanded group including a large number of congressional leaders—would negotiate these options into what the Congress can accept and the parties of Puerto Rico still want. Then Congress would approve a joint resolution representing this compromise on the three options, and after presidential approval, sovereign powers would be transferred to Puerto Rico. Assured that the United States will accept the option that the people of Puerto Rico choose, the people will then vote after a three-month electoral period.

Summary: Costs and Benefits of Movement

In 1973, two decades after the United States thought it had removed the issue of Puerto Rico from the international agenda, Michael Reisman wondered whether Puerto Rico "may be in the process of becoming an international issue." Today, Puerto Rico has indisputably become one of the remaining international, colonial issues. The United Nations debates the issue annually; it is raised in the Organization of American States (OAS); the Socialist International and the NAM do not miss an opportunity to reaffirm their support for Puerto Rico's independence; and new organizations like COPPAL emerge and embrace the issue to prove their progressive credentials.

Still viewing Puerto Rico as an internal matter, the U.S. government has had to double its efforts just to keep from falling backwards. The costs of defending the status quo in Puerto Rico mount and argue for a reassessment of strategy and policy. In this chapter, I recommend three changes in strategy: The United States should try to return to the Committee of 24 and try to influence its composition; the United States should testify before the committee whenever the issue arises; and the United States should try to reshape the agenda of the committee so that it grapples with genuine issues, which do not always leave the United States in a defensive position.

The decision by President Reagan and the Republican party to endorse statehood diminishes the meaning of self-determination and weakens our international position. The U.S. government and both political parties ought to support self-determination and remain neutral on specific status options. The president and Congress should reaffirm their willingness to accept and support whatever the people of Puerto Rico decide—in conjunction with the people of the United States.

The international costs of defending the political status of Puerto Rico may be high, but they should not be grounds for retreating from a policy of respecting the self-determination of the Puerto Rican people. However, self-determination is not the issue. Since Congress will make the ultimate decision on political status, and no one can say with certainty what Congress will do, Puerto Ricans are understandably reluctant to commit themselves by taking the first step. Therefore, the debate has degenerated into a question of who should take the first step toward resolving the stalemate on political status—Puerto Rico or the United States?

I propose a process of mutual determination—a joint, bicameral, and bipartisan approach—whereby both sides walk together toward resolving the problem. The major motive for movement is not the international cost of defending the status quo, but the cost to our political values of permitting institutionalized inferiority under the democratic roof of the United States. Thus, U.S. support for self-determination should require that it stop denying that Puerto Rico's status is strictly an internal matter and begin to work with the people of Puerto Rico to address the status issue.

Notes

Acknowledgments

This chapter was first presented as a paper at a conference on Puerto Rico sponsored by the World Peace Foundation, September 19–20, 1980, in Washington, D.C. The participants of the conference, and especially Juan M. García-Passalacqua, Richard Bloomfield, José Sorzano, and C. William Maynes offered extremely useful comments on that paper.

I owe a considerable debt to the following people who have shown, over the years, considerable skill and wisdom, but mostly patience, in trying to educate me to the Puerto Rican reality and dilemma: Arturo Morales Carrión, José Cabranes, Maurice Ferré, Franklin D. Lopez, and most especially to Juan Manuel and Ivonne García-Passalacqua. They are all welcome to take credit for anything in this paper that they recognize or like since many of my ideas are the product of our conversations. At the same time, they should not hesitate to blame my own continued obtuseness for any errors in this paper or points of disagreement.

I would also like to express my gratitude to the following people for granting me extended and productive interviews: Miguel Lausell, Carlos Gallisa, Roberto Rexach Benitez, Hector Ramos, Hernan Padilla, Ruben Berrios Martinez, Fernando Martin, and officials in the United Nations and in the U.S. State Department, who asked not to be identified.

Finally, this paper has benefited enormously from a large number of excellent works, especially the following: Jorge Heine, "The Commonwealth of Puerto Rico, 1952–1982: An Assessment," in *Time for Decision: The United States and Puerto Rico*, ed. Jorge Heine (Lanham, Md.: North-South, 1983); Jeffrey Puryear, "Puerto Rico: An American Dilemma," in *Puerto Rico's Political Status*, ed. Pamela Falk (Lexington, Mass.: Lexington Books, 1984); José Cabranes, "Puerto Rico: Out of the Colonial Closet," *Foreign Policy* 33 (Winter 1978–1979); several works of Juan Manuel García-Passalacqua, especially Chapter 8 of *Puerto Rico: Equality and Freedom at Issue* (New York: Praeger, 1984); and the very good reports prepared by the General Accounting Office (GAO).

1. In 1967, in Puerto Rico's only plebiscite on political status, independence received 0.6 percent of the votes; commonwealth received 60.4 percent; and statehood received 39.0 percent. However, the major proindependence parties boycotted the plebiscite, and the voter turnout was much lower than normal (66 percent versus the usual more than 80 percent). In the gubernatorial elections from 1952 to 1980, those parties favoring independence received the smallest percentage of the vote, but these ranged from 19 to 12 percent in 1952 and 1956 to 6.4 and 5.7 percent in 1976 and 1980. See the Comptroller General of the United States, *Report to the Congress: Puerto Rico's Political Future: A Divisive Issue With Many Dimensions* (Washington, D.C.: General Accounting Office, GGD-81-48, March 2, 1981), pp. 36–39.

2. The U.S. ambassador to the UN even went to Puerto Rico for consultations before the UN General Assembly met in 1982. Pressing business kept her from making a trip in 1983, but the counsellor to the U.S. mission went instead.

3. I am indebted to Ben Stephansky's recollection for this marvelous quip.

4. This was Resolution 23 of the constitutional convention. See W. Michael Reisman, *Puerto Rico and the International Process: New Roles in Association*, Report for the Conference on Puerto Rico and the Foreign Policy Process, held at the Carnegie Endowment for International Peace, October 1973 (Washington, D.C.: American Society of International Law, 1975), p. 42.

5. Ibid., pp. 173–183, Appendices 4–6. See this note for the text of Resolution 748, as well as UN Resolutions 1514 and 1541.

6. For this vote and others at the UN, the following sources were used: *U.S. Participation in the United Nations: The President's (Annual) Report to Congress; Yearbook of the United Nations*, 1953, pp. 533–539; and for a summary of action before August 26, 1974, UN General Assembly, Special Committee on the Situation with regard to the Implementation of the Declaration on the Granting of Independence to Colonial Countries and Peoples, Question of the List of Territories to which the Declaration on the Granting of Independence to Colonial Countries and Peoples is Applicable, 26 August 1974, A/AC.109/L.976. Also see Robert Pastor, "The International Debate on Puerto Rico: The Costs of Being an Agenda-Taker," *International Organization* 38, 3 (Summer 1984).

7. For a brief review of these, see the Comptroller General of the United States, *Report to the Congress: Experiences of Past Territories Can Assist Puerto Rico Status Deliberations* (Washington, D.C.: General Accounting Office, GGD-80-26, March 7, 1980), pp. 61–62. Also, see statement by Honorable Maurice Ferré, mayor of Miami, speaking as a U.S. citizen born in Puerto Rico before the Special Committee on Decolonization, at UN Headquarters (New York, August 29, 1978), p. 7.

8. David A. Kay, "The Politics of Decolonization: The New Nations and the United Nations Political Process," in *The Process of International Organization*, ed. Robert S. Wood (New York: Random House, 1971), p. 401. Also see David W. Wainhouse, *Remnants of Empire: The United Nations and the End of Colonialism* (New York: Harper and Row, 1964).

9. See, for example, statement by Eleanor Roosevelt, U.S. Representative to the General Assembly, "Communist Charges Against U.S. Territorial Policies," *Department of State Bulletin* 27, 705 (December 29, 1952):1032–1033.

10. Reisman, *International Process*, p. 46.

11. My emphasis. For the negotiations leading up to Resolution 1514, see Kay, "Politics of Decolonization," pp. 403–407. The U.S. delegation was very upset by Eisenhower's decision, and several openly expressed their disagreement. Harold J. Lidin reported that Juan Mari Bras, who established the proindependence movement in 1960 and later the Cuban-aligned Socialist party, persuaded his contacts in the UN to insert the underlined phrase. "UN has Long History of Interest in Puerto Rico Status," *San Juan Star*, August 15, 1977, p. 6.

12. For the resolutions, see Reisman, *International Process*, pp. 176–183.

13. Juan M. García-Passalacqua, *Puerto Rico: Equality and Freedom at Issue*, Hoover Institution Latin American Series (New York: Praeger, 1984), p. 128.

14. Austin Linsley, "U.S.-Cuban Relations: The Role of Puerto Rico," in *Cuba in the World*, ed. Cole Blasier and Carmelo Mesa-Lago (Pittsburgh: University of Pittsburgh Press, 1979), p. 122.

15. William E. Ratliff, *Castroism and Communism in Latin America, 1959–76* (Washington, D.C.: American Enterprise Institute for Public Policy Research, 1976), pp. 195–198.

16. Linsley, "Role of Puerto Rico," p. 123.

17. Reisman, *International Process*, p. 47.

18. Linsley, "Role of Puerto Rico," p. 124.

19. Ibid.

20. Daniel Patrick Moynihan, *A Dangerous Place* (Boston: Little, Brown & Co., 1978), pp. 111–112.

21. For an excellent analysis of the political and economic changes that occurred in Puerto Rico in the last thirty years, see Jorge Heine, ed., *Time for Decision: The United States and Puerto Rico* (Lanham, Md.: North-South, 1983), Introduction. The statistics on Puerto Rico's economic growth and increased dependence on the United States are from Government Accounting Office, *Puerto Rico's Political Future*, March 2, 1981, pp. 26–30. That report confirmed one of Heine's conclusions—that "all of the island's political parties are dissatisfied with this relationship [the current commonwealth status]" (p. ii).

22. In the spirit of Governor Muñoz, who used to stress the continuity of commonwealth to mainland audiences and the changes to Puerto Rican audiences, the Puerto Rican leaders who sold this statement to the White House insisted that it represented only a restatement of the U.S. position, but later described it as "a political bombshell and a milestone of considerable significance" or as "the abandonment of the defense of the status quo" and as an "opening up of a policy of 'alternative futures.'" José Cabranes, "Puerto Rico: Out of the Colonial Closet," *Foreign Policy* 33 (Winter 1978–1979):84; Juan M. García-Passalacqua, "Decolonization in the Caribbean: The U.S. and Puerto Rico" (Paper presented to a Conference on the "International Relations of the Contemporary Caribbean," Caribbean Institute and Study Center for Latin America of Inter-American University of Puerto Rico, April 22–23, 1983), p. 10.

23. Cabranes, "Out of the Colonial Closet," p. 67.

24. Statement of Maurice Ferré before the UN Special Committee on De-Colonization, August 29, 1978.

25. Cabranes, "Out of the Colonial Closet," p. 69.

26. García-Passalacqua, *Equality and Freedom at Issue*, p. 130.

27. *U.S. Participation in the United Nations: The President's Report to Congress for the Year, 1980*, pp. 314–315.

28. *U.S. Participation in the United Nations: The President's Report to Congress for the Year, 1981.*

29. Michael J. Berlin, "U.S. Wins UN Vote on Puerto Rico," *Washington Post*, September 25, 1982, p. 1; also, "U.N. Supports U.S. Over Puerto Rico," *New York Times*, September 25, 1982, p. 3.

30. UN General Assembly, September 24, 1982, A/37/PV.4, September 27, 1982, in Spanish.

31. Both cited in García-Passalacqua, *Equality and Freedom at Issue*, p. 134.

32. For an analysis of the Socialist International's policy on Central America, see Robert A. Pastor, "Mirror Images: The Socialist International and the U.S. in Central America," *The New Republic*, May 16, 1983, pp. 13–15.

33. Interview with Ruben Berrios Martinez, April 26, 1983.

34. John Vinocur, "Socialists' Stand on Puerto Rico Angers the U.S.," *New York Times*, May 6, 1983, p. A6.

35. Carmen Delgado Votaw, "Puerto Rico: A Pawn or an Option for Governance in the Western Hemisphere's Future" (Paper prepared for the Aspen Institute Project on Governance in the Western Hemisphere, June 1981), p. 3.

36. Frank J. Prial, "Puerto Rico Should Be Independent, Venezuela Says at the U.N.," *New York Times*, September 28, 1982. Also, Harold J. Lidin, "CRB Blasts Venezuela Role in U.N. Resolution," *San Juan Star*, August 28, 1980, p. 6.

37. The Puerto Rican Nationalist party also became the first organization to gain accredited-observer status at the UN, but that status was revoked in 1950 after the attempted assassinations and uprising. Harold J. Lidin, "U.N. Has Long History of Interest in Puerto Rico Status," *San Juan Star*, August 15, 1977, p. 6.

38. Moynihan, *A Dangerous Place*, p. 111.

39. Linsley, "Role of Puerto Rico," pp. 127–128. The banner headline of the Puerto Rican newspaper *El Nuevo Día*, September 1, 1978, contained the following message from Juan Mari Bras, former head of the PSP and ally of Cuba: "La Estadidad, Sólo Sobre Nuestros Cadaveres [Statehood Only Over Our Dead Bodies]."

40. Interview with Ruben Berrios Martinez, president, Independence party, and with Carlos Gallisa, secretary general of the Socialist party of Puerto Rico, April 1983.

41. García-Passalacqua, *Equality and Freedom at Issue*, p. 134.

42. Interview with Hernan Padilla, mayor of San Juan, April 26, 1983.

43. Carlos Romero Barceló, "Puerto Rico, U.S.A.: The Case for Statehood," *Foreign Affairs* 59 (Fall 1980):64. For a further analysis of the diplomatic costs and a strategy for reducing them, see Robert Pastor, "The International Debate on Puerto Rico: The Costs of Being an Agenda-Taker," *International Organization*, vol. 38, no. 3.

44. For Ford's statement, see *New York Times,* January 1, 1977, p. 1. President-elect Carter's response came the next day: "Until the Puerto Rican people themselves express a preference for statehood . . . the Congress should not take the initiative." *New York Times,* January 2, 1977, p. 2. For the 1978 proclamation, see *Presidential Papers,* July 25, 1978, p. 1336; for President Reagan's statement, see *Presidential Papers,* January 12, 1982, p. 19; for his campaign promise, see Ronald Reagan, "Puerto Rico and Statehood," *Wall Street Journal,* February 12, 1980; *Republican Platform,* Proposed by the Committee on Resolutions to the Republican National Convention, July 14, 1980, Detroit, Michigan, p. 68; for Bush's speech, see Robert Friedman, "Bush, at San Juan Rally, Calls for 'Statehood Now,'" *San Juan Star,* September 28, 1981, p. 1.

45. The final quote is from Cabranes, "Out of the Colonial Closet," p. 91. See also Juan M. García-Passalacqua, "The Caribbean, Puerto Rico, and the United States" (Paper written as Visiting Scholar of the Latin American Program of the Woodrow Wilson International Center for Scholars, Smithsonian Institution, Summer 1982), pp. 73–85. García-Passalacqua packaged this perspective with a single phrase: "Ahora le toca al Yanqui [Now it's the Yankee's turn to move]."

46. With Vice President Bush's strong speech urging "Statehood Now" as a backdrop, a senior prostatehood delegation from Puerto Rico came to the White House in January 1982 to request that the president initiate statehood legislation. President Reagan apparently had second thoughts, as his statement on January 12 lacked the enthusiasm of Bush's speech, and instead of initiating legislation as he had promised, he merely reaffirmed his support for statehood.

47. In a poll taken by Yankelovich, Skelly, and White for *El Nuevo Día,* the people of Puerto Rico were asked what issues concerned them most. Puerto Ricans ranked the status issue next to last—ninth of ten issues—with only 38 percent mentioning it. *El Nuevo Día,* June 2, 1983, p. 2.

48. Interview with Maurice Ferré, mayor of Miami, April 27, 1983.

49. Carlos Rangel, *The Latin Americans: Their Love-Hate Relationship with the United States* (New York: Harcourt Brace Jovanovich, 1977), p. 50.

50. Many useful recommendations have been offered by Jorge Heine, Jeffrey Puryear, José Cabranes, and Alfred Stepan ("The United States and Latin America: Vital Interests and the Instruments of Power," *Foreign Affairs,* America and the World, 1979). My proposal for mutual determination benefits from those recommendations, but it is more of a product of a dialogue with the leaders, representing all of Puerto Rico's major political parties, whom I interviewed in San Juan in April 1983. For the complete proposal see Robert Pastor, "The United States and Puerto Rico: A Proposal," *Washington Quarterly* 7, 3 (Summer 1984).

51. I am indebted to Juan M. García-Passalacqua for this point.

Comment

Ambassador José S. Sorzano

Robert Pastor challenges current U.S. policy on Puerto Rico in two major areas: the U.S. position at the United Nations—a procedural question—and the U.S. position on Puerto Rico's political status—a substantive question. I find myself closer to Dr. Pastor's substantive arguments than to his procedural views. Given my current responsibilities in the U.S. mission to the UN and at the risk of appearing to be in greater disagreement with Dr. Pastor than is really the case, I will concentrate the bulk of my remarks on the question of U.S. tactics at the UN.

Dr. Pastor begins his analysis by describing accurately the position that U.S. delegations invariably have taken in the UN when confronted with any attempts to include the question of Puerto Rican status in deliberations before that body. These activities, which Dr. Pastor terms "a summer ritual," are repeated year after year not because of a congenital lack of imagination but simply because the U.S. view is demonstrably correct. The facts are as follows: (1) The UN General Assembly first removed Puerto Rico from the list of non-self-governing territories in 1953 and since then has twice ratified this decision by overwhelming margins. (2) The status question is for the Puerto Rican people to decide for themselves without outside interference. Puerto Ricans have repeatedly demonstrated that they have the political institutions, ability, leadership, and experience to engage in self-determination. (3) U.S. administrations and Congresses over the last thirty years have consistently maintained that the United States will abide by whatever decision is made by the Puerto Ricans. Departure from this "catechism" may be more provocative and exciting than its periodic reiteration, but it would diminish the strength and cogency of the U.S. position.

Dr. Pastor argues that the U.S. position succeeds in convincing fewer nations every year. Furthermore, he stresses that Puerto Rico receives increasing international attention and probably engages more American attention than most other UN issues. He asserts that to continue present U.S. tactics in the UN carries with it political and diplomatic costs that the United States does not need to bear. Based on all this, Dr. Pastor concludes that the United States should change its UN strategy. His recommendations are that we should rejoin the Committee of 24 (C-24), seek to influence its membership and agenda, and fully participate in its deliberations. I disagree with the conclusion and the arguments advanced by Dr. Pastor in support of that conclusion.

Contrary to the view that U.S. arguments convince fewer nations every year, Dr. Pastor's own evidence (see Table 7.1) shows a slight growth in UN support for the U.S. position over the past thirty years. This growth is *despite* the enormous increase in the UN membership of former colonial nations sympathetic to decolonization, the increased radicalization of many third world nations, and the undeniable decline of U.S. influence in the UN over the last twenty years. In fact, during a period in which the United States was on the defensive in the UN, losing most votes by large margins, last year's vote on Puerto Rico, which gave the United States a lopsided victory, clearly demonstrated the strength of international support for the U.S. position.

As Dr. Pastor points out, the Non-Aligned Movement (NAM), prompted by Cuba, can be counted on to write periodic communiqués attacking the U.S. stand on the Puerto Rican question. But the same nations that support the "consensus," nonbinding NAM declarations, vote in the UN against the NAM position on Puerto Rico. Thus, in the last General Assembly the United States not only defeated Cuba in the number of total votes, but, even *within* the NAM, the United States received nearly double the number of votes received by the Cuban position. Voting with Cuba were only the hard-core Soviet bloc (about 30 nations). This hardly suggests a weakening of the U.S. position.

As Dr. Pastor points out, the Socialist International (SI) recently issued a number of communiqués that included calls for Puerto Rican independence. But these were the views of *political parties,* and as the cases of France and Australia suggest, they were not necessarily binding on governments, even governments dominated by socialist parties.

Nor is it accurate to say that the United States expends more diplomatic energy on the issue of Puerto Rico than on most other issues in the UN. Because of objective international factors, the composition of UN membership, and the bloc basis of the political process, about 80 percent of the organization's work is devoted to just two issues: the Middle East and southern Africa. In fact, in the normal hectic conditions of a General Assembly, Puerto Rico is hardly a noticeable issue, since it is submerged in the Committee of 24 (a committee within a committee). When it appears that the issue may attain some prominence, the United States begins its preparations—as Dr. Pastor recommends—well in advance. To prepare for the vote in 1982, Ambassador Kirkpatrick visited Puerto Rico twice to consult with Puerto Rican political leaders, and the selection of a prominent, elected Puerto Rican official (Dr. Hernan Padilla, mayor of San Juan) as a public delegate to the thirty-seventh General Assembly was not mere coincidence.

Dr. Pastor is correct in arguing that continuation of present U.S. tactics in the UN has diplomatic and political costs associated with the trade-offs, bargaining, IOUs, and arm twisting undertaken in support of our policy. But such costs are inextricably linked with any issue within a political process that has quasi-legislative features. Furthermore, I do not believe—as Dr. Pastor suggests—that U.S. lobbying on the Puerto Rican issue was the indirect cause of the election of Nicaragua (which the U.S. opposed) to the Security Council. Instead, Nicaragua beat the Dominican Republic because its NAM membership, its international presence in various forums, and the Falklands issue gave it an insurmountable advantage.

I willingly concede that the first question that arises when observing UN affairs is why is the United States always on the defensive? The answer requires a conference of its own, but suffice to say that in a process where "one nation, one vote" is the basis of electoral participation, the third world has an overwhelming advantage that allows it to control the agenda, the deliberating process, and the outcome. Where this process has become particularly politicized, the United States has opted to stop participating, as in the International Labor Organization (ILO) (temporarily), the council of Namibia, the recent Palestinian conference, and the Committee of 24. With respect to the committee, this was not an exclusively U.S. decision; only two Western states remain involved (Norway and Australia), and even they may not remain long because of the highly politicized manner in which the committee conducts its business.

But let us assume that, as recommended by Dr. Pastor, the United States decided to rejoin the Committee of 24 and undertook to influence its membership, agenda, deliberations, and decisions. I submit that this very ambitious agenda could not be successfully implemented without playing a good deal of political "hard ball," in other words, without incurring the diplomatic and political costs that Dr. Pastor associates with our current stance in the UN. Therefore, the evidence strongly supports the continuation of the current U.S. posture in the UN with regard to the Puerto Rican question.

My disagreement with Dr. Pastor on procedural matters in the UN does not carry over into substantive questions. I wholeheartedly agree that self-determination is an American core value and that the United States should willingly bear the costs incurred in its defense. Where I disagree is how to best defend this sacred value. By involving the UN in the status debate on Puerto Rico we will only diminish the ability of Puerto Ricans to decide their own future without outside interference. Self-determination, however, would seem to require that the Puerto Rican people take the first step; the initiative must be theirs. Furthermore, a final decision would require something similar to what Rousseau termed a "social contract." Such decisions, however, can only be taken when the conditions have matured. We should resist firmly the natural temptation to speed the maturation process.

8
The Puerto Rican
Status Question:
Changing the Paradigm

Juan Manuel García-Passalacqua

Introduction

The United States of America does not have a policy on Puerto Rico. The Digest of U.S. Practice in International Law dutifully includes, in its section on "Self-Governing and Non-Self-Governing Territories," the July 25, 1978, proclamation of President Jimmy Carter on "alternative futures" for Puerto Rico.[1] That is all.

In 1950, after two Puerto Rican nationalists tried to kill the president of the United States, George F. Kennan wrote: "Recent events have surely been eloquent enough to cause us all to ask ourselves whether we have really thought through all the implications of a relationship so immensely important, so pregnant with possibilities for both good and evil, as the colonial tie between our country and the people of Puerto Rico."[2] That was more than a quarter-century ago.

The Analytic Paradigms

It must be understood at the outset that the nature of this problem is paradigmatic. A paradigm is the entire constellation of beliefs, values, and techniques shared by the members of a given community.[3] Graham T. Allison has emphasized the role of paradigms in the formulation of U.S. national policy.[4] As a precondition for solving the Puerto Rican dilemma we must examine the reasons for the nonexistence of a policy and avoid repeating past mistakes. In this respect, Allison's theories are valuable.

The first lesson is that the *nation* that is to produce the *policy* is not a centrally coordinated, purposeful individual. The makers of policy in the United States are a conglomerate of factors, sectors, and actors.[5] To untie the Gordian knot of nonpolicy we must examine the *assumptions* of each one of those factors, sectors, and actors that have led to this state of affairs. Allison's models of "rational actor," "organizational process," and "bureaucratic politics" are useful when applied to the case of Puerto Rico.

We will use the analytic paradigms to explain the problem in three different, but perfectly consistent, ways. The United States was the economic metropolis of Puerto Rico as early as 1850. It became the island's military metropolis in 1898; it has been its political metropolis for the last eighty-five years. However, the United States has consistently refused to recognize it has a colony in the Caribbean Sea. The essence of the problem is that paradigm. For the sake of analysis, let us apply Allison's "working synthesis of the models"[6] to the case of Puerto Rico.

Model I—The Rational Actor

In this model, policy is regarded as the outcome of a single, purposeful entity—a rational actor. What is the problem? The relationship between Puerto Rico and the United States. What are the alternatives? The status quo, statehood, independence, or an improvement of the present status. What are the costs and benefits of each alternative? They have been studied recently by a U.S.–Puerto Rican status commission[7] and by the General Accounting Office.[8] What is the observed pattern of national axioms? They have gone from outright colonialism in the 1900s,[9] to legitimation of the status quo after 1952,[10] to recent strong support for self-determination for the Puerto Ricans.[11] What are the pressures in the international marketplace? Support for decolonization and independence from adversaries[12] and friends[13] of the United States. Thus goes the traditional, most popular analytic paradigm. We will attempt to get away from its simplicity and elaborate.

Model II—Organizational Process

In this model, the theory of the behavior of large organizations, as first applied by Herbert Simon and others to the private firm, is used to explain policy outcomes as the result of organizational routine. What organizations in the U.S. government deal with Puerto Rico? The Congress, the U.S. Armed Forces, the Federal Bureau of Investigation and other intelligence agencies, all U.S. departments, the U.S. judiciary, and the White House.[14] Which organizations traditionally act on a problem of this sort and what is their relative influence? The army,[15] the Interior Department,[16] and the House and Senate Committees of Interior and Insular Affairs[17] and Public Lands[18] have all lost power to act on the problem as the relative influence of the Department of State,[19] the U.S. Navy,[20] the Federal Bureau of Investigation, other intelligence agencies,[21] and the White House has increased in recent years. The key organizational change occurred in 1961 when President John F. Kennedy issued an executive order transferring all matters relating to the status question to the White House, where they have purportedly remained for the last two decades.[22]

What are the standard operating procedures (SOPs) of these organizations for gathering information and generating alternatives on the problem? They have implemented their policies individually, and they seldom coordinate or exchange information. The three branches of the U.S. government have developed reactive, not active, SOPs that are put into effect when pressured by external events. The judiciary, of course, reacts only when important *cases* arise in the courts and has mostly affirmed the ample power of Congress under the territorial clause of the Constitution.[23] The executive agencies have preferred *internal staff studies* (War and Interior in 1937, Interior in 1945, HEW in 1976–1977, State in 1975–1981),[24] joint *metropolitan-insular committees* (on independence in 1936, on changes in the Jones Act in 1943 and 1946, on examining all facets of the relationship in 1964),[25] and much more recently, White House *interdepartmental commissions* (Carter in 1977, Reagan in 1981).[26] The congressional committees have traditionally favored *hearings* held on the island, particularly in winter.[27] None of the five traditional SOPs has ever produced a single, coherent U.S. policy on Puerto Rico.[28]

No alternative, except support for the status quo, has ever been offered. What SOPs do these organizations have for implementing alternative courses of action? Each one goes its own way, implementing its own piecemeal policy on Puerto Rico. Thus, under the second analytic paradigm, the organizational process of the government of the United States has *no* tradition for dealing with the problem, since essentially it has not been recognized as such.

Model III—Bureaucratic Politics

In this model, politics—the struggle for power among the various actors in the policymaking process—is added to the organizational model. Emphasis is placed on the channels within government, trade-offs among the players, and politically forced deadlines. These factors are used to explain the resulting outcome. What are the channels for producing action on this problem? None.

In the past twenty years, since legal responsibility was transferred from the Department of the Interior to the White House, a status commission,[29] two ad hoc committees,[30] and two interagency task forces[31] have been created by the White House, and none has produced any result. Which players in what positions are centrally involved? During the period between 1961–1976 the problem was dealt with by middle-level bureaucratic officials in each individual agency. The Puerto Rican decision after 1976 to involve the two major Puerto Rican political parties in the U.S. presidential nomination process elevated the issue to the level of campaign committees and White House staff reports. This power play added additional political content and impact to the issue.[32]

How do different pressures affect the central players? A cursory description of the situation today will include officials of the U.S. Armed Forces (concerned with strategic and naval considerations), the Domestic Council and the Office of Management and Budget (concerned with costs and effectiveness of social programs), the Foreign Service (deals with the issue at the United Nations and other international forums), and the Federal Bureau of Investigation and other intelligence agencies (concerned mostly with domestic and international terrorism); and more recently, the politicians in the staffs of incumbents or candidates for the presidency and the vice-presidency (nurture intraparty allegiances in the expectation of Puerto Rico's role in the nomination process). Also playing a role are several committees in the Congress. Each of these crucial players has different assumptions about the Puerto Rican "reality," operates under different pressures and priorities, and obviously represents varied and contradictory positions.

What are the deadlines that will force the issue to resolution? At present, none is urgent. Yet the increasing strategic importance, the need for cuts in social programs, the increasing pressures from the international community, the escalation of armed struggle—such as Fuerzas Armadas de Liberación National (Armed Forces of National Liberation) or FALN— and the impending scramble for delegate votes from Puerto Rico to the national conventions, *all* are factors increasing the pressure on the different sectors and actors to act during the 1980s. Where are foul-ups likely? The most critical potential foul-up is the adoption of uncoordinated policies by the different sectors.

The Allison models, when seen from a third world perspective, require improvement by including nongovernmental factors, sectors, and actors that influence the formulation of U.S. policy. One must include a fourth parallel model that will take into consideration the financial and corporate sectors in the United States and the think tanks and the public-opinion apparatus, particularly the press. Even if we acknowledge the presence of these influences, they lie outside the scope of this essay, which deals strictly with governmental actors, sectors, and factors.

The utilization of Allison's working synthesis of models produces a concise and more complete description of the problem than the traditional approach.

The Congress, responsible under the Treaty of Paris and U.S. Constitution[33] for U.S. policy on Puerto Rico, has acted with great *conservative restraint*[34] in all the years of the relationship. The rational-actor model, used to interpret the problem in the last two decades, has proved insufficient, since the essential, unitary actor does not exist in this case. Increased attention has to be paid to the organizational process and bureaucratic politics models if a solution is to be found. The alleged policy of self-determination, if understood as the American will to leave the matter to be decided by the Puerto Ricans, is a fallacy.[35] To prove this point, let us examine how the United States has ignored the will of the Puerto Ricans, as part of its incompetence to produce a true U.S. policy on Puerto Rico.

Improvements in the Status Quo

On July 25, 1952, the United States and Puerto Rico established the present relationship of commonwealth status.[36] A few months later, legislation was introduced in the U.S. Congress by Puerto Rico's resident commissioner to clarify what had been done.[37] In 1959 a second effort was made by the Puerto Rican Legislative Assembly to propose to the U.S. Congress "clarifications and modifications."[38] In 1962 the Legislative Assembly again proposed to Congress a procedure to establish the "ulterior final political status" of Puerto Rico.[39] The U.S. Congress *never* acted on *any* of the three formal "improvement" proposals.

An analysis of the organizational process and the bureaucratic politics exercised in the attempt to improve the status quo between 1958 and 1960 provides an excellent case study of what has been wrong. Pursuant to a resolution from the Legislative Assembly, Resident Commissioner Antonio Fernós Isern introduced H.R. 5926 in March 1959, a bill to provide for amendments to the compact between the people of Puerto Rico and the United States. The chairman of the House Committee on Interior and Insular Affairs requested the views of the various departments of the executive branch. A brief survey of their reports contained in the record demonstrates the relevance of the organizational/bureaucratic models.[40]

The Department of Defense delegated to the U.S. Navy the responsibility for expressing its views, a significant step in itself. The Navy opposed the bill "because of the magnitude of problems that this legislation could create for the military departments in the land and water areas." It was the only department to take a clear position. Furthermore, this position prevailed.

The Department of Interior recognized that it no longer had responsibility for, or supervision over, Puerto Rico, "deferring" to other departments because of the "specialized matters" in the bill. Its reports lauded congressional recognition since 1947, of the "maturity" of the Puerto Ricans and expressed "the responsibility of the United States" to give them self-government "in accordance with their capacity." Apart from insisting that "the question of Puerto Rico's ultimate status be left open," the department avoided taking a position on the bill.

The Department of State favored "clarification and strengthening of self-government," recalling the presentation it had made before the United Nations in 1953. However, it refused to surrender its responsibility to conduct all foreign affairs for Puerto Rico and expressed doubts as to the "request and consent" powers of the people of Puerto Rico in the relationship.

The Department of Health, Education and Welfare deferred responsibility to Interior, State, and Justice on the basic policy questions in the bill. It insisted that Puerto Rico should not exercise any power that could properly be exercised by the United States in the several states of the Union and expressed doubts about the proposal of U.S. property or functions.

The Agriculture Department opposed the bill because it transferred federal functions to the island.

The Justice Department was the last to react, issuing an extensive statement insisting on the absolute power of the Congress over Puerto Rico, refusing to take a position on the bill, and emphasizing "technical amendments" on income tax laws, naturalization and citizenship, federal properties, ports and navigable waters, and other matters. The judicial conference reported opposition to the use of the Spanish language in the U.S. District Court for Puerto Rico.

In essence, the Fernós-Murray Bill of 1959, drafted in accordance with the electoral will of the people of Puerto Rico and with the Puerto Rican leaders' assumption as to what commonwealth status was and should be, encountered completely different assumptions in the departments of the U.S. government. Interior and HEW deferred to other unnamed departments. State and Agriculture limited themselves to defense of their turf. Justice defended the congressional turf. Only the Navy took an unequivocable position and it was against the bill. There was no coordinated position. It was a veritable clash of paradigms. The resulting gap made consensus impossible and the bill was allowed to die.

Robert J. Hunter in a report prepared for the members of the House Interior Committee stated: "U.S. Government opposition could well prove more formidable than insular objections," and concluded: "Already there is an obvious trend which demonstrates that Federal executive and legislative branches will tend to be far more cautious and conservative in their approach to this revision of the compact than they were nine years ago in its original adoption."[41]

In summary, several times in the last thirty years the Legislative Assembly of Puerto Rico has attempted to get the U.S. Congress to improve the status quo, representing the will of the people of Puerto Rico. When taking the legislative road, the efforts have been derailed by the opposition and objections of the executive departments, each based on its own assumptions and each for its own parochial reasons. After the 1960s, the government of Puerto Rico opted for another strategy and went first to the executive branch. A misunderstanding arose on the efforts to afford permanence for commonwealth status, a position opposed by the Bureau of the Budget on behalf of the administration.[42] The resulting stalemate has since led to the creation of the status commission, two ad hoc committees, and two interagency task forces, none of which has obtained any action from Congress. Finally, the initiative of President Gerald Ford for a unilateral grant of statehood did not receive consideration from the Congress either.[43] This brief historical survey demonstrates that *all* previous efforts to improve or change the status quo have ended in failure.

The reason for this failure seems evident from the instances summarized. Unless and until a clear unified policy is adopted by *all* branches of the U.S. government on Puerto Rico, the situation will continue to deteriorate. The existing assumptions have led to a situation in which, in the absence of a policy, U.S. executive agencies, the Congress, and the judiciary, each has an equal right to determine (and in effect protect its turf) the future of the territory.

The only solution previously proposed for the problem—by Senator Henry Jackson, among others—is to centralize the coordination of all Puerto Rican matters in a White House aide.[44] Although historically such a presidential initiative has been needed to get Congress to act on Puerto Rico,[45] such an aide would certainly become a colonial proconsul for the island. We have proved that the issue has important bureaucratic elements but not a bureaucratic solution. The issue is much more complex, and thus it needs a much more serious effort to solve it.

The basic reason for the present crisis is economic collapse. The economic crisis has resulted from the colonial structure.[46] The policy paralysis is due to the assumption that since Puerto Rico is not a colony, there is no need to decolonize. The paradigm must be changed.

A Program for Decolonization

Having examined the reasons for the absence of a U.S. policy on Puerto Rico, and having described the pitfalls of past experience, let me propose a policy on the completely new assumption that what is needed is a program for decolonization.

Policy Assumptions

The proclamation issued by President Jimmy Carter on July 25, 1978, opened a new era in U.S.–Puerto Rican relations. In effect, it abandoned the status quo and faced alternative futures for Puerto Rico.

1. Essential to that position is the understanding that the 1952 referendums and the 1967 plebiscite are now inoperative (more than half of the voters in the lists today were not electors then) and that a new process of self-determination for Puerto Rico is required.

2. The creation of commonwealth status in 1952 and its concomitant recognition by the United Nations in 1953 did not solve Puerto Rico's political status problems.[47] Both processes must be recognized as historical facts but deserve no further defense. The present situation must be taken as it now exists.

3. Puerto Rico is legally a territory of the United States. As the first General Accounting Office report recognizes, the problem to be addressed is one of "territorial transition."[48]

4. To avoid semantic traps, it must be understood that three different concepts now in use by different actors mean the same thing:

(a) territorial transition under the constitutional and treaty power of the Congress to *dispose of the territories;*

(b) *decolonization* under the precepts of Resolutions 1514 and 1541 of the General Assembly of the United Nations;

(c) *self-determination* as understood in the United States and Puerto Rican political circles.

5. If all four new assumptions are accepted, the U.S. government, the international community, and the Puerto Rican electorate and politicians, by close and continuous consultations, can design a program for Puerto Rican self-determination to be executed during the 1980s.

Alternative Futures

In essence, this description implies that Puerto Rico is still a colony and that, in this case, the United States is a colonial power. The proclamation of July 25, 1978, means (when read in this context) that the United States is ready and willing to decolonize in terms of the will of the Puerto Rican people.

1. The case can no longer be treated as an internal matter between the U.S. and Puerto Rico. To ignore or refuse to recognize the legitimate interest of the international community in the self-determination or disposition of the territory is to complicate, rather than facilitate, a solution to the problem.

2. It can no longer be argued that the matter is "completely in Puerto Rican hands." The glaring fact is that under our constitutional system the U.S. Congress deals with at least 485 areas of Puerto Rico's life,[49] and Congress will make the final decision regarding Puerto Rico. Reality militates against this cosmetic position. As a colonial power the United States does have—as recommended by Arthur Borg in his seminal paper for the State Department—an important role to play, from beginning to end, in the decolonization and self-determination process.[50]

Procedure, Not Substance

The substantive solutions to the Puerto Rican issue can be, in the words of the proclamation of July 25, 1978, independence, statehood, or mutually agreed changes in the present status. However (apart from the role the U.S. government can play in clarifying the true conceptual and legal possibilities of each solution) no effort should be made to incline the balance toward any of them. The facts regarding each alternative future should speak loudly and clearly for themselves.

The U.S. government should approach the Puerto Rican question at this time in strictly *procedural* terms. The question should thus be framed: What is the procedure to guarantee true self-determination? On this matter, we can search for and obtain a consensus between forces in the United States, Puerto Rico, and the international community. We may not be able to agree on which of the substantive alternative futures is desirable, but we can design a procedure that will offer guarantees to reach a goal recognized and accepted by all.

The List of Non-Self-Governing Territories

If the previous argumentation is followed, it is necessary to face the question of whether Puerto Rico should be put back on the UN list of non-self-governing territories. In any event, the United States should file an intended plan for decolonization or self-determination and invite the decolonization committee to observe it—probably in terms offered by Ambassador Andrew Young's 1978 statement to the decolonization committee.[51] This gesture of international comity and good faith would be a first step in the process, leading to a final resolution years later. It could be undertaken as a U.S. initiative or accepted as a response to the initiative of a friendly nation—such as Venezuela (which sponsored its own decolonization resolution at the UN in 1984). There is reason to believe that Cuba would welcome such an initiative in the committee, permitting it to take a more constructive position.[52]

Academic and Technical Studies

In recent years we have witnessed the release of the interagency committee report on Puerto Rico and the two GAO reports.[53] We have also seen the important resolutions on Puerto Rico adopted by the Mexico City, Oaxaca, Santo Domingo, and Portugal meetings of international party organizations.[54] These developments have been accompanied by forums held on the issue at Harvard University, the Wilson Center of the Smithsonian Institution, Yale University, the Lehrman Institute, the Americas Society, and the World Peace Foundation among others.[55] Also important is the attention given to Puerto Rico by *Foreign Policy* (in an article by José Cabranes)[56] and *Foreign Affairs* (in an article by Alfred Stepan).[57] All these developments point to what Cabranes terms "coming out of the colonial closet." In the context of this surge of interest, it is essential that the emerging debate be channeled not to a fruitless discussion of the advantages and disadvantages of the alternative futures, but to the factual clarification of their implications.

National Party Platforms

The president's July 25, 1978, proclamation should be adopted as a bipartisan U.S. policy in the platforms of the Republican and Democratic parties.

1. The Puerto Rican delegation to Democratic national conventions has been and henceforth will be divided between statehooders and commonwealthers. Each will push his choice. Independence is not represented. If these factions fight to have their status preferences included in the platform, the results could damage the existing position on self-determination.

2. The Republican party should not paint itself into a corner by endorsing only statehood.[58] In this context it is pertinent to examine Ronald Reagan's announcement of his candidacy for the 1980 election and his subsequent modifications on the status issue in Puerto Rico.[59] An effort must be made to convince the Republicans to support the alternative futures policy as a bipartisan decision of the United States.

UN Debate

The UN decolonization committee and the General Assembly will continue to address the Puerto Rican question each year. Failure to adopt a self-determination platform by the political parties will hurt the United States. On the contrary, a bipartisan platform based on the 1978 proclamation can be transmitted to the UN as a signal of positive support for that body's role.

1. If this important procedural step is taken, there is reason to believe (after Venezuela's resolution of 1984) that a consensus resolution can be obtained giving the United States the opportunity to announce the procedure for decolonization and self-determination.

2. The Puerto Rico Bar Association's constitutional law committee, the only institution in the island where lawyers of the three ideological persuasions have achieved consensus on the status issue,[60] can be offered a role in the effort to articulate U.S.–Puerto Rican–UN attitudes on the matter. Members of that committee have made that effort with the State Department, the National Security Council, Latin American delegations, and Sweden among others in past years after reaching consensus in the island. Even if those efforts did not prosper, they have created the conditions for possible success.

3. No effort should be made to insist on the position of "no-jurisdiction" by the committee or by the General Assembly. The U.S. position had only one member willing to espouse it in the committee in 1982 and a dwindling majority in the General Assembly.[61] It reflects a lack of sensitivity on the part of the United States to the realities of the case to insist that Puerto Rico is not an international issue.

Presidential Leadership

Early in the presidential term beginning in January 1985, the president should announce a new policy toward Puerto Rico based on recognizing its international relevance and the principle of self-determination. This policy should consist of a program of procedural steps toward a final solution of the status question.

First Procedural Option: The Plebiscite

There are two main procedural options; they are not incompatible but complementary. Others may arise, but on the basis of years of analysis of this problem, these two seem the most logical.

The plebiscite method, used in 1967, is somewhat in disrepute in Puerto Rico and in the international community. The FBI report on how it was conducted should be reread and the conclusion will be obvious: It is better forgotten.[62] This scenario does have the advantage of posing the issue squarely and immediately. However, as Alfred Stepan has pointed out, plebiscites are historically won by their proponents, thus leading to the possibility that the prostatehood party may go to a plebiscite alone (with a nominal "citizen group" opposing statehood and favoring independence but without official party support). This approach will lead to about 48 percent participation of the electorate and about 90 percent triumph for statehood. A plebiscite thus held will be condemned by all minority parties, by the international community, and by members of Congress (Congressmen Ronald Dellums and Mickey Leland, and Senator Bennett Johnston have already expressed reservations). Even if the margin of participation is above that of many state elections in the United States, the role of abstention will be overplayed to discredit results. The United States will be blamed, wrongly, for having promoted a process that has such drawbacks. It seems obvious that before any vote is attempted, preconditions or previous procedural steps should be designed to prevent such a negative outcome.

Second Procedural Option:
The Constitutional Conference

The context in which any vote by the people of Puerto Rico occurs is, in a sense, more important than the result, and can dictate its acceptance by all interested sectors. The medium may be the message. Thus, once again, procedure is more important than substance. This would suggest an alternative method, of which the plebiscite would be only one element, albeit the most relevant.

1. The situation in Puerto Rico, minus a civil war, is somewhat similar to that in India during colonial times or in Rhodesia in recent years. Several political leaders vie for power within the community; the issue on which they disagree is how to end colonialism.

2. It is in the interest of the United States that a consensus be reached by *all* local registered parties on how to go about *exercising self-determination,* or *decolonization,* or *disposing of the territory* (the terms favored by each of the three ideologies), all really being the same process. Such a consensus will work toward eventual acceptance of the result of the process, particularly if seen as an open-ended one in which the initial triumph of one substantive alternative *does not preclude eventual consideration of others,* depending on the reaction to the winner's demands by the U.S. Congress.

3. It seems obvious from our analysis of past experience, that the search for such a consensus must be an initiative of the president of the United States. With the Camp David and Lancaster House experiences as models, the president should call the Puerto Rican party leaders to a constitutional conference on the future of Puerto Rico. Initiated by the president, it can be subsequently conducted by the vice-president or other senior White House official, with the aid of the State Department. The agenda would be a search for precedural consensus and guarantees to solve the problem.

4. Essential to the discussions would be the design of a *process* in which the expression of *the people's will,* when conducted, can be *informed and free.*

5. As the constitutional conference progresses, informal consultations should be conducted with other governments, particularly those of Latin American nations, on their reaction to diverse proposals. Although the advice of friendly nations has often been to "leave the whole thing in the hands of the Puerto Ricans," that advice is uninformed and perilous. The advisors of today may become tomorrow's critics.

6. If the Puerto Rican leaders agree on a decolonization process, well and good. If they do not, they will not have anyone to blame but themselves if the matter is finally taken out of their hands at the federal level by the United States.

The Preconditions

It seems clear from the preceding arguments that there would be several preconditions to holding a status plebiscite or a local constitutional convention (as preferred by the PNP and the PDP, respectively).

1. The precondition favored by the Socialist party, which has close ties with Cuba, is the "transfer of all powers." Congressman Ronald Dellums has filed a bill to that effect in Congress.[63] Its thrust is that Congress will have to legislate to divest itself of all power over Puerto Rico. The proposal as presently described has no chance of acceptance by the U.S. Congress. If the proposal's impracticality is carefully explained to both Cuba and the Socialists, they might be able to offer a more reasonable definition of the *transfer of powers*.

2. An option for the *transfer of powers* by the Congress has been carefully defined by the Puerto Rican Bar Association committee. Such a definition deserves study.[64]

Congressional Enabling Act

The logical extension of the 1978 proclamation on self-determination and alternative futures would be the adoption by the U.S. Congress as a result of a presidential initiative, of *an enabling act of Puerto Rican self-determination*.

1. There is ample precedent for an act of Congress, in the exercise of its power under the Constitution, Article 4, Section 3, paragraph 2, to "dispose of—the territory—of the United States." The GAO report points out that this power has been exercised to admit thirty-seven states and to grant independence to one territory (the Philippines). Nothing prohibits the Congress from designing and adopting *alternative ways of disposition of a territory*, dependent exclusively on the choice by the people of said territory.[65]

2. The assumptions of the proposed enabling act of Puerto Rican self-determination are that the island is indeed a U.S. territory and that Congress intends to dispose of it either by making it a state or an

independent republic, or by improving the present commonwealth relation toward eventual statehood or independence.

3. *The proposed act would define the three options as Congress is willing to grant them, thus clarifying the real choices to the Puerto Rican people before the plebiscite.*[66]

4. The definition of statehood should include the position of Congress regarding: (a) terms of imposition of federal taxation; (b) assumption of the territorial public debt; and (c) English language requirements in government and schools. The models here could be the admission acts of Hawaii and Alaska, or the Ford administration's Puerto Rican statehood bill.

5. The definition of independence should also include the position of Congress regarding tariffs, immigration and citizenship, public debt, economic aid, and military bases. The model here could be the Philippines' independence act.

6. The text of the ad hoc committee report on commonwealth status could be an acceptable definition of the mutually agreed changes to commonwealth status.[67]

7. The U.S. Congress should also define what it would understand to be a clear expression of the popular will, in terms of both participation and the margin of a majority.

8. The adoption by Congress, after a presidential initiative, of such an enabling act of self-determination would demonstrate good will and help prevent violence in Puerto Rico and the United States on the issue, by showing a true will to decolonize Puerto Rico. It would also enhance the chances of international acceptance of the result.

9. A UN decolonization committee resolution after the enactment of the bill would probably accept the process as decolonizing and set the stage for a final decision.

The Issues of the Public Debt and Economic Assistance

Two essential elements of such a proposed enabling act of self-determination would be the assumption by the United States of Puerto Rico's debt (now calculated at $12 billion) and the guarantee of a "maintenance of effort" in economic aid for the island (now amounting to $4 billion a year) *regardless* of which of the three substantive choices is made by the people of Puerto Rico. No better sign of the true will to afford self-determination can exist.

1. The implications of these two commitments for U.S. national security are clear. They would guarantee that regardless of the outcome of the plebiscite and the subsequent action by Congress, Puerto Rico would remain solidly in the Western camp before the world, and any temptation

to explore other ideological alternatives would be eliminated. Freed from the spectre of future economic want, Puerto Rico would then be in the forefront of the Caribbean ideological plurality debate, on the side of democracy.

2. The clearest and logical justification for the economic-aid commitment would be reciprocity for the permanence of U.S. military bases in the island.

The Puerto Rican Self-Determination Exercise

The process, flowing from the 1978 proclamation to the party platforms to the self-determination enabling act, could culminate with a vote by the Puerto Rican people themselves that would then be informed, massive, and free. The plebiscite, instead of being an initial bone of contention, would then be the logical result of the conditions created for its success and acceptance.

The Constitutional Convention

Whether the choice of the people is statehood, independence, or an improved commonwealth, a local constitutional convention will be required in Puerto Rico to adapt the present constitutional structure to the changes previously found acceptable by Congress.

1. The convention could then remain in session until the negotiations with Congress end, *keeping the other options as available alternatives in case Congress should refuse* (since one Congress cannot constitutionally bind another) *to grant the preferred option.*

2. The electorate would know that the delegate to the convention for whom they vote will represent one option but will be able to choose another if the negotiation for the preferred formula with Congress fails.

The U.S. Congress Vote

If the aforecited processes are achieved, bills would be presented in the U.S. House and Senate to ratify the will of the Puerto Rican people.

1. At this point, it would be made clear to the Congress that the U.S. president will not lobby for any one solution, but will leave the matter entirely in the hands of the majority of Congress. This policy is suggested (even at this late stage) to maintain the position of substantive neutrality on behalf of the president and also keep the options open in case Congress should reject the substantive solution favored by a Puerto Rican majority.

2. It should be pointed out to the Congress that procrastination in considering the issue can lead to the further destabilization of Puerto Rican society.

3. In the expectation of a statehood triumph, U.S. analysts predict civil disruption in the metropolis.[68] A careful study of the precedents of Quebec, Ireland, and Algeria should be made to educate policymakers in this eventuality.[69]

The Solution

It has been my intention to propose the consideration of the Puerto Rican issue as a continuum of proposed events that conceptualizes the issue as a *process* capable of producing a coherent, consistent, and articulate sequence of events leading to a solution.

1. A probable scenario is as follows: The commonwealth option may have become economically and politically inoperative. A majority of the people will probably opt for statehood over independence, by an 80 to 20 margin if the option is posed in those terms. The U.S. Congress might not be inclined to grant statehood in terms acceptable to the Puerto Rican people. In that case the irresistible force may meet the immovable object on the Puerto Rican issue in the 1980s.

2. According to important U.S. analysts, this scenario points out that the option of independence should be kept open at all times, since it may end up being the only truly final solution.[70]

I have proposed a program for decolonization. By accepting its paradigms and new assumptions, this procedure becomes a strategy to assure readiness for any eventuality. The plan can serve as a model for solving the status debate. It, or something like it, is needed as a U.S. policy on Puerto Rico. The goal is to provide procedural, not substantive, guidelines for the decolonization of Puerto Rico.

Notes

1. The proclamation states: "Whatever decision the people of Puerto Rico may wish to take—statehood, independence, commonwealth status, or mutually agreed modifications in that status—it will be yours. . . . I will support and urge Congress to support whatever decision the people of Puerto Rico reach." *Digest of U.S. Practice in International Law* (Washington, D.C.: Government Printing Office, 1980), pp. 171–172. This was the first such unequivocal statement in history.

2. George F. Kennan, *American Diplomacy 1900–1950* (Chicago: University of Chicago Press, 1951), p. 18.

3. Thomas Kuhn, *The Structure of Scientific Revolutions*, 2d ed. (Chicago: University of Chicago Press, 1970), p. 175.

4. Graham T. Allison, *Essence of Decision: Explaining the Cuban Missile Crisis* (Boston: Little, Brown & Co., 1971).

5. Rafael Hernandez, "La Estructura de Poder en Estados Unidos: Notas Sobre un Model de Análisis," Mesa Redonda Internacional Sobre Estados Unidos en los '80, Centro de Estudios de América, La Habana, 1983.

6. Allison, *Cuban Missile Crisis*, pp. 256–257.

7. Status de Puerto Rico, Informe de la Comisión de los Estados Unidos y de Puerto Rico Sobre el Status de Puerto Rico (Washington, D.C.: Government Printing Office, August 1966).

8. Comptroller General's Report to Congress, "Puerto Rico's Political Futures: A Devisive Issue With Many Dimensions," mimeographed (Washington, D.C., 1981).

9. See, for example, Simeon E. Baldwin, "Constitutional Questions Incident to the Acquisition and Government by the United States of Island Territory," *Harvard Law Review* 12(1899):393; and Senator J. B. Foraker (R.-Ohio), U.S. Congress, Senate, Congressional Record, March 8, 1900.

10. See, for example, Chief Justice Earl Warren, who labeled the relationship "the newest and perhaps the most notable of American governmental experiments in our lifetime." Address on the Dedication of the New Supreme Court of Puerto Rico, mimeographed, 1956. *El Mundo*, February 6, 1956, p. 1.

11. See, for example, U.S. Ambassador to the UN Henry Cabot Lodge's promise of more autonomy or outright independence. Official records of the General Assembly, Eighth Session, Plenary Meetings, September 15–December 9, 1953 (New York, 1954), p. 311. Distinguish from Carter's proclamation in *Digest of U.S. Practice in International Law,* that extended the offer to *all* alternatives.

12. Loida Figueroa, *El Caso de Puerto Rico A Nivel Internacional* (Rio Piedras: Editorial Edil, 1979), describes the efforts by revolutionary Cuba since 1960.

13. See Juan O. Tamayo, "Alliances Shift in Caribbean as U.S. Friends Turn Away," *Miami Herald*, October 1, 1982, int. ed., p. 3-A; and "Socialist International Backs Puerto Rican Independence," a *New York Times* story from Paris, reproduced by the *San Juan Star*, May 6, 1983, p. 13. See also the speech by Jorge Illueca of Panama, president of the General Assembly, *Claridad*, September 27, 1984, p. 3.

14. Listings of U.S. agencies and programs operating in Puerto Rico are contained, respectively, in *Status of Puerto Rico, Selected Background, U.S.-P.R. Commission on the Status of Puerto Rico* (1966), pp. 894–970; and in U.S. Department of Commerce, *Economic Study of Puerto Rico* (Washington, D.C.: Government Printing Office, 1979), pp. 331–339.

15. The Department of War was responsible from 1898, and its Bureau of Insular Affairs operated from 1909 to 1934 with full powers. Surendra Bhana, *The United States and the Development of the Puerto Rican Status Question, 1936–1968* (Kansas City: Kansas University Press, 1975), p. 13.

16. President Franklin D. Roosevelt transferred the island's administration to the Interior Department in 1934. Ibid., p. 13, n. 27; p. 119.

17. The Interior and Insular Affairs Committees assumed jurisdiction in 1898 and exercised strong supervision particularly from 1934 to 1952 and again in the 1960s. Ibid., pp. 37–71, 147–159.

18. Ibid., pp. 101–132, n. 38.

19. The State Department began to exercise important influence after 1943 because of the post–World War II decolonization movement in the United Nations. Ibid., pp. 50, 101, 117.

20. The U.S. Navy was the main promoter of the 1898 invasion because of Admiral Alfred Thayer Mahan's geopolitical theories, and its intervention and influence have always been very strong. Bhana, *Status Question*, pp. 107–108, nn. 73–74. Jorge Rodriguez Beruff, "Antecedentes de la Expansión Militar Norteamericana en Puerto Rico," *Claridad*, June 24–30, 1983, En Rojo, pp. 19–23; see also *San Juan Star*, February 1, 1980, p. 23; January 20, 1980, p. 1; and January 29, 1980, p. 1.

21. Bhana, *Status Question*, p. 48, n. 53; p. 136, n. 6; and Carmen Gautier Mayoral and Teresa Blanco Stahl, "COINTELPRO en Puerto Rico 1960–1971" (Verano: *Pensamiento Crítico*, 1979). For an interesting novelistic description, see Tad Szulc, *Diplomatic Immunity* (New York: Simon & Schuster, 1981), pp. 94–100, and its review in the *New York Times Book Review*, September 27, 1981, p. 13.

22. A Memorandum For the Heads of the Executive Departments and Agencies, The White House, Washington, July 25, 1961, read: "All departments, agencies, and officials of the executive branch of the Government should faithfully and carefully observe and respect this arrangement in relation to all matters affecting the Commonwealth of Puerto Rico. If any matters arise involving the fundamentals of this arrangement, they should be referred to the Office of the President." *Documents on the Constitutional History of Puerto Rico*, 2d ed. (Washington, D.C., 1964), p. 206. Federal Register, July 27, 1961.

23. The most important cases have been: *Downes* v. *Bidwell*, 182 U.S. 244 (1901), on "unincorporation"; *Balzac* v. *People of Puerto Rico*, 258 U.S. 298 (1922), on the grant of U.S. citizenship not incorporating the territory; *Granville Smith* v. *Granville Smith*, 75 S. Ct. 553 (1955), taking note of the creation of the commonwealth in Puerto Rico; *Calero Toledo* v. *Pearson Yatch*, 416 U.S. 663 (1974), analyzing the development of commonwealth status; *Califano* v. *Torres*, 435 U.S. 1 (1978), reiterating the power of Congress over Puerto Rico under the territorial clause; *Torres* v. *Puerto Rico*, 442 U.S. 665 (1979), limiting the powers of the commonwealth; and *Harris* v. *Rosario*, 446 U.S. 651 (1980), permitting Congress to discriminate between U.S. citizens residing in the states and in the territory, *avoiding* Justice Thurgood Marshall's dissenting admonition that "the case raises the serious issue of the relationship of Puerto Rico, and the United States citizens who reside there, to the Constitution." Ibid., p. 656.

24. Bhana, *Status Question*, p. 37, nn. 56–59; p. 80, n. 44. See also note 70 below for an enumeration of recent State Department studies.

25. Bhana, *Status Question*, pp. 23, 59, 95, 182.

26. *San Juan Star*, March 3, 1977, p. 1, and June 22, 1983, p. 2.

27. Bhana, *Status Question*, pp. 53, 101, 178.

28. For an excellent example of the ensuing confusion, see Antonio Fernós Isern, *Estado Libre Asociado de Puerto Rico Antecedentes, Creación y Desarrollo Hasta la Epoca Presente* (Puerto Rico: Editorial Universitaria, 1974), pp. 413–536, specifically pp. 471–472, 493–517.

29. For history, see Juan M. García-Passalacqua, "Antecedentes e Historical Legislativo de la Comisión de los Estados Unidos y de Puerto Rico Sobre el Status de Puerto Rico," 24 *Revista del Colegio de Abogados de Puerto Rico* 3, May 1964, pp. 357–462. For its report, see Status de Puerto Rico, Informe de la Comisión de los Estados Unidos y de Puerto Rico Sobre el Status de Puerto Rico.

30. Ad Hoc Advisory Group on the Presidential Vote for Puerto Rico, Hearings, March 1–3, 11–12, 1971, Report, August 1971 (Washington, D.C.: Government Printing Office, 1971), 26 pages; President's Ad Hoc Advisory Committee, Transcripts of Proceedings ACE-Federal Reporters, Inc. (Washington, D.C., 1975); and Administración de Servicios Generales, Compact of Permanent Union Between Puerto Rico and the United States, Report, October 1975 (Washington, D.C.: Government Printing Office, 1975), 124 pages.

31. The first task force was created by President Carter on March 2, 1977, and produced an economic report (see U.S. Department of Commerce, *Economic Study of Puerto Rico*, vols. 1 and 2). The second was created by President Reagan in 1981 and held hearings in Puerto Rico but issued no report. *San Juan Star*, March 14, 1981, p. 1, and June 23, 1981, p. 15. It met in late June 1983 to hear Puerto Rican political leaders and the U.S. Navy Caribbean Frontier Commodore Diego Hernández speak on an increase in defense spending in Puerto Rico. *San Juan Star*, June 22, 1983, p. 2.

32. The decision in Puerto Rican political circles to intervene actively in the process for nominating the candidates for president of the United States has not been adequately documented; see "Ley de Primarias Presidenciales Compulsorias del 24 de septiembre de 1979," 16 Leyes de Puerto Rico Anotadas (L.P.R.A.), sections 1321–1353, and Harry Turner, "The Puerto Ricans Who Walked D.C.'s Halls of Power," *San Juan Star*, December 20, 1980, p. 22.

33. *Documents on the Constitutional History of Puerto Rico*, pp. 47–52; 1 Leyes de Puerto Rico Anotadas, pp. 169–182.

34. Pedro Munõz Amato, "Congressional Conservatism and Puerto Rican Democracy in the Commonwealth Relationship," 21 *Revista Juridica de la Universidad de Puerto Rico* 4, May-June 1952, pp. 321–336. See also Bhana, *Status Question*, pp. 65, 93, 106, 208, and 211, for examples.

35. The best elaboration of this argument is that by Jeffrey M. Puryear in "Puerto Rico: An American Dilemma," Americas Society (March 16, 1983), mimeographed, 24 pages. See also Bhana, *Status Question*, p. 216, nn. 8, 16, for the expert opinion of Commissioner Fernós Isern, and Jorge Heine and Juan M. García-Passalacqua, *The Status Question*, Foreign Policy Association Headline Series (New York, 1984).

36. The literature on the status issue is voluminous but mostly irrelevant. For a bibliography, see Comptroller General's Report to Congress, "Puerto Rico's Political Future: A Devisive Issue With Many Dimensions," Appendix E, pp. 243–282. Also see Paquita Vivó, *The Puerto Ricans: An Annotated Bibliography* (New York: Bowker, 1973).

37. H.R. 252 of 1953. See Fernós Isern, *Estado Libre Asociado*, pp. 357–370. For proof that the paradigms of congressional and Puerto Rican leaders differed

completely as to what they were doing, see Bhana, *Status Question*, pp. 168–171.

38. Fernós Isern, *Estado Libre Asociado*, pp. 413–536. Twelve proposals have been made to "improve" the status quo since the approval of the Jones Act, that involve thirty-five different issues in the relationship (see Heine and García-Passalacqua, *Status Question*, Table 1, pp. 18–19).

39. Fernós Isern, *Estado Libre Asociado*, pp. 555–572.

40. House Committee on Interior and Insular Affairs, Robert J. Hunter, *Puerto Rico: A Survey of Historical, Economic and Political Affairs* (Washington, D.C.: Government Printing Office, November 25, 1959), pp. 63–99. See also Fernós Isern, *Estado Libre Asociado*. Quotes of reports are from these two sources.

41. Hunter, *Economic and Political Affairs*, p. 62.

42. See, for an elaboration, Juan M. García-Passalacqua, *La Crisis Política en Puerto Rico*, 2d ed. (Rio Piedras: Editorial Edil, 1983), pp. 35–40. See also Fernós Isern, *Estado Libre Asociado*, pp. 562–566, and Bhana, *Status Question*, p. 126.

43. Office of the White House Press Secretary (Vail, Colorado), Statement of the President, December 31, 1976; Text of Letter from the President to the Speaker of the House and the President of the Senate, January 14, 1977, mimeographed.

44. In a speech before the Puerto Rico Chamber of Commerce when he was a presidential candidate, Senator Jackson stated that the island was "war booty," that statehood was impossible without English as the official language, and that independence also was impossible without a constitutional amendment. He then promised he would introduce legislation to create a White House post. His position won him the title "eminent troglodyte." *San Juan Star*, April 18, 1974, pp. 1, 37, and April 1, 1976, p. 1.

45. Truman R. Clark, *Puerto Rico and the United States 1917–1933* (Pittsburgh: University of Pittsburgh Press, 1975), pp. 23, 83, 90. The author's final chapter is appropriately entitled "The Policy of No Policy." He concludes: "As Whitney Perkins has suggested, by formulating no stated policy for empire, the people of the United States could successfully deny to themselves that their nation was an imperial power," p. 175. See on this issue, Juan Manuel García-Passalacqua, *Puerto Rico: Equality and Freedom at Issue*, ed. Robert Wesson, Latin American Political Series, Hoover Institution (New York: Praeger, 1984).

46. The best brief description of the crisis is found in José J. Villamil, "Puerto Rico 1948–1976: The Limits of Dependent Growth," in *Transnational Capitalism and National Development*, ed. Villamil (England: Harverster Press, 1979), pp. 241–260.

47. Jorge Morales Yordán, "The Constitutional and International Status of the Commonwealth of Puerto Rico," 8 *Revista del Colegio de Abogados de Puerto Rico* 1, November 1957.

48. Comptroller General's Report to Congress, "Experiences of Past Territories Can Assist Puerto Rico Status Deliberations," mimeographed (Washington, D.C., 1980).

49. U.S. Department of Commerce, *Economic Study of Puerto Rico*, vol. 1, pp. 331–339.

50. C. Arthur Borg, "The Problem of Puerto Rico's Political Status," Senior Seminar in Foreign Policy, U.S. Department of State, 17th Session, 1974–1975, mimeographed.

51. U.S. Mission to the United Nations, Press Release USUN-78 (78), August 28, 1978, mimeographed, 3 pages. See also Adrian Pelt, *Libyan Independence and the United Nations: A Case of Planned Decolonization* (Yale University Press, 1970) for an overview of such a process.

52. See Juan Manuel García-Passalacqua's lecture, "Las Perspectivas de la Política Norteamericana Hacia Puerto Rico el Decenio del Ochenta," in Mesa Redonda Internacional Sobre Estados Unidos en los '80, mimeographed transcript of proceedings, La Habana, 1984.

53. See notes 14 and 48, respectively.

54. The latest by the Socialist International in 1983. *Puerto Rico Libre*, April, 1983, p. 9. Also see *San Juan Star*, May 6, 1983, p. 13, and June 21, 1983, p. 27.

55. For example, see *Ford Foundation Letter* 13, 1 (February 1, 1982):1–2.

56. José Cabranes, "Puerto Rico: Out of the Colonial Closet," *Foreign Policy*, Winter, 1981, pp. 66–91.

57. Alfred Stepan, "The United States and Latin America: Vital Interests and the Instruments of Power," *Foreign Affairs*, 1980, pp. 672–680.

58. This advice has been afforded, among others, by *Christian Science Monitor*, January 29, 1982; *Washington Post*, January 15, 1982; *New York Times*, January 15, 1982; *Wall Street Journal*, February 3, 1982; and *St. Louis Post Dispatch*, January 18, 1982.

59. *U.S. News and World Report*, November 26, 1979, p. 48; *Wall Street Journal*, February 11, 1980; *San Juan Star*, January 10, 1982, p. 1; *El Nuevo Día*, November 1, 1980, p. 2; and *San Juan Star*, January 13, 1982, p. 12; *San Juan Star*, August 18, 1984, p. 31.

60. "Informe Sobre Requisitos Procesales Esenciales Para la Descolonizacion de Puerto Rico," 39 *Revista del Colegio Abogados de Puerto Rico* 4, November 1978, pp. 647–650.

61. Naciones Unidas, Asamblea General, A/37/PV.4, 27 de septiembre de 1982; 30mo Periodo; Acta Taquigrafica de Cuarta Sesion, 24 de septiembre de 1982, pp. 7–62. The same situation was repeated in 1983 and 1984.

62. Gautier Mayoral and Blanco Stahl, "CIONTELPRO en Puerto Rico 1960–1971."

63. *Claridad*, August 8–14, 1980, pp. 18–19.

64. 39 *Revista del Colegio Abogados de Puerto Rico* 4, November 1978, pp. 647–650.

65. This proposal has a historical precedent in the Tydings-Piñero Bill of 1945. 8 *Revista de Derecho Legislacion y Jurisprudencia del Colegio de Abogados de Puerto Rico* 3, July-September 1945, pp. 237–240, 269–291. In early 1945, the impending UN conference in San Francisco mobilized the White House and the Congress on Puerto Rico. Colonial Governor Rexford G. Tugwell proposed in his message to the legislature that the Congress define the options it was willing to grant and the Legislative Assembly approve a resolution to request

said definition. Secretary of the Interior Harold Ickes agreed, adding the requirement that the economic consequences of each option be explained. Interior
prepared an internal memorandum on the options and rejected independence
because of economic dependence. Luis Muñoz Marín, chairman of the local
legislative commission, insisted on several options, each with economic guarantees. (If carefully examined, the economic conditions then specified will be
recognized as precursors of the Caribbean Basin Initiative.)

In consultation, the local legislative commission and Senator Myllard Tydings
drafted a bill that was co-sponsored by Puerto Rican Resident Commissioner
Jesus T. Piñero, offering to Puerto Rico the options of independence, statehood,
and autonomy, each with economic guarantees. Truman sent a message to
Congress on October 16, 1945, to that effect. However, there was no support
for statehood in Congress or for the Tydings-Piñero Bill. In the face of congressional
conservatism, the Puerto Rican legislature approved a similar bill and called for
an immediate plebiscite. Truman sustained Tugwell's veto of the bill. In March
1946, Muñoz was told by White House staffer Ben Dorfman that neither statehood
nor independence could be offered by Congress with adequate economic guarantees. *Congressional conservatism in refusing to offer the three options with
adequate economic guarantees led to the policy of the legitimation of the status quo
as the only option, the origin of today's crisis.* Bhana, *Status Question*, p. 216, nn.
8, 16.

66. For detailed elaboration of the reasons for such policy, see Puryear,
"Puerto Rico: An American Dilemma."

67. *San Juan Star*, August 12, 1975, pp. 14–15.

68. International Strategic Issues, ed. Constantine C. Menges, vol. 1, no. 7,
October 1980, mimeographed, 4 pages.

69. Royal Commission on Bilingualism and Biculturalism, *Final Report*, Ottawa,
October 8, 1967, on Quebec; Alistair Horne, *A Savage War of Peace* (New York:
Viking Press, 1977), on Algeria; George Dangerfield, *The Damnable Question*
(Boston: Little, Brown & Co., 1976), on Ireland. For the danger in Puerto Rico's
case, see *El Nuevo Día*, September 1, 1978, p. 1.

70. Robert Wesson, "Freeing Puerto Rico," *New York Times*, May 25, 1978;
Albert N. Williams, "Puerto Rico: Commonwealth, Statehood or Independence?"
National War College, April 1977; Eric Svendsen, "Puerto Rico Libre," Open
Forum No. 20, Spring/Summer 1979; Dolores Wahl, "Puerto Rico's Status: A
Problem for the Eighties," Executive Seminar in National and International
Affairs, 22nd Session, April 1980; David E. Simcox, "The Future of Puerto Rico:
Self-Determination for the Mainland," Open Forum, 1981.

9

The Puerto Rican Parties Speak: What We Need from the United States

The Path to Statehood: Puerto Rico Is No Exception

Héctor Ricardo Ramos Díaz

In the collective Puerto Rican subconscious the term *status* has become equivalent to the term *problem*. I will try to show the ease with which the island could become a full-fledged state of the Union and thereby extricate itself from the present problem. What would be necessary for a transition to statehood in Puerto Rico? The General Accounting Office (GAO) has issued a report showing that the arrangements between Puerto Rico and the federal government to facilitate a smooth transition are minimal. In fact, the internal political and constitutional organization of the government of Puerto Rico is identical to that of any state of the Union. Puerto Rico is a politically organized community. Since 1917 the island has had a popularly elected senate and house of representatives. In 1948, the governor became an elected official. In 1952, our local constitution was approved by a constitutional convention. The similarities between Puerto Rico and any state of the Union, as far as internal political organization is concerned, are remarkably advantageous for a transition toward statehood.

The only requirements for any territory to be admitted to the Union are those contained in Article IV, Section 3, of the U.S. Constitution: "New states may be admitted by the Congress into this union; but no new state shall be formed or erected within the jurisdiction of any of the states; nor any state be formed by the junction of two or more states, or part of states, without the consent of the legislature of the states concerned as well as of the Congress." Obviously, the Constitution allows Congress a great deal of flexibility in defining the specific conditions for Puerto Rico to be admitted to the Union.

The only economic concession that Puerto Rico would require is a transition period before the federal tax structure is applicable. Individuals and corporations currently exempt should not have to pay federal taxes for a specific period, say, twenty years. Economic concessions—lands and money—have often been granted to newly incorporated states. For example, Florida and Louisiana were given a special maritime jurisdiction, and New Mexico and Arizona each received more than 1 million acres of land to help their territorial debts. In sum, the different historical, political, geographic, economic, and social circumstances of the territories have traditionally been taken into consideration by the Congress in the transition to statehood.

Puerto Rico's alleged inability to meet statehood's financial requirements has been raised as an obstacle. I should point out here that the American Revolution could hardly have been justified in economic terms. In fact, it should not be difficult to understand that our aspiration to political equality should overshadow material concerns. We hold that to achieve our goal of social and economic equality it is our duty to attain political equality, just as many ethnic and racial groups have done in the past or are attempting to do today. Once we have obtained political equality, Puerto Rican and U.S. corporations located in Puerto Rico should pay their share of federal taxes.

Statehood will immediately make the island a more attractive place for investment. In the business world potential profit is seen as a direct function of risk. The political security and stability offered by statehood will reduce the perceived risk of investing in Puerto Rico. Statehood will reduce the current demand of corporations for a larger return on investments in Puerto Rico than on the mainland.

The so-called advantages of the present colonial status are at best fragile and at worst nonexistent. The Congress's insistence in overturning section 936 of the IRS code has shown that tax exemptions are not intrinsic to firms that operate within U.S. possessions. Those firms cannot count on such advantages permanently. Indeed, statehood offers the only status alternative that would lead to the orderly withdrawal of these exemptions, rather than their sudden loss.

The position of the New Progressive party (NPP) is that statehood and the phase-out of federal tax exemptions over a transitional period of some twenty years will avoid any "tax shock." Puerto Rico will be able to slowly reduce its tax rate to approximate the average rates of other states.

In other areas as well, negotiations can define and facilitate the transition to statehood. A phase-out of federal custom duties and excise taxes, some type of formula to facilitate the expiration of federal tax exemptions tied to the expiration of the Puerto Rican exemption, and the assumption by the federal government of all or part of the Puerto Rican public debt are all matters that can be worked out between the federal and Puerto Rican governments. The United States should be willing to smooth the path to equality for a community of U.S. citizens that have shared the stigma of political inferiority and economic discrimination, while, at the same time, 200,000 of its men have been inducted into the U.S. Armed Forces and have served with both pride and gallantry in the defense of our collective liberties alongside fellow Americans from the mainland.

Contrary to a widespread myth, Congress should not be an obstacle to Puerto Rico's gaining statehood. Historically, Congressional inquiries into the economic conditions of territories seeking statehood have been intended to identify those transitional measures that would better assist the change in status to statehood. These investigations have never functioned as a barrier to the attainment of political equality. Other than being able to support its own state government and provide its share of the total cost of the federal government, no state has ever been required to have achieved a specific level of wealth or to make any kind of payment to the federal treasury. Special economic concessions have been the norm when territories have become states.

The Constitution does not endow the federal government with powers in the cultural area. Congress cannot encroach upon the sovereign powers of the states by requiring an official language. This doctrine was firmly established in *Coyle* v. *Oklahoma* (1911). Therefore, any clause of the enabling act that specifically restricts the right of Puerto Rico to adopt Spanish as its official language would be unconstitutional.

A special element in Puerto Rico's road to decolonization is obtaining an electoral mandate in favor of both decolonization and statehood. A mandate does not require an overwhelming percentage of voters; it simply means a solid majority obtained through a truly democratic process. Clearly the responsibility to carry out this process in a fair and impartial manner rests with Puerto Rico.

The federal Constitution gives Congress the authority to admit states into the Union. The specific means that Congress considers appropriate, as long as they are framed within its vested powers, are wholly discretionary. The Senate committee report accompanying the most recent admission act sets forth the following standards:

The Constitution of the United States provides that new states may be admitted into the Union by the Congress, but it sets forth no specific requirements. However, a study of American history, with particular attention to the facts and circumstances surrounding the admission of each of the 37 states that have come into the Union since its founding, shows that the requirements have been: (1) that the inhabitants of the proposed new state are imbued with and sympathetic toward the principles of democracy as exemplified in the American form of government; (2) that a majority of the electorate desire statehood; and (3) that the proposed new state has sufficient population and resources to support state government and to provide its share of the cost of the federal government.

Puerto Ricans are clearly imbued with the principles of democracy. Our history of the last 85 years, indeed the last 400 years, clearly demonstrates our unwavering commitment to democratic institutions. Furthermore, our republican state government embodies the values of the U.S. system of government and the egalitarian principles of the federal Constitution. Moreover, we have one of the highest voter turnouts in the hemisphere—around 85 percent.

In regard to the second criterion, the support of the Puerto Rican electorate for statehood has grown from 12.9 to 47 percent in less than thirty years. During the same period, support for the parties favoring independence has declined from 19 to 6 percent and for the party supporting the continuation of the colonial situation from 64.8 to 47 percent.

We began this chapter by inquiring into the necessary conditions for the transition of Puerto Rico from its present status to statehood. The single most important prerequisite to solve the status problem is the cooperation of the U.S. government. The Congress must show its determination to face this issue constructively and assist in solving the problem of Puerto Rico's political status.

Although Puerto Rico must ultimately be responsible for choosing its own political destiny, Congress should guarantee that the will of the Puerto Rican people will be respected. Indeed, Congress has supreme authority in dealing with a territory that belongs to the United States. Puerto Rico yearns for and urges action. We do not ask Congress to impose on us a specific status alternative. Instead, we hope that Washington will live up to its historic responsibility. Change in the political status of Puerto Rico is inevitable.

Give Commonwealth the Tools to Work

Miguel Lausell

The Popular Democratic Party Position on Status

The United States should honor the will of the Puerto Rican people by permitting growth within the present political framework. That will was expressed by the people of Puerto Rico in the plebiscite of July 23, 1967. The Popular Democratic party (PDP) does not seek a change in the island's political status; instead, we are asking for more tools to deal with the problems of Puerto Rico within the context of the present political relationship.

In the early months of 1964 the U.S. Congress created a status commission to study the political relationship between Puerto Rico and the mainland. The commission concluded its report on the status question by emphasizing that

> an expression of the will of the citizens of Puerto Rico by popular vote on the question of whether they wish to continue the commonwealth status capable of growth and development or to change to either statehood or independence would be helpful to all concerned. The Commission recognizes, however, that it is for the people of Puerto Rico to decide when, and in what manner they wish to express their preference. Such an expression should precede any change in status.

The Puerto Rican legislature responded by passing a law calling for a plebiscite, which was held on July 23, 1967. Three choices were possible: commonwealth, statehood, and independence.

More than 60 percent of the votes cast were in favor of commonwealth status. This proposition was defined on the ballot as follows:

> A vote in favor of the Commonwealth shall mean: (1) The reaffirmation of the Commonwealth established by mutual agreement under the terms of Act 600 of 1950 and Joint Resolution 447 of 1952 of the Congress of the United States of America; (2) The inviolability of common citizenship as the primary and indispensable basis of the permanent union between Puerto Rico and the United States; (3) The authorization to develop the Commonwealth in accordance to its fundamental principles to a maximum of self-government compatible with a common defense, a common market, a common currency, and the indissoluble link of the citizenship of the

United States; (4) That no change in the relations between the United States and Puerto Rico shall take place unless previously approved by a majority of the electors voting in a referendum held to that effect.

In accordance with the wishes of the people as expressed in the plebiscite a compact of permanent union between Puerto Rico and the United States was eventually presented to the U.S. Congress in 1975. The compact clearly stated the need for growth within the commonwealth status. Indeed, the text of the compact included several petitions from the government of Puerto Rico to the U.S. Congress. The following are some of the most important:

1. To grant Puerto Rico the right to enter into international agreements, such as commercial treaties with foreign countries.
2. To allow Puerto Rico to impose tariffs and other controls on products imported from foreign countries.
3. To apply U.S. defense and national security laws to Puerto Rico in accordance with their terms, having the president and the governor consult and cooperate to facilitate their objectives.
4. To allow duty-free importation of materials and articles to Puerto Rico for subsequent shipment and sales to U.S. customs territory provided that free-at-side shipping prices contain at least 35 percent of the value added in Puerto Rico.
5. To allow Puerto Rico to have control over immigration of aliens to the island.
6. To allow Puerto Rico to have control over all labor-management regulations, salaries, and all labor conditions in its economy.
7. To have all assigned federal funds to Puerto Rico disbursed in the form of block grants.
8. To allow Puerto Rico to regulate local ecology.
9. To allow all procedures in the U.S. district court for the District of Puerto Rico to be conducted in Spanish.

Nine years later Congress has still not acted upon this compact. What possible justification can there be for this lack of action? President Ford's sudden and inexplicable proposal supporting statehood in 1976 was tantamount to blatant interference in an issue that should properly be left to the people of Puerto Rico to decide. Furthermore, the Congress has chosen to ignore the recommendations of its own status commission and several UN resolutions. The continued inaction of Congress shows a complete disregard for the rights of the people of Puerto Rico to self-determination. It implies that, by deciding which proposals to ignore and which to acknowledge, for all practical purposes Congress exercises unilateral power to determine the political future of Puerto Rico.

The necessity for congressional action has now become imperative: President Reagan's Caribbean Basin Initiative fundamentally threatens the progress of Puerto Rican economic and social development. Combined with the recent amendment of section 936, the Caribbean Basin Initiative constitutes a moral breach by the United States of the existing political pact between Puerto Rico and the mainland.

The behavior of the U.S. Congress is contradictory. On one hand, Congress has acted positively toward the petitions of the Marshall Islands and the Federate State of Micronesia by granting those possessions even more political power than has been requested by Puerto Rico. On the other hand, it has ignored repeatedly the petitions of Puerto Rico, and even compounded our present economic and social problems by supporting legislation that adversely affects us.

Sixteen priceless years of development have already been wasted since the 1967 plebiscite. The PDP maintains that Congress must act upon the 1975 compact by enacting the pertinent legislation or at least indicating under what terms these proposals are feasible.

Alternative Futures

The PDP does not favor holding another plebiscite unless the U.S. Congress guarantees that the various status alternatives will be defined beforehand. No one will gain from a repetition of the past. Furthermore, by following this modus operandi we will avoid further waste of government funds and time.

If the will of the people, expressed in the 1967 plebiscite, is not honored by Congress various alternatives are possible. One alternative is to create a permanent constitutional convention. The delegates to this convention would be elected by direct vote of the people of Puerto Rico and remain in session until a final solution to the status issue is obtained. The constitutional convention would be empowered to submit concrete petitions to the U.S. Congress on the political status of Puerto Rico. Congress would have the obligation to approve, deny, or modify the convention's proposals. After Congress has taken action the petition would be returned to the constitutional convention, where any changes by Congress would be examined before presenting the compact for final ratification by direct vote of the people of Puerto Rico. Once ratified, the U.S. and Puerto Rican Congresses would be obliged to enact the necessary legislation to produce the desired compact.

Another alternative is to create a direct petition from the Puerto Rican legislature to the U.S. Congress. The petition would request the necessary political powers to save Puerto Rico from the pending socioeconomic crises. Indeed, the Puerto Rican legislature has already taken this step. On March 21, 1982, the legislature presented a resolution to Congress that contained a fifteen-point program in a petition designed to deal adequately with the island's social and economic problems.

The program asked Congress to grant Puerto Rico powers that would increase the commonwealth's ability to regulate its own commerce and otherwise promote economic development. Such powers would include the right to impose tariffs and controls on imports from foreign countries, to enter into trade agreements with foreign countries, to impose controls to protect local farm production from imports, to use foreign flagships in commerce with the mainland United States, to receive block grants of federal aid to provide the local government greater autonomy and flexibility in the use of federal transfer payments than under current specific programs, to change section 936 tax credit legislation to enhance investment opportunities on the island, and other development measures. The thrust of this resolution was to provide for a stronger, more autonomous commonwealth government that would have the policy instruments to pursue development objectives without the present excessive dependence on Washington. Once again Congress has been given the opportunity to act. A commonly held maxim of U.S. politics is that Congress reacts only to crises. Puerto Rico is now in crisis. This Congress has no more excuses; it must take action on the problems of Puerto Rico.

A New Approach to an Old Issue

Luis Batista Salas

The issues involved in the Puerto Rican status debate are both complex and divisive. Yet everyone on the island agrees, no matter what their ideology, that the United States should focus more attention on the political future of Puerto Rico. Years of neglect have fostered the political stalemate that currently exists on the island.

The recent political history of Puerto Rico has been dominated by intense factionalism. The struggle for power between Carlos Romero Barceló and Rafael Hernández Colón, and the control of the legislature by one party, the PDP, and the executive by another, the PNP, has made partisan conflict the norm on the island. Meanwhile, pressing economic and social problems have been ignored as the two political parties have concentrated on outmaneuvering each other.

The results of the 1980 election showed a growing feeling of dissatisfaction with the political parties of the island. The results reflected more a concern for local and ephemeral issues, imbued with petty partisan rivalries, than a popular mandate for any particular political status.

When San Juan Mayor Hernán Padilla announced in March 1983 that he would seek the Progressive party's nomination for governor, Governor Romero reacted by closing the nomination process to the rank and file. As a result, Mayor Padilla formed a new party, the Puerto Rican Renewal party (PRP), to contest the 1984 election. How does the PRP differ from the old parties? What is its position on the status issue? First, the party responds to the growing concern among many people about the direction that Puerto Rico's politics has taken in the last twenty years. The daily personalistic battles between the major political parties have drained needed human and political resources from the more immediate and pressing problems facing our island: unemployment, crime, government mismanagement, education, and health care. The present political parties are no longer capable of addressing the island's socioeconomic problems because they cannot provide the necessary leadership.

The Puerto Rican Renewal party commits itself to working for a resolution of the economic and social problems that currently constitute the real issues facing the electorate. *When progress has been achieved in these areas, the party will then concern itself with solving the issue of status.*

First, we must begin with the economy. For more than two decades Puerto Rico enjoyed one of the highest rates of annual growth in the world. For the past decade, our economy has been stagnant. In 1982, Puerto Rico experienced its worst annual economic performance in the postwar era. Unemployment is currently 24 percent. Government control of the economy is too extensive: An amazing 55 percent of the island's gross domestic product is contained in the budget of the commonwealth government. Per capita income is only one third the U.S. national average. In addition, there has been a significant decline in new private investment in Puerto Rico in each of the past four years. Greater cooperation is needed between the island's private and public sectors to create a strong economic recovery. We must not let time run out. As the U.S. economy improves in the months ahead, Puerto Rico risks by inaction the possibility of being left in a state of permanent recession.

At the same time, violent crime has been increasing dramatically. Allegations of government corruption, including misuse of public monies, are widespread. Poor government administration has resulted in a general decline in the quality of commonwealth public services. Other urgent problems include a lack of decent housing for all our citizens and an educational system that needs fundamental changes to provide the next generation with the necessary skills for a more productive work force.

These real issues facing the Puerto Rican electorate are the issues that will decide its future. After progress has been made in these areas, the island can focus its attention on resolving the status issue once and for all. When that time comes, Puerto Ricans will be able to petition the United States for a change in status—from a position of pride, dignity, and accomplishment—rather than from economic or social need.

The Puerto Rican Renewal party was made up of a broad coalition of citizens and crossed traditional ideological boundaries. It counts statehood, commonwealth, and independence advocates among its members. This new pluralist political movement is committed to the principles of immediate socioeconomic reform and to the creation by legislation of a plebiscitary commission with representation from the main political parties of Puerto Rico. This commission would be entrusted with forming a multipartisan procedural consensus to solve the status problem. In turn, it would ask the federal government, both the Congress and the president, to provide a mutually agreed upon definition on the substantive content of each formula before the decision is posed to the voters in Puerto Rico.

Therefore, the PRP wants the U.S. government to give it a free hand to search for a local consensus through the plebiscitary commission and the U.S. Congress to define for it the substantive elements of statehood, independence, and improved commonwealth status.

In that context, the Puerto Rican Renewal party has viewed with great interest proposals made from time to time for the creation of a Senate select committee on Puerto Rico. While the PRP seeks to create a consensus in Puerto Rico and to solve urgent economic and social problems, a select committee would begin to study ways to immediately improve our critical economic situation and to spell out the conditions under which the U.S. government would be willing to grant statehood, independence, or improved commonwealth status.

The creation of the PRP is a landmark on the road toward definition. For the first time in history, a political party has crossed ideological barriers and gone beyond the fruitless three-ring-circus debate on the merits and drawbacks of the substantive status options. For the first time in Puerto Rican history a party proposes to implement a change in status, based on concrete procedural and substantive realities.

This new and equitable approach can divest the Puerto Rican status debate of its platitudes, helping the present leadership and the members of each party to initiate a real dialogue concerning the method for solving the issue. This, in turn, will help the United States take affirmative action in defining the status of Puerto Rico. Once the federal government, with the active participation of the local parties, has expressed its terms, the local parties will have to promote their respective status solutions, not on speculative promises, but on the hard facts and figures of what the federal government has announced as the options.

U.S. and Puerto Rican leaders have the historic responsibility of setting in motion fundamental changes to our present situation. The process we defend can keep the status issue from being used by the political parties as an electoral tool to keep their constituents involved in an emotionally charged, but fruitless, debate. That debate has diverted attention from the most pressing problems of our island.

Independence:
The Only Permanent Solution

Fernando Martín

This book could be a useful step toward beginning the process of decolonization if it succeeds in educating U.S. policymakers on the nature of colonization in Puerto Rico and on the urgency of its liquidation. Introspection about the values and principles at stake could lead to a reevaluation of the U.S. role in Puerto Rico. On the other hand, this book could merely compound the mistakes of the past if its net effect is to mystify the present reality of subordination and dependence or if it manages only to deflect the growing consciousness concerning Puerto Rico into an alternative paradigm, just as false, though even more pernicious, than its predecessor.

One can already hear the rumblings of the approaching paradigm. They are noticeable on the mainland and in Puerto Rico; they are the sounds of a new language, a colonialist version of "doublespeak." The formulas are familiar by now. They include words such as *alternative futures, procedural consensus,* and of course, *self-determination.*

Several authors have stated, like an incantation uttered by a would-be alchemist, that the problem of decolonizing Puerto Rico is not a substantive one, but instead a procedural one. To avoid the conceptual and political traps that the forces of colonial inertia will once again set in our way through the medium of well-intentioned men, we must not lose sight of the core of our dilemma.

Puerto Rico is a Latin American nation in the Caribbean, which has been occupied militarily by the United States since 1898 when it was demanded as booty of war from Spain. Sovereignty rests with the Congress of the United States, which has seen fit to maintain Puerto Rico as a colony, subject to the rule of Congress and exercising only limited powers of internal self-government.

In the sociohistorical sense, Puerto Rico is no mere territory or parcel of real estate; it is a people, a *pueblo*. It is a full-fledged nation that has been denied the exercise and enjoyment of its sovereignty by a foreign country that has jealously guarded its power over Puerto Rico and has never shown the slightest inclination to renounce it.

What the Puerto Rican Independence party wants from the United States is for it to renounce its sovereignty over Puerto Rico so that the Puerto Rican people, as an independent nation, may manage and direct their affairs as they see fit.

Puerto Rico, as a distinct and separate nation, has an inalienable right to its independence, and the United States, as a colonial power, has an absolute obligation to renounce the sovereignty it exercises over its colony. The problem is far from being procedural; it is inescapably substantive. The principle involved is not self-determination as a method, but self-determination as the effective and continuous enjoyment of sovereignty so that a nation can rule itself.

Whether the people of Puerto Rico, once a free and independent nation, should want in the future to propose to the United States of America, or to the United States of Mexico for that matter, some form of economic or political agreement consistent with accepted principles of international law is something quite different from the proposition that the present colonial condition can be legitimately transmuted into something other than an independent republic.

Some say that for Congress to proceed to grant independence to Puerto Rico *ex parte* would be an exercise in imperialism. I recommend that they reexamine the premises of their position. Indeed this argument demonstrates that they have so internalized a subconscious contempt for the Puerto Rican people that they are conceived as being the proverbial "white man's burden."

If Congress proceeded to recognize the independence of Puerto Rico, such a decision would not be imperialistic; instead it would be the termination of U.S. colonialism on the island. The devolution of sovereignty and the recognition of independence can never be considered an imposition unless one believes that Puerto Rico is either unworthy or incapable of exercising its powers as a nation. Have we become so jaded that we are willing to characterize the emancipation of the slaves as an imposition? Or to think that emancipation should have been subject to a method of self-determination in which the slaves might have opted to renounce their right to freedom? Freedom is an inalienable right; therefore, it is also irrevocable.

When a full-fledged nation is a colony of another the question of colonialism, like the question of slavery, is not one of procedure but of substance. Therefore, any argument that obscures the obligation of the United States to proceed with the devolution of sovereignty to Puerto Rico and to recognize its political independence is little more than a back-handed denial of the existence of a colonial relationship or an attempt to convert the principle of self-determination into an obstacle to the attainment of independence by the colony. Beware of liberals bearing gifts.

In very general terms, our proposal is simple. The U.S. Congress should approve a resolution setting a specific date for the granting of independence to Puerto Rico. At the same time it should express its willingness to negotiate the conditions that shall accompany the devolution of sovereignty as well as the treaties and arrangements that will prevail, at least initially, between the two countries. The Puerto Rican leadership, advised of this fait accompli, would proceed to the various negotiations and hold a constitutional convention that would lead to independence.

This moment is not appropriate for setting down the long list of matters that must be discussed at the negotiating table; they go from the pedestrian to the sublime. After eighty-five years of colonial rule, they include every aspect of our economic and institutional life. Yet the common objective should be ensuring continuity and stability within change.

One of the great advantages of independence is that it allows the maximum flexibility of any of the so-called status options. Virtually no arrangement concerning trade, citizenship, taxes, foreign aid, currency, or defense cannot be agreed upon by both parties if it is mutually beneficial. The only parameters in this nation-building exercise would be the imagination and the good will of both parties. Other than the withdrawal of the jurisdiction of the United States over Puerto Rico no preconditions or precedents would be needed to limit future relations between both countries. In trade matters alone, for example, the Caribbean Basin Initiative has gone a long way in destroying atavistic notions about forms of access to the U.S. market for the exports of Caribbean republics.

We would be underestimating both sides if we believed that the obstacles to a transition to a viable and prosperous Republic of Puerto Rico are technical in nature; there will be technical problems, both difficult and novel, but none that could not be overcome if the U.S. government developed the necessary political will to discharge its responsibility toward the Puerto Rican nation by granting it its independence; our real commonality of vital interests is our best mutual guarantee.

Unfortunately, the United States has given no indications that it is on the verge of acting upon its responsibility under the principles of international law by taking this historic step. The United States will not leave Puerto Rico until the combined costs of colonialism are perceived to be too high. For to be right is very important, but unfortunately it is not enough. In the nature of colonialism rationality and even enlightened national self-interest are not prevalent; the colonial reality spins a complicated web of relationships and interests that serve to maintain its existence against the true long-range interests of both the colonizer and the colonized. This web of strategic, bureaucratic, economic, and social interests generates powerful political forces that feel comfortable, if not secure, in the colonial context. The longer the colonial relation, the more difficult they are to uproot. In turn they generate a language and an imagery that seek to make legitimate the colonial condition, and in times of stability, to glorify it; thus servitude is extolled while independence is made a bogeyman.

These political forces, the true expression of colonialism, must be fought on all fronts to expose them in an effective manner. If rationality is to prevail, the forces of darkness must be defeated.

This is why the Puerto Rican Independence party is engaged in the political process in Puerto Rico; that is why it is active in the Socialist International and in the Conference of Latin American Political Parties; that is why we are promoting the debate on the colonial status of Puerto Rico in the United Nations. We will not rest until independence is achieved.

Our secret weapon, however, is not any of the above: Our principal ally in this struggle for our independence, for our right to be masters in our own home, is the deterioration of the colonial structure in Puerto Rico and the impossibility of any serious consideration by the United States of statehood as an option for Puerto Rico. Colonial status has failed to provide the required stability in Puerto Rico; it is after all the colony of Puerto Rico that is in crisis.

The mere fact that this book is being written is a prologue to the inevitable epitaph of the pathetic attempt to legitimize colonialism in

Puerto Rico—the Estado Libre Asociado—an associated free state that was neither associated, nor free, nor a state. The virtual collapse of the colonial economic model has already been amply documented. Socially, a short visit to Puerto Rico will suggest, even to the uninitiated, the alarming symptoms that anticipate the development of a tropical South Bronx.

As colonial status begins to shudder in the throes of its helplessness, statehood will be examined and found wanting. Statehood is an unacceptable status, not only because it would cost too much or be culturally unacceptable or offensive to Latin America and international opinion, or because a sufficiently large majority in favor of it in Puerto Rico might never develop. It is unacceptable for another, more profound reason: Although a large enough reservation camp could be found to place the 100,000 *independentistas* who are today the political tip of the nationalist iceberg, one cannot predict how many more will be in the next generation or in the one after that, because as long as Puerto Rico is a proud and distinct nation, surrounded by water on all sides, with its own language and sense of collective destiny, it will find its way to independence sooner or later in the same way as the meandering river will always reach the sea. The digestive system of American federalism is much too delicate to swallow a Latin American nation whole.

What the Puerto Rican Independence party wants is the independence of Puerto Rico; to this end the U.S. government should proceed with all deliberate speed lest both our nations risk the inevitable turmoil and bitterness of being overtaken by events. In politics, as in life in general, an ounce of prevention is worth a pound of cure.

About the Contributors

Luis Batista Salas is the Chairman of the Board of the Aqueduct Authority of Puerto Rico. He was the vice-mayor of San Juan, Puerto Rico.

Richard J. Bloomfield has been director of the World Peace Foundation since 1982. A career foreign service officer from 1952–1982, he served as ambassador to Ecuador, 1976–1978, and ambassador to Portugal, 1978–1982.

E. Thomas Coleman is a Republican congressman from Missouri. He is a member of the Agriculture Committee and the Education-Labor Committee.

Nelson Famadas was the chairman of the Governor's Financial and Economic Council under Governor Carlos Romero Barceló (1980–1984).

Bertram P. Finn is vice-president and manager, Corporate and Municipal Finance Department, A.B. Becker, Puerto Rico. From 1979–1981 he was the executive director of the Economic and Financial Advisory Council of the Governor of Puerto Rico. From 1970–1971 and again from 1977–1979, Dr. Finn was with the Economic Development Administration of Puerto Rico.

Juan Manuel García-Passalacqua, an attorney, is also a political analyst for the *San Juan Star*. He was an assistant to the former governors of Puerto Rico, Luis Muñoz Marín and Roberto Sanchez Vilella. He served as a member of the National Hispanic Advisory Group to President Jimmy Carter.

Miguel Lausell is chairman of the Telephone Company of Puerto Rico. In 1973 he was appointed undersecretary of the Treasury of the Commonwealth of Puerto Rico in charge of legal affairs. Among his areas of responsibility were supervision of the Industrial Incentive Act, the Petroleum Law, tax reform, section 936 legislation, and banking law.

Mr. Lausell also has served as assistant to the governor of Puerto Rico, Rafael Hernández Colón.

Fernando Martín is professor of law at the University of Puerto Rico. Mr. Martin is secretary for International Affairs of the Puerto Rico Independence party and was the party's candidate for governor in the 1984 elections.

Peter R. Merrill is an economist with the Joint Committee on Taxation of the United States Congress. He has worked as an economic consultant and in federal and local government.

Arturo Morales Carrión has been executive director for the Puerto Rican Endowment for the Humanities since 1977. He was president of the University of Puerto Rico from 1973–1977 and was deputy assistant secretary of state for inter-American affairs in the Department of State during the Kennedy administration. His most recent book is *Puerto Rico: A Political and Cultural History* (W. W. Norton, 1983).

Randolph Mye is a senior policy advisor for South America in the Department of Commerce. He was the deputy director of the Puerto Rico staff for the Inter-Agency Report on the Puerto Rican Economy issued in 1979.

Luis Nieves Falcón, a sociologist, is on the faculty of the University of Puerto Rico.

Robert A. Pastor is currently on the faculty of the School of Public Affairs, University of Maryland, College Park, where he is teaching and doing research on U.S. policy toward the Caribbean Basin. He was the senior staff member responsible for Latin American and Caribbean affairs on the National Security Council from 1977–1981.

Héctor Ricardo Ramos Díaz is an attorney in private practice. He was secretary of the Department of Consumer Affairs in Puerto Rico under Governor Carlos Romero Barceló (1977–1984).

Guy F. Smith is an advisor to the mayor of San Juan. He was a special assistant to the resident commissioner of Puerto Rico (1977–1984).

José S. Sorzano is the deputy permanent representative of the United States to the United Nations. He is on leave from Georgetown University where he is associate professor of government.

Index